# Walking to Woot

## A Photographic Narrative Discovering New Dimensions for Parent-Teen Bonding

# Walking to Woot

A Photographic Narrative
Discovering New
Dimensions for
Parent-Teen Bonding

By Jackie Chase

AdventureTravelPress.com

*Walking to Woot* A Photographic Narrative Discovering New Dimensions for Parent-Teen Bonding

Copyright © 2016 by Jackie Chase

All rights reserved. No part of this publication may be reproduced, distributed or transmitted in any form or by any means, including photocopying, recording, or other electronic or mechanical methods, without the prior written permission of the publisher, except in the case of brief quotations embodied in critical reviews and certain other noncommercial uses permitted by copyright law. For permission requests, E-mail the publisher, addressed "Attention: Permissions Coordinator," at the address below:

AdventureTravelPress.com. FL, USA
Publisher@AdventureTravelPress.com

Ordering Information:

Quantity sales. Special discounts are available on quantity purchases by corporations, associations, and others. For details, contact the "Special Sales Department" at the E-mail address above.

Jackie Chase: Walking to Woot: A Photographic Narrative Discovering New Dimensions for Parent-Teen Bonding

Color Print: ISBN- 978-1-937630-57-7 [2016]

***Grayscale: ISBN-978-1-937630-59-1 [2016]

E-book: ISBN- 978-1-937630-54-6 [2016]

Publisher's Cataloging-In-Publication Data (Prepared by The Donohue Group, Inc.)

Names: Chase, Jackie, author, photographer.

Title: Walking to Woot : a photographic narrative discovering new dimensions for parent-teen bonding / Jackie Chase.

Description: AdventureTravelPress.com, [2016]

Identifiers: LCCN 2016950653 | ISBN 978-1-937630-57-7 (color print) | ISBN 978-1-937630-59-1 (grayscale print) | ISBN 978-1-937630-54-6 (ebook)

Subjects: LCSH: Chase, Jackie--Travel. | New Guinea--Description and travel--Pictorial works. | Indigenous peoples--New Guinea--Pictorial works. | New Guinea--Social life and customs--Pictorial works. | Parent and teenager--Pictorial works. | Mothers and daughters--Pictorial works. | Travel--Social aspects--Pictorial works.

Classification: LCC DU739 .C43 2016 (print) | LCC DU739 (ebook) | DDC 919.5--dc23

## PRAISE FOR "WALKING TO WOOT":

"The numerous, full-color photographs are the book's strongest attribute, as they document a wide swath of jungle and village life." **Kirkus Reviews**

"'Walking to Woot' is an inspiring story that succeeds on many levels. At its core this is a story of mother-daughter bonding through travel, which has been done plenty of times before, but seldom for a month-long trip through such a wild environment. In case it all seems too fantastic to believe, the book is loaded with color photos taken along the way, penis gourds and all." Tim Leffel, author of "Travel Writing 2.0"; editor: eZine: **PerceptiveTravel.com.**

"Not only is the book an engaging read, but it is inspiring and, I found, an encouragement to try new things and to escape the trappings and bindings of the modern world. It's a story of grit and determination that will motivate readers to explore the many layers that exist in the world around them." Five-star review from Mamta Madhavan for **Reader's Favorite**

"Chase portrays the jungle in a picturesque and figurative style; she uses exquisite descriptions, drawing from her keen photographic eye." Five-star review by Cheryl Rodriguez for **Reader's Favorite**

"Some of us might have chosen a less hostile environment for their journey of self-discovery, but all credit to this mother and daughter whose incredible experiences enabled them to discover their own true selves. Not only is the book an engaging read, but it is inspiring and, I found, an encouragement to try new things and to escape the trappings and bindings of the modern world." Five-star review by Jane Finch for **Reader's Favorite**

"First of all, I must say how impressed I was with the quality of the story. The descriptions of the journey and adventures are first class. We often take our lives here in the United States for granted." **Vermont Reviews**

"Chase's memoir is a compelling and well-written non-fiction offering that reads like an adventure tale. Walking to Woot: A Photographic Narrative Discovering New Dimensions for Parent/Teen Bonding shows how a mother and daughter bonded during their jungle adventure, but even more so, it gives the reader a look at a tribal culture that's far removed from modern times and places. This travel memoir is most highly recommended." Five-star review by Jack Magnus for **Reader's Favorite**

"Jackie Chase's craving for adventure, knowledge, and an in-depth understanding of ancient wisdom led her to discover what people really need…a closer connection to those we love. This amazing journey shared with her teenaged daughter has brought them together in special ways in which they'll be bonded for the rest of their lives. It is in such deep connections with our children that we all thrive, such as the family found among the indigenous people of New Guinea. My life-long quest has been observing parent-infant & toddler relationships in traditional cultures. Just as Jackie has discovered with teen relationships, by watching how these people cherish each other and honor the earth, we find what has been missing in our own constantly busy materially focused lives." Charlotte Peterson, PhD, Child Psychologist and author of **"The Mindful Parent: Strategies from Peaceful Cultures to Raise Compassionate, Competent Kids"**

"Walking to Woot is gripping. This book is so appealing in part because it includes the reader. Not only are the experiences vividly described, but the author is open about her thoughts and feelings throughout. It inspires people to see every day as an adventure of its own and every person as a unique treasure, to be valued for their own sake. Even a non-traveler will enjoy an exciting story of travel, family, and creepy crawlies. This honest

reflection helps add context and relevance to the experience as a whole, allowing the reader to understand the benefits and costs of exotic travel."
**Online Book Club**

*Complete Review by US Review below:*
"How can one even begin to grasp the simple yet complex evolution of tribal society that exists much the same today as it did thousands of years ago? ... Katherine and I had many questions and few answers; but determined, we tried to grasp every concept blown our way."

Some of us long to take trips into the unknown. We wish to leave behind our material possessions, and live simpler lives. Jackie Chase did just that, for one adventure-filled month. Jackie is no stranger to travel. She's spent much of her life flitting from one place to another in search of a deeper understanding of the world's cultures. In Walking to Woot, Jackie takes the reader with her to live among the Dani people in New Guinea, Indonesia. Despite being a seasoned traveler, Jackie had her apprehensions about the potentially dangerous trip. She had good reason to: This time, she was bringing her 14-year-old daughter, Katherine, with her.

Jackie recounts the month-long trip using descriptive, informative, and often reflective writing. As readers, we feel like we make every bug-infested, often uncomfortable step with her. Jackie's strong writing brings the foreign surroundings alive and brings readers closer to nature and the Dani tribe. Her writing is accompanied by dynamic photographs that document the trip. The photographs are full of personality. These are not mere vacation snapshots: Jackie has a knack for capturing the moment and an eye for shape and color. Photos of incredible mid-action moments, the individuals they encounter, and an over-abundance of penis gourds illustrate the magnificent journey Jackie and Katherine make. Together, the words and photos weave a tale of the wilderness and the people who live among it.

Information about the Dani tribe and their traditions is included throughout the book, making it a learning experience as well as an adventure. This information comes from conversations with their guide, Julius, from the Dani people themselves, or from research done by the author. The inclusion of these knowledge bites transforms this book from a mere photo travel tale. Instead, Walking to Woot is an informative foray into a tribe barely touched by modern civilization.

The Dani tribe are described as nothing but welcoming everywhere they go. The villages they visit invite the mother and daughter to watch and participate in their celebrations, festivals, and traditions. Yet despite the overwhelming kindness that greets them, Jackie remains apprehensive about the dangers of the trip and her daughter's safety. The author's fearfulness and distrust is a stark contrast to the tribal people's open curiosity and wonder. The experience leaves Jackie and Katherine and, by extension, the reader marveling at how much Westerners take for granted and how little we really know.

Through learning about the Dani, Jackie and Katherine learn about themselves. This self-exploration leads to a clearer understanding of what the world has to offer and what they have to offer the world. The Dani's sense of community and family also help strengthen Jackie's relationship with her teenage daughter. For Jackie, this is just another adventure in a string of many. But for Katherine, this is an experience of a lifetime. Jackie includes an interview with her daughter years after the mother-daughter duo returned from their adventure. The interview offers an insightful glimpse at the way Katherine, as a teenager, processed the surroundings she was exposed to at the time. This conversation, as well as a few pages of Katherine's journals included in the back of the book, show what a profound impact the Dani people had on Katherine. What we see in front of us is not all there is. Walking to Woot is sure to ignite the itch to uncover the world's secrets in anyone who reads it. Reviewed by Yuliya Geikhman: **Recommended** by the **US Review.**

"Your writing is so descriptive. I can picture & feel what you experienced in a culture so foreign to our own. Your pictures are absolutely crystal clear." (Even on the Kindle version) **Sharyl Mount Hunter Booth**

To Katherine, whose desire for living on the edge matches my own.

| Page | Contents |
|---|---|
| 1 | Introduction: Hidden Riches of Secret Places |
| 3 | Chapter 1: Throwim Way Leg |
| 9 | Chapter 2: Runway into the Stone Age |
| 25 | Chapter 3: Wrapped Like Birthday Presents |
| 61 | Chapter 4: The Mysterious Spear |
| 82 | Chapter 5: Women Fully Clothed |
| 89 | Chapter 6: Goose Bumps |
| 105 | Chapter 7: Arrow Aimed at My Heart |
| 121 | Chapter 8: What Is a Ghost Story? |
| 129 | Chapter 9: A Gathering of Pigs |
| 157 | Chapter 10: Walking to Woot |
| 179 | Chapter 11: Leaving the No-Name Village |
| 189 | Chapter 12: Off to See a Mummy |
| 209 | Chapter 13: Ring around the Rattan Hoops |
| 223 | Chapter 14: Removing Our Cultural Masks |
| 229 | Chapter 15: Cannibals Hide and Seek |
| 237 | Chapter 16: Impossible to Leave-Impossible to Stay |
| 245 | Chapter 17: Before the Trip, a Volcano under My Feet |
| 247 | Chapter 18: Trading Free Travel for Family |
| 249 | Chapter 19: Dancing Your Own Dance |
| 251 | Chapter 20: Pieces of My Self-Portrait |
| 253 | Chapter 21: Reality Better Than Dreams |
| 255 | Chapter 22: Barefoot in a New Guinea Hospital |
| 259 | Chapter 23: Which Color to Slide Down on the Rainbow |
| 261 | Afterglow: The Rest of the Story |
| 269 | A Teen's Notes: Youthful Landscapes |

290 Appendix: Two Approaches to Packing

292 Author Page and What's in other books?

*"The edge of the world does not look far away.
To that I am on my way running."* **Papago Indian Song**

# Introduction: Hidden Riches of Secret Places

*Mom & daughter outside Sentani Airport*

The wilds of the New Guinea jungle were the catalyst for a Midwest mother and her fourteen-year-old daughter to grow their relationship and personal potential. There were no road maps or landmarks to guide this internal exploration. Walking to Woot shares a taste of raw adventure traversing both the inner and outer geography of two women's courage as they become sensitized to a deeper reality about the direction of their lives.

The world is full of diversity. How it impacts a life depends upon attitude and reaction. An open approach gives participating observers the opportunity to merge into and feel the ways of living within. This exposure works with almost any culture, from the appreciation of diversity in ethnic neighborhoods at home to the practices of tribal customs abroad. For some observers, reality is hot water, electricity, favorite foods, friends, music, technology and comfortable beds. Remove these and it is possible to drench the participant in the customs of little-known cultures to discover strengths not known before. In the story that follows, courage becomes a two-way contagion as both mother and daughter face fears and overcome them while building the spiritual muscle and determination needed to cope with today's challenges.

In addition to the adventure tale and the mom-and-teen bonding story, there is a larger picture that stunned the author and gives pause to the reader: the rapidly vanishing traditional cultures that collide with Western modernization. She questions in Chapter Two, Was the runway the ribbon of life for the developing village of Wamena, or the beginning of the end for the primitive villagers?

That loss of centuries-old cultural traditions seems to expand when we fail to welcome, appreciate, and enrich our lives with neighbors who are different. The resulting wars, refugee dislocations, or local prejudice might diminish if enough readers catch the contagion of smiles, open thought, and friendship expressed by this Western mother and teen.

*"But what do dreams know of boundaries?"* **Amelia Earhart**

# Chapter 1: Throwim Way Leg

Distant voices drowned the stillness in the air. Rustling through the jungle growth, we entered a clearing of burned wild grass, which destroyed any means of concealment or protection. We stopped dead in our tracks within seconds of hearing the swishing sound of flying arrows.

"Did you hear that sound?" Katherine whispered frantically, grabbing my arm.

"Yes, but where did it come from?" I said.

"I'm scared and don't like this," she said with hesitation.

"Katherine, will you ever forgive me if we do survive this?" I said.

She took a few steps backwards but I would hear her say, "It's okay Mom. We'll be okay."

*Hiding during war games*

*Sneaking up on the enemy*

Our eyes caught two groups of local tribal men called Dani crouching in the yellow grass. Crudely carved spears protruded above bodies, glistening with pig grease. Muscled arms waved bows while calloused fingers manipulated arrows. The opening between the groups equaled the distance of a short arrow shot. The warriors watched with eyes empty of expression and lips drawn in straight lines. The men's silence led us to believe it was imperative we remain still. Opposite the smallest group, a warrior rose to his full height. He reached for an arrow and shot toward us, high over the heads of the crouched warriors. Lime-powder paint, pig grease mixed with soot, and curly plumes of the bird of paradise decorated the warrior's body.

*Dani warrior ready for a kill*

A form of paralysis swept over my entire body. Sounds of the jungle diminished beneath the drum-like beating of my heart.

My bare knees didn't feel the thorn bushes that I noticed later had left scratches on bare skin. My brain rushed into a state of crisis.

My thoughts came more rapidly when I thought I was going to die. I had to summon the courage to be stronger than my fears.

My mind, fully alert, sensed my body detached. My eyes searched for Katherine's position. Safe and secure?

Our first day in the jungle, and my expectations and foregone conclusions were dissolving.

The sudden yelling, which came from every direction, alarmed me even more. Streams of nervous sweat ran down my cheeks.

Were these cannibals out looking for their dinner or just angry warriors out to rape and kill anything in their sight?

I glanced around but could see only our guide, Julius, above my thorn-bush cover. My body felt heavy like one of those cement statues in a garden. About six feet behind me, branches from a fallen tree hid slivers of blond hair covering eyes tightly squeezed shut. I could barely see the tips of Katherine's fingers covering her ears.

I remembered about ten years ago finding Katherine as a small child standing beside a squished frog in the driveway. Her eyes closed so tightly they were nothing more than thin lines.

Her knuckles were white from pressing her hands hard against her head. I asked her why she covered her ears.

"My eyes can close, but my ears can't," she said.

Without any doubt, I expected our imminent capture. Although against government rules, cannibalism exists in the well-hidden forests of the Asmat tribes.

I knew they fought battles mainly over women, food, and land. Maybe we had trespassed on a sacred burial ground.

My trembling fingers, damp with sweat, untangled the strap of the camera, my witness to the extraordinary scene.

*Aiming spears ready for action*

*Waga Waga husband and wife hiding from enemy*

Would the movement from lifting the camera to my face trigger a barrage of arrows and spears? Ignoring us, several Dani leaped away, whooping and yelling, leaving a curtain of dust in the chaos. They never looked back and didn't seem to care about the startled intruders interrupting their war games. Laughing and singing, warriors chasing warriors crashed exuberantly down a steep embankment of loose rocks.

A group on the far side of the field ran in the opposite direction, moving their spears and bows up and down to the sounds of their chanting. There were no captives or wounded or even cries for help.

Both sides appeared content with the outcome of the battle. I looked across the field of flattened grass where minutes ago, men had crawled like lions on a hunt. I sighed with relief. Close inspection of an arrow under my boot revealed a long stem of a plant. In lifting my leg, I realized the tightness in my muscles.

Could I take another step? Katherine and I both were breathing hard as if we had just run a mile race. Instead of using the extra adrenaline filling my body for fighting or escaping, I felt satisfied facing that unsettling event. By not screaming or attacking the warriors with the pepper spray attached to my belt, I may have set a good example for my daughter.

Every exhausted muscle in my body felt the adrenaline rush dissipate. I managed enough steps backwards for my shaking hand to reach for Katherine's, cold but clammy.

"It's over. Are you all right?" I said. I hugged her with all the strength I had left to give.

She wrapped her arms around my back and squeezed. And with a half-smile said, "We survived our first real encounter with adventure, didn't we?"

A mock warfare battle between rival villages is an integral part of Dani life. I knew that mock warfare games were common, but when it was actually happening it felt real.

The men play the pretend games to impress their opponents and their women, with much time spent on making weapons and decorations to wear during the battles.

Pig grease covers their entire bodies with a coating of soot. Boar's teeth hang from their noses and bird feathers and flowers intertwine to make their head garlands. Paint and plumage transform their faces into masks.

The Dani have a legend about a snake and a bird. The race between the two was to determine the life of humans. If the snake won the race, then man should shed his skin and live forever like snakes. If the bird won the race, man must die. The bird won the race.

Using feathers, the Dani decorated their bodies, their armbands, hair, and the holes in the nose, illustrating their close spiritual relationship with birds.

Katherine later said, "The whole scene looked like a movie set, so the reality of the experience frightened me less because it didn't seem real."

Oh, to be a teen again, I thought. At that moment, I came to realize my assumptions of Katherine's maturity were correct. Acting with discrete confidence, as if nothing threatening had transpired, I absorbed a bit of her teenage courage.

I felt blessed with a new awareness of my own body to summon the strength to move forward. Throwim way leg in New Guinea pidgin language translates to "taking the first step in a long journey."

*"Travel is flight and pursuit in equal parts"* **Paul Theroux**

# Chapter 2: Runway into the Stone Age

Backpack and straw hat in place, I reminded myself that after a difficult first step, distance does not matter.

As I shifted the unbalanced weight on my back, my snail's-pace walk slowed further on the asphalt corridor that stretched lazily into the fringe of the mountains. I glimpsed a mirage of thatched huts, the sunlight playing with inquisitive eyes, spying through wood slats, cloaked in yellow.

I stepped out of the line of passengers, leaving the crowded plane, and paused for a second glance.

Flowering vines laced an enclosure around tribal huts. A brown-skinned child, wearing nothing but a smile climbed over the fence using a tree-branch ladder. When I waved, he vanished.

Someday, perhaps, I would comprehend the extraordinary sight, flanking the peculiar runway; at that moment, neither Katherine nor I knew the significance of the bamboo huts with their umbrellas of dark golden thatch, growing gourds of various shapes.

**Wamena runway**

Women went about their daytime chores without noticing the interruption of the modern world, landing nearby. Hiding behind the fence rails, Dani children's curious eyes peered out at the modern intrusions.

I stared at their small brown faces and wondered: *Do I see a culture on the brink of incalculable change? Do these children view the runway as a glimpse of their future as they watch the trail of strange-looking passengers disappear to the opposite side?*

Preoccupied, I flinched as a man, mumbling short syllables, lightly touched my shoulder and pointed to the end of the line. The airport employee wanted me to proceed toward the baggage and customs area. I looked back to find Katherine, fourteen, drifting like me out of the line of passengers. Her look of disbelief matched my feelings. *Do we sense triumph to see tribal people so soon after deplaning or alarm for what the next month might bring,* I thought?

"Get back in line," I shouted to my daughter, above the roar of an incoming plane.

"Wait for me," she yelled.

We had twenty-nine days to live experiences of a lifetime.

While enthralled with the odd juxtaposition between the ancient huts and the runway, I forgot that I had put my camera gear down on the hot asphalt. I caught myself before tripping over it with all its straps and locks. After untangling my pile of carry-on luggage, I adjusted my hat and wondered if my decision to search for a simpler existence had gone too far. Would a dream, transitioned to reality, end as a nightmare? For a moment, insecurity and fear swept over my body like shadows cast by vultures.

Then it happened. My life flashed before my eyes: a vivid moment between breaths. Walking on that runway, I felt an anticipatory glow melt all my inhibitions and fears. I saw that glow not as one of desire or lust for adventure and independence but the emergence of my dimly lit self-confidence. Each step forward caused the light of my assurance to burn brighter. Calm replaced my fearful perceptions. I had no idea of the event's significance. The runway experience helped me face the decisions that waited ahead.

My vision returned to my surroundings. An open-air building with a corrugated tin roof bordered the opposite side of the runway. The reflection from the roof blinded me, but I sensed some scrambling, dark movements in that direction. I turned toward the ancient grass huts standing in a cloud of peacefulness. I looked back at the buildings encompassing the bustle of activity, and observed uniformed men loading trucks with crates of tires while yelling at children, struggling under the weight of oversized boxes. Was the runway the ribbon of life for the developing village of Wamena, or the beginning of the end for the primitive villagers?

Walking from the plane, I felt my lightweight nylon pants filling with air like balloons. Wind or Dani spirits tugged, almost lifting me off the ground as if pulling me back in time. Spirits circle the remote Dani tribe's lifestyle, and the spirits' greeting to include me came as a surprise. My life was slowly sifting through an upside-down hourglass, and its predictability had vanished.

Katherine and I shared the common denominators of living on the edge and balancing where one challenge stopped and another began. Our extensive travels in Mexico, Guatemala, and Ecuador had taught her how to deal with primitive living. Recognizing her courage and enthusiasm after a month of disguised uncertainties in the Amazon, I believed she could face the challenges of a trip of this magnitude, exploring the jungles north of the Baliem Valley nestled and protected on the island of New Guinea, Indonesia.

I hoped to introduce her to a simpler lifestyle in a world without the distractions of our complicated lives. A place less westernized opened the possibilities for relying on our means and intuition. After reading about the Dani, whose sustenance came from the land, we became intrigued, and we wanted to observe life different from our own. To get to know ourselves better, we had decided to give up the conveniences of electricity, hot water, and fully stocked grocery shelves. I wanted nothing to fall back upon except my mind and spirit for exploration.

Those who surrounded us at the airport could not even dream of our world of superficial layers of materialism--a materialism so prevalent in our society, so common, so expected, that it has caused people living in advanced countries to react to it with indifference. Repetitious chores blurred my true objectives of discovering who I am in addition to being a mom, like a dusty road that clouds the windowpanes. This made it more difficult for me to see the light within, a light which illuminates the qualities of self-confidence and which nurtures the needs of mind and spirit.

For me, this trip meant the discovery of my inner self, a sort of self-identification. More conscious of time and not wanting it to control, I took deeper breaths. My mother taught me to live life striving for more accomplishments than I thought possible. She believed that changing our pace--through simplifying our lives--gives us a better sense of time to examine the expectations others place on us.

She once said, "Distractions, good and bad, consume our time and emotional energy. They blind us from seeing a clear path toward finding the answers to the meaning of life and self-discovery."

Leaving the excess baggage of distractions and our need for material things allowed us the opportunity to learn the art of living in unpretentious ways. I had filled my sixteen years of married life with trying to make others' lives fulfilled. I believe we must paint an image of the life we hunger to live. We can research the facts, prepare for the emotional changes, open our hearts to self-confidence, and resolve to face the challenge. The timing felt right.

I can't say for sure what pushed me forward into such primitive worlds. Perhaps I harbored a basic curiosity, a desire to reclaim my real identity, an eagerness to get back to nature, or a need to satisfy my infatuation

for understanding how primitive cultures survive. The anthropologist inside me sang her song while my spirit danced to her tune.

Research into the ancestral heritage of the Dani people enticed us to explore this unexampled valley. Unlike our society, which encourages and develops individualism, the Dani rely on a cohesive society. Traditions of the Dani define their legacy; close-knit families living with contentment take pride in their ancient customs. Their culture of cooperation, timed by centuries of experience, serves as a lifeline for their future. The Western world shares fragments of the Danis' religious beliefs, parenting skills, leadership qualities, and characteristics such as honesty and kindness.

The Dani people have a rare and irreplaceable recognition of their environment. Tribal people developed most of the world's staple crops. Both traditional and modern drugs originate from undeveloped tribal areas and the locals who are often experts with herbal remedies. As one scientist said, "When a medicine man dies, it's like a library has burned down." I thought often of the impact of that kind of loss when Luis, our guide in Ecuador, misplaced his journal, full of teachings from his father, a local medicine man. Our modern society, with its scientific, advanced culture, produces one type of progress. But there are many remote cultures with alternative living patterns that have developed, over centuries, different ways of coping with life's challenges.

Past travels with indigenous peoples taught me that differences could turn into similarities. This secret of acceptance allowed Katherine and me to integrate into the primitive lifestyle. I had been woolgathering, dreaming, as I stood in that customs line with my daughter, the blazing sun baking our skin. I heard the customs agent speaking to us. The officious little man rambled in untranslatable phrases. He then waved us into a shouting arena of guides and taxi drivers, all trying to compete for our attention. We focused on the alluring busy market across the road.

We remained alert for pickpockets and their distracting partners. Suddenly Katherine jumped sideways. The crowd had forced her backward into a pile of green limes next to a woman squatting over the dirt whose expression looked as blank as the stones under her blackened feet. A net bag hanging over the woman's naked back framed the matted plaits of her hair.

*Selling Limes*

Coils of fiber from her skirt touched the ground. A woven mat, caked with black hairs and mud, ready for the next customer's count of limes, clung to the dirt, edging the woman's dust-covered toes.

"Someone pushed me!" Katherine protested.

I answered, "Blond hair and blue eyes will attract a lot of attention here. Everyone is just trying to get a glimpse of us as we are of them."

Katherine recovered from her encounter with the tumbling limes, but her face still harbored a look of surprise and indicated her need for a hug. The brief incident jostled my normal "travel alone" state of mind. Katherine's presence with me on the journey made it imperative that I make wise decisions--and the majority of them. She needed to experience some independence and discover her own strengths, though our adventure, lived separately together, would form a bond between us, unrealized at that time. The remote cultural journey laid bare our weaknesses and apprehensions, enabling us to draw on each other's strengths. In a few days, the osmosis of the cultural ways of the Dani would filter into our mother-daughter relationship, creating changes that would last a lifetime. The strengthening of our relationship would provide the incentive to overcome the challenges and barriers of the days ahead.

As I watched the Dani woman squatting near her little store of limes, and looked around the outdoor market at the diversity of the people circling us, I knew that life has more variety than I ever dreamed. Wonder lay around every corner. Warped stands held up by tree branches held alien articles for sale.

"Mom, hurry," Katherine said. She pointed to a group of gourds overflowing with grubs, crawling over and under each other.

"Ouch, what was that?" I said.

"The guidebook called those little creatures cuscus, and a claw must have scratched you as you walked by," she said.

Cuscus, or possums, held on to their tree limb cage with the scaly end of their prehensile tails, catching their curved claws on neighboring cages full of squawking chickens. Large birds scared smaller ones from the kernels of rice spilling out of twenty-pound rice sacks, soggy with mold from lack of customers.

Horim, or penis gourds were everywhere. Neat rows, ready for wearers to insert over penises, lay stacked like firewood. A tangled pile of gourds curled around each other, hiding below on crumpled sheets of newspaper. The merchandise risked getting kicked and stepped on by all who approached. Piles of unknown objects and my shock exposed my narrow perceptions of the world.

Months of research, preparation, and planning failed to make me aware of my limited understanding of how this culture lived. The reality of what lay ahead displayed itself before us. In our homeland, hosts rolled out red carpets for dignitaries, and those carpets signaled the importance of the people who walked on them. But such splendors are not found on this distant isle. Katherine and I received a more meaningful reception as Dani people rolled out the carpet of their hearts, enabling us to walk into their lives.

*Squatting keeps the chill off*

"I can't wait to see what is inside the market!" Katherine said. A group of gray-haired men huddled for warmth and caught my attention until I felt a squeeze on my arm.

"Mom, let's go into the market," Katherine said with determination.

"We need to get rid of our luggage and check into the hotel and find a guide before we take time to look around," I said.

A loud siren startled us. Days later, we discovered the siren from the Wamena airport warns villagers crossing the runway to and from their jungle huts of an approaching plane.

After settling on a two-door taxi, we pushed and shoved our month of necessities into the four-passenger vehicle without a trunk, counting and recounting each item. We had squished everything needed for the next month into two large carry-on duffel bags. Writing materials, camera, first aid kit, books for long nights inside huts, and sixty protein bars filled our backpacks. We each had a duffle bag, backpack, jacket, and hat. Packing for the Amazon trip gave us some ideas of what to pack and what to leave at home. Research had taught me that the Dani people live on sweet potatoes. The protein bars, packed full of vitamins and twenty grams of protein, would even out that diet.

The vehicle's back seat held the sustenance of our lives, reduced to essentials.

Raw sewage trickled through mud ditches in front of rusty, tin-roofed shacks. Naked men, wearing only penis gourds, formed a single line along the edge of the road, avoiding our taxi as the driver swerved to miss potholes. The taxi tires kicked up dust that colored the men's bodies grey. My face felt glued to the window, and I couldn't form words. I wanted to say, Stop and let me open the door and take pictures or get some sign to prove seeing these tribal people wasn't a dream. The men driving the taxis came to this island from bigger cities on islands like Java with dreams of better lifestyles. Taxis were used for business officials, patrons of small stores and restaurants in Wamena, and government staff and policemen.

"Quick, look at that one!" Katherine said.

I turned to her side of the car and did a double take. "Oh my gosh! The pictures in the books never showed anything like that," I said.

"What if he'd been driving this taxi?" Katherine said.

I laughed.

"Maybe we would still be in shock and staring at him instead of outside the windows," I said.

The man, naked except for a long gourd touching his chest on one end and attached somehow to his penis on the other end, ran toward the car to get a look at us. Seeing him in real life caused both of us to stare without blinking.

Most penis gourds measure about ten inches long, maybe two inches in diameter at the base. A thin bark string, wrapped around the testicles, holds the gourd in place. Another thin string of bark attached at the narrow tip and circled around the waist or, depending on the length, up and around the neck. Anthropologists describe the Dani as phallocrypts, or penis-sheath wearers.

What kind of souvenirs would we bring home from a trip like this? My children would love showing off a stuffed cuscus or wave around some cassowary feather headdress. But penis gourds? I overheard Allie, my six-year-old, say one day to her dad, "Why does mom have all these weird things in our house?"

"Your mom loves showing off her souvenirs of how other people in the world live," her father would say.

Tribal carvings, feather headdresses from the Amazon, blowguns from Borneo, and photographs unfamiliar to a child invaded our family space, making it look like a museum. Brennan, my ten-year-old son, loved showing off to friends the normally off-limit photos magnetized to the refrigerator. The bare-breasted woman standing next to her husband, whose penis gourd almost touched his chin, giving him the appearance of having a permanent erection, made my kitchen a favorite hangout that summer. I wanted Katherine to get comfortable with the custom of men wearing penis gourds. I'm sure my friends thought the idea of having naked men in full view while reaching for some ice cubes was entirely inappropriate.

"Can you believe my sister gets to go see these people in real life?" he said to his friend Tommy, who covered his mouth, trying to hide giggles.

Tommy said, "Why aren't you going with them?"

Brennan lifted his eyebrows with, "Are you kidding? I would miss a whole month of sailing and lessons for bare-foot skiing."

We had conditioned our emotions to think of life in minimal terms, but we had jumped off the bridge without knowing how to fly. We had an insatiable appetite for the unexpected, not knowing what waited around the next corner.

Young men posing as guides flocked to our hotel, forming a ring around us as we exited the cab. Did they come to interview for a paying job or did two women traveling alone arouse their curiosity?

During previous travels, I found that young men would congregate outside airports and in front of hotels, hoping to meet with foreigners needing guides. Their knowledge of the best places to wait for work came from experiences with previous clients. The owners of the Hotel Sri Kandi enforced a rule of no visitors inside the lobby unless invited by a paying guest; however, the young, hopeful entrepreneurs followed us right into the lobby, feigning innocence of any rules. An Asian woman tried to get them to leave before giving us a room, but tireless after traveling many days to get halfway around the world, we busied ourselves asking questions as we invited the young men inside one by one.

*Downtown Jayapura*

 The two days of flying, the day lost crossing the time zone, and the three days in Jayapura awaiting a flight into Wamena, faded into minor memories. It was now the fifth day, and we had not even started our trek into the unknown. Compared to the events ahead of us, we minimized the inconveniences and the hardships we had endured. I had anticipated adventure, so my feelings wavered when our first job of hiring a guide, cook, and porters to carry our gear stared us in the face. We watched different routes ambiguously scribbled on crumpled paper during the interviews. With hand motions and little-understood English, I tried to explain our test for all the guides. They needed to comprehend our wanting, not a temporary peak moment, but a high that would last a lifetime. We sought not a place but rather discovery, exploration, and a new way to look at life.

 Older than most, a thirtyish man named Gerald seemed the most knowledgeable about the area. His infrequent, appealing smile was infectious, and he exuded a deep confidence. Somehow during the conversation, intuition told me that he might not like living in huts and eating like natives. His price of twenty-five dollars a day, plus ten dollars a day each for porters and a cook, sounded like triple the going rate. It was too early to make a decision and his fees sounded high compared to guide prices in other countries.

 "You have much money," Gerald said after I wrinkled my forehead at his prices.

Some guests in the hotel laughed. I pulled the pockets in my pants inside out like I have seen men do when telling a homeless person they have no money. "Do you see money?" I asked.

"You rich." Gerald said, "You American."

He had priced himself out of the market, and I wondered how he could afford to shine his shoes.

A boy, Indonesian, not a Dani, talked to us about taking several day trips with a few of his English-speaking buddies tagging along. Short trips to nearby villages would give us only a visual awakening to tribes, living as their ancestors had taught them. These nearby tribes gave up trying to push back the modern world of automobiles, plastic containers, soda pop, clothing, and generators for television, intruding into their lives from Wamena. Katherine and I sought a deeper palette of experiences to force confrontations with ourselves.

"I would like a trip without diversion that would allow us to experience isolation," Katherine said.

I have read that teenagers lack judgment, along with the aptitude to weigh future consequences; yet the idea of risky activities bewitches them. Katherine's abilities to memorize, forecast, and accomplish always startled me.

Isolation invites unfiltered exposure. Cut off from Western society, we would acknowledge these people with a more open mind. Open to vulnerabilities for survival, we could allow the culture to permeate through our shell of existence to our deep inner selves. As we navigated toward the unexpected, fires of exhilaration burned within. We wanted the Dani people to take us by the hand and educate us in their ways, allowing us to enter their villages, help with daily chores, and accept us as friends.

Without a clue as to what the next month would bring, we decided that before we made any definite decisions about a guide, we needed to find a nourishing meal. Afterward, we would check out the friendliness of the villagers in the market.

Past the market, we found an obscure restaurant. The unlit room inside looked clean. "On previous trips, you always warned not to eat in places that didn't have several customers," Katherine said.

"Yes, when we have more than one option, which is the best idea? Customers generally mean good, safe food. I don't see any other places to eat around here, and we want to eat before it gets too dark outside," I said.

Caution always pulled us toward the well-cooked choices on the menu, and we didn't know many words from the 185 Dani languages of the valley, but a couple of color photographs on the menu helped out.

Probably the last Western type of food for us for the next month and for sure no more meat of any kind," I said.

"We tasted monkey and snake in the Amazon last year. I want to taste some different kinds of foods while I'm here," Katherine replied.

"I'll remember that when our guide offers something unusual to eat and you're shaking your head no," I said.

We chose spaghetti, with something called chicken. The only utensils were tiny little spoons like we use to feed a baby. Kind of like a short knife with a rounded end and a shallow well for holding food. Great for twirling spaghetti. The waitress-cook dropped a white saucer on the table and oily pieces of meat toppled on the torn plastic tablecloth. We both had heard the meat frying in the hot grease as well as our stomachs growling for protein. We tried to pull the dark meat off the bones but without much luck. We were on day five of our trip, and the only protein we had had so far was eggs. The food washed down well with warm, strawberry soda. One glass had a crack all the way down the side, and the other had two chips on opposite sides of the rim, so we drank the soda from the bottles.

Every tiny shack selling groceries offered bottled soda, a common sight in fourth world countries, which are now called LDCs or Least Developed Countries. After hiking all day in the jungles of Borneo, I could not believe the unusual greeting coming toward me. A boy carried a washtub of cold river water and orange soda pop in glass bottles. The language barrier kept me from finding out how and why those sodas came to that roadless place so high in the hills.

It never ceases to amaze me the impact our Western culture of conveniences has upon the most remote and distant places. Maybe within our lifetime, we will destroy the natural evolution of remote societies. Then again, the introduction of technological advances also brought positives such as better sanitation, more access to health care, and modern medicine to save the lives of many in LDC countries.

Our visit to the outdoor market offered us the rare opportunity to appear as the observed instead of the observers. Hundreds of Dani moved about in the chaotic square, selling or buying vegetables, chickens, and every kind of body ornament imaginable. Carcasses of rats, cuscus, and birds created a stench so putrid I said to Katherine, "Take a deep breath while we walk past this area."

She said, "Why?"

Within a few seconds, she pushed me aside and took giant steps to the next set of wood planks, outlining more tables of goods for sale. A crowd she passed laughed so hard I turned to see if they were laughing at us. One woman, her bare breasts bobbing up and down from the laughing, pointed to Katherine and me, nodded, and smiled. When I caught up to Katherine I found her trying on dozens of bracelets made from strings of tree bark. I promised we would come back on our way back from our month-long trek for take-home treasures. Overwhelmed, and wanting not to be the center of attention, we kneeled against a wall. We noticed the beautiful similarities of the brilliant bird feathers between the Dani market and the markets of the Otovalo Indians of Ecuador and the Mayans of Guatemala.

An uneasy feeling followed us back to the hotel. A weakness of self-confidence materialized. No streetlights lighted our way. Children ran by, trying to touch our white skin or Katherine's yellow hair.

"Ouch," Katherine said.

"Did you step on something?"

"No, one of those boys pinched me!" she said.

The sky was so black I could hardly see her expression to know if she was scared or maybe sorry for making the decision to travel so far from home.

"Maybe they just wanted to make sure you were real," I said.

Grizzly-haired beggars extended deformed hands. Groups of men lined the gutters of disease.

"Doesn't it mean when people paint their naked bodies that they are ready for war? In western movies, the American Indians always had painted bodies," Katherine said.

I thought for a few seconds. "All the photographs I found of this culture showed men with painted bodies as if maybe it's an everyday occurrence." The locals paid no notice to the malarial mosquitoes, buzzing about the ditches filled with raw sewage.

How did we know whether our apprehensions reflected reality or the frequent urban horror stories from home? Perceptions of safety affect a person's psychological state of mind. At the moment, fearful and threatening feelings caused anxiety. Both of us were isolated from the world.

"Are we on the right road for the hotel?" I said.

"Your sense of direction is always right on, Mom," Katherine said.

"Too many distractions when we left the hotel to find the restaurant and then the market," I said.

Did personal safety boundaries of trust exist? How could we shed ingrained warning signals?

"Mom, look. Someone is waving like they want us to hurry. Maybe another guide wants us to interview him," Katherine shouted.

Answers did not come, but we returned to the hotel unharmed. This short excursion into the nighttime scene of Wamena taught me quickly that I wanted to find a guide who would diminish feelings of powerlessness and mistrust.

After waiting patiently in front of our hotel, another young boy eagerly greeted us. His boundless energy meshed with his wide smile, instilled in us a welcomed sense of trust. We needed affirmation at the end of a somewhat hurried return to a secure hotel. We talked in the lobby, often not able to comprehend with words, resorting to hand motions or drawing pictures on paper. Laughter needed no interpretation. I took to him at once. Our requirements of a guide matched the needs for any new foreign friendship: trustworthiness, patience with our questions, and the ability to understand a little English along with some of the village languages.

"How old are you, and what is your name?" I asked him.

He obviously understood English, as he shook his head, lifted his shoulders and then said, "Mama says this many." He held up fingers to equal eighteen, but he looked to be in his early twenties. I wondered if villagers kept records of births and deaths. We did not want our trip overshadowed by guide problems. Persons stranded in an unknown location in America feel frustrated and uncomfortable, but eventually, those challenges resolve themselves with a return to safety. A guide's disappearance in a remote jungle, however, could pass unnoticed, and a careless step could cause a fall or an improper gesture insult a tribal chief, which could lead to a catastrophe.

Julius, the boy, questioned me, "My help wear penis gourds?"

"Honesty and dependability wear better than clothes," I replied before realizing he might not understand what I meant.

My sign language explained walking up and down hills, along with shaking my head and repeating the word "No." Weighing less than anyone in the hotel lobby, he walked over and motioned for me to get on his back. While carrying me around the room in front of other guests, Julius laughed, and his good humor covered my embarrassment.

The Chinese hotel owner watched with a smile, so I said to her, "Okay, it's your turn."

Her lack of English caused her to shake her head, not for saying no, but probably in disbelief that her American guest would act so foolishly.

I thought, what a typical American woman's response, feeling embarrassed. I wanted to think that by leaving the traditional female boundaries at home, I gained confidence in myself; however, the thought of a slender young man carrying me up some tiny little hill made me realize a trip like ours needed physical as well as emotional strength. Might a woman in a man's job need to overcome her femininity?

The village of Wamena sank deep between two mountain ranges, which created the Baliem Valley. The reality of my simplistic back-to-the-basics adventure included hills, and I knew I would summon that energy when the time came. Making Julius aware of my climbing abilities seemed important; but in the end, I knew any grumbling would fall on Mother Nature, not Julius.

Julius shook his head and with hand motions suggested no hills. How encouraging! "Do you think Julius would make a suitable guide?" I asked Katherine.

"He is an attentive listener, has talked about hiring a cook who can prepare safe food, and is knowledgeable about the customs of the area, important for ensuring the safety of our welfare," I said.

Our previous month-long adventure in the jungles of the Amazon taught us the importance of someone who knows the area, the people, and the potential dangers of the jungle. Katherine and I soon developed a peer relationship more like best friends, rather than mother-daughter. We began to share our feelings and develop strengthened trust and respect toward each other's judgments and opinions. I minimized verbal discussion. We got close enough to read the signs of each other's thoughts through mere expression and body language.

Katherine scooted the heavy chair close to me and leaned her exhausted body against my shoulder. "He makes me laugh, plus he knew the location of all the villages on your list of places to see."

She giggled. I felt a sense of relief to see her accepting of our situation. In an ancient token of agreement, we shook hands with Julius.

By leaving the next day during the morning darkness, Julius, the four porters, Katherine, and I would find the market still asleep, an interesting contrast to the organized chaos of the twilight hours. Neither Katherine nor I could contain our excitement about starting our trek before sunrise.

I turned and squeezed Katherine's shoulders. She shivered.

"Are you ready for this or do you want to go home? We can easily change our plans and pay the penalty to fly back early?" I said.

"Are you kidding? I feel nervous but not afraid," she said.

Anticipation killed all possible hope for sleep. I looked at Katherine.

"Do you think you could deal with another walk back to the market? We could buy some rice and vegetables for the journey."

She tapped on Julius's shoulder and said, "Could we go to the market now for food and utensils for the journey, since we are leaving when it will be dark in the morning?"

The darkness suggested a quick unpacking, searching for jackets. Ignoring insecurities or apprehensions, I followed behind Katherine along the lightly graveled path and moved deeper into the journey.

The darkened market with rotted, falling-down structures intimidated me. The people next to the night sky blended with a mountain of chicory beans piled on the dirt. The market, full of hard-to-identify fruits and crude tools, begged for business. Shapes of people stood, squatted, or moved under the cover of huge blankets of banana leaves. Shadows of bird wings and bat heads from dim lanterns played on the sides of flat pieces of tin walls, separating families. The hard-packed dirt floor comforted children, sleeping between piles of cut wood and claws of birds' feet. Naked men lay curled over mattresses of sweet potatoes. Julius used his bargaining power to obtain our twenty pounds of rice, two red bowls, one wok for cooking, two cups, and two spoons. "Not much food for a month in the jungle," I said to Julius, standing maybe too far for him to hear my comment.

He pointed to a blue washtub, full of wiggling sago palm maggots. He plopped one in his mouth and extended his cupped hand with several toward Katherine. She grabbed my arm and squeezed like a silent signal to protect her.

"You said you wanted to try some local foods," I said. I hugged her with a look of not even if you wanted to try them would I let you.

I waved Julius away and said, "We no eat!"

Without pause I pointed to both of us and made motions in a horizontal mode with my hands and then pointed to my mouth. I turned back to Katherine and said, "Are you okay? Maybe we should have brought more peanut butter and protein bars?"

"We can eat rice so we won't starve. Maybe along the way some villages will have fresh vegetables we can buy," she said.

"I remember reading about the protein, fat and vitamin content of insects in a scientific article and in cases like grubs and caterpillars, it's higher than soy protein. The tribes cut down a sago palm tree and cut open the trunk and let it sit for three months. When they come back, hundreds of grubs or maggots fill the trunk," I said.

"You mean they eat them raw? In the Amazon, they cooked them in oil. I remember trying them and they were crunchy not gooey," she said.

"The strange thing is how they clean their ears with the worms," I said.

"No way and I don't want to hear this," she said.

"They put the worms in their ears. The worms eat their ear wax, and then they remove the worms and eat them!" I said. Back home in Missouri I thought about how to prepare for the dramatic change in quality and amount of food our journey might offer. Well-cooked foods like pasta, rice, soup, and scrambled eggs won our votes over the stranger and more unusual fare that research told us to expect as normal. Locals chose the larvae of Capricorn beetles or the sago weevil as favorites. Various caterpillars, snakes, crickets, and grubs steamed in taro leaves caused me to shudder, thinking about our potential diet for the next four weeks.

An uneventful march took us back to Hotel Sri Kandi for a long anticipated sleepless night. We pondered what might lie ahead.

I lay in bed thinking aloud, "We have almost a whole month ahead of us in a jungle full of unknowns. Do you think Julius has ever guided anyone before?

Do you think the cook he hires will understand our need for safe food? Long days of walking from village to village require time for rest. Will we be able to communicate our needs to these people?"

"Mom, go to sleep!" Katherine mumbled. "You showed the government permit we had to get into Jayapura a few days ago to the hotel owners, so they know where we are going and when to expect us back here. Julius watched as they copied that information into their notebook, so try to enjoy sleeping on a mattress for the last time in a long while."

I had forgotten about the travel permit required to travel in remote areas of New Guinea. We had to apply for the permit in Jayapura, with our photographs and travel documents. The document cost nothing and had limitations of a thirty-day visit. We had to return it on our departure. I didn't feel any sense of security, though, thinking an official would come looking for us if we didn't return.

An adventure had found its way into our lives. Our reassurance came from Helen Keller's quote, "Life is either a daring adventure or nothing."

*"I soon realized that no journey carries one far unless, as it extends into the world around us, it goes an equal distance into the world within."* **Lillian Smith**

## Chapter 3: Wrapped Like Birthday Presents

**Streets in Wamena**

    Our first day in Wamena gave us the opportunity to ease into the Dani lifestyle, giving us a taste of the laid-back attitudes of the people there.
    Women wearing four-inch wide strips of tree skin and sago fiber skirts covering only their privates, and men wearing only penis gourds added to our culture shock.
    The lack of western food, hot showers, or tourists along the way heightened my excitement on the eve of our journey.

*Porters waiting for hire*

Hours before sunrise, any misgivings I developed while organizing my gear lasted less than a minute at the sight of the porters and cook standing in a line on the hotel porch. Their appearance signaled the beginning with no time for second thoughts about whether to move forward or go home. This journey removed any anchors to the reality we left back in the United States.

"It's colder than I thought it might be during the early morning hours," I said.

Katherine said, "Are you cold or scared or both?"

"Let's do this," I said as I looked at her for a sign of approval.

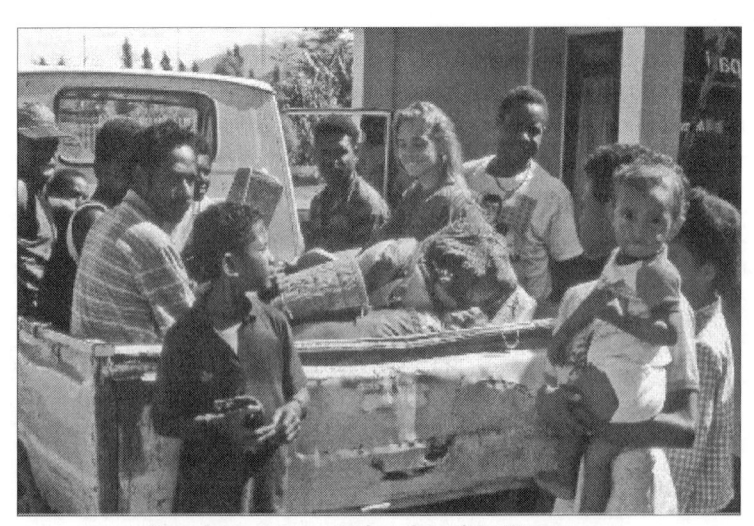

*Truck transportation leaving Wamena*

An old pickup truck pulled up to the porch of the hotel. I said, "That looks like it was rescued from a junkyard."

No comments or smiles came from anyone as each member of the trekking party climbed aboard the truck to take us ten kilometers away from food we recognized, electricity, and beds with mattresses.

"Katherine, let's sit on my bag. Nothing breakable inside," I said.

Our luggage took up half the space of the truck bed, compared to Julius's child-sized ragged backpack.

"Julius, why is your bag so small for a month trek?" I said.

In broken English, he said, "I only need one shirt, one pair of jeans, one pair of socks and my sunglasses."

After a while, the gravel road abruptly ended as if the powerful jungle controlled its destiny. Mountains painted with watercolor-like strokes of chestnut trees and evergreens stood wrapped in the midnight blue of the sky. Katherine, the five strange men, and I jumped to the ground, signaling the beginning of our month-long trek. A haunting wind touched our arms, legs, and faces. Katherine and I ignored the questioning look on each other's face. The challenge lay ahead as we walked in a shadowy dream, waiting for the night colors to dissolve. My feet, reminding me of the stiffness of my new hiking boots, endured their suffering while I considered the significance of the moment. The claustrophobic jungle, my new home for the next month, surrounded me. Four strange men walked ahead of Katherine and me: one, wearing only a penis gourd, walked behind. I wanted the words in my journal to reflect the strangeness of our new encounter, not hurting feet.

The porters conveyed uneasiness with the weight of our packs on their backs. The Dani people carry heavy loads balanced on their heads, but the floppy duffel-type luggage had straps for the shoulders, and I encouraged with hand motions for the porters to use them.

"Mom, you need to show Coughin how to carry the backpack so the weight doesn't hurt his back," Katherine said with a mischievous, almost daring look.

"How do you reach the straps and pull them forward to adjust the buckle in front on a stranger wearing only a penis gourd?" I said. A real test.

"I can figure this out. Just watch me," I said as I wondered how spoiled they must think we are with all this stuff.

Coughin's face and muscles looked strained. I motioned for Coughin to take the bag down from the top of his head and helped him with the shoulder straps. I pointed to the waist straps and made signs to pull them forward which he did but, of course, he had no idea of how to buckle the straps.

"Julius, would you help buckle the waist straps so this pack is more comfortable for him?" I said.

Katherine and I adjusted our small packs. "My pack feels heavier than when we went out walking every night at home with the packed bag on our back, trying to get used to the weight," I said.

"We're going to be in such good shape by the end of this journey," Katherine said.

And we were on our way. Katherine and I listened uneasily as the porters chanted in monotone. I did not know if they were attempting to wake the birds or scare off possible predators, lurking on the path ahead. Sweeping treescapes, concealing our path, persuaded nature to display its haunting riches in the jungle. The overlapping vegetation included velvet mosses and fungi on the ground and blue bamboo canes swaying thirty feet above. Those canes selfishly used sunlight for their own growth and created a tangled web. A profusion of plant species clung to vines for support and filled the void with a natural chaos.

"Julius, what are those?" I questioned, looking high in the canopy. Brown pods like corn on the cob without kernels decorated tree branches like Christmas-tree ornaments.

"Mucuna," he said. He then added, "Don't touch," as I bent over to pick one up that had fallen. He squinted and pointed to his eyes and said, "Poison."

I learned after returning home that the mucuna pods are covered in microscopic hairs that cause burning if they get in your eyes.

Each step taken dissected a new layer, and Julius helped interpret instead of just letting us stare at the wonder of its splendor.

Twisted vines seized every opportunity to wrap themselves around our bare legs. Breathing in the clammy dead air made me cringe.

Far removed from city noises, fresh-cut park paths, and access to life's take-for-granteds, I looked at Katherine while pulling a spider web from my hair and said, "Do you think we will get used to this?"

"I feel like a kid again, sloshing through the swampy woods behind our house, searching for the hermit who hid in that little cabin with the roof falling in. Did someone really live there, Mom? Or did you just make up that adventure for us?" she questioned.

Her brow wrinkled with concern for my discomfort and my obvious show of uncertainty. Had we been in the comfort of our own home, I could imagine Katherine's reply: an exasperated "Oh, Mother!" Here in this land of unknowns, she seemed to have grown up overnight. Or did both of us grow together? We could sense our developing bond; we were already beginning to rely on each other for mutual support.

We started out knowing this trip would last for one month. At first I had thought the responsibility of assuring Katherine's safety and continual involvement would cascade in on me; yet, I did not want my mother's instinct or my over-protectiveness to oppress or burden her. Aware of her intrepid spirit, I left the unfounded concerns behind, worries such as we might starve on only one bowl of rice a day or how uncomfortable we might feel when sleeping with strange men in our grass huts.

Months of reading books from anthropologists contributed to my understanding of the various indigenous tribes I wanted to meet. Sharing all I'd learned with Katherine gave her the understanding that this trip would offer incredible experiences. My research, or a selfish desire to escape the stresses of society, did not reveal the true magnitude of the potential dangers I placed before us. Had I foolishly put my daughter in danger? Did widening her horizons justify the risks we were taking?

Katherine's compassion for humanity, plus her level of patience and adaptability, gave her a head start, compared to most girls her age. My friends described their daughters as overly dramatic and stressed about even little things. Their daughters were money-oriented, needed immediate gratification, and were me-centered. Katherine didn't have the need to do things to fit in or to be cool by smoking or drinking.

Sometimes teens, including Katherine, do reckless and dangerous things just for the fun of it. As adults, our experiences alter the paths we choose to follow. Adulthood produces barriers we accept as parents, such as becoming protective.

Over-involvement ruins the opportunity for discovery and independence. Every decision a parent makes is one fewer for the teenager to make for himself/herself. Each day a parent keeps a teenager dependent on him/her is one fewer day the teen has to become independent.

My best friend, Hallie, when she found out about my upcoming trip said, "How can you take your daughter on such a dangerous journey?"

I said, "If I had had the chance for a trek into the jungles at age fourteen, and my mother said, 'Sure let's go,' I wonder how that would have changed my life. What if she would have said no to the opportunity? Would that negative answer have changed my attitude about my mother?"

My parents were good role models, never answering all my questions, opening a search for my own journey. I wanted to allow Katherine to learn and grow and accept who she is, not whom I felt she should be. Back home there was a need to be in control by making decisions for her based on what I believed was right or wrong. By my asking questions and listening to her answers, I hoped she would begin to make her own mistakes and achieve her own successes. As Katherine's guide, I found myself tapping into her youthful spirit which helped me in the process of letting go of previous restraints. Katherine's father and I set high expectations for our children. Parenting is deeply transformative and constantly changing. Leaving three of my four children at home gave me an unknown freedom for sleeping late, reading all night, singing out of key, or wearing my socks inside out without explanation. Pride and admiration for the daughter I had raised filled my mind as I thought of her willingness to leave her teenager's social life to bathe with piranhas in dirty rivers in the Amazon. This fact alone convinced me of her yearning to understand the forgotten people and select some of their virtues to implement in her lifestyle.

Neither Katherine nor I understood what facts of life we would uncover about the Dani people and ourselves. Most people visualize tribal people wearing clay or wooden masks. Medicine men and tribal dancers used masks to interpret religious and burial ceremonies for protection from disease, infertility, and famine. People of civilized cultures wear masks as well. Our invisible masks disguise our real individuality.

The outer layers of our character consist of the masks we use to conceal our real selves. We wear these faces to protect ourselves from the judgment of others. Pretending to take the role of something or someone else makes us a better version-- or even a persuasively different version--in order to be accepted. Masks of a classy dresser, domineering boss, close friend, sports enthusiast, submissive wife, helpful neighbor, or hotshot driver all protect us from neglect by others. We wear masks to influence our associations with the people of the world in which we live.

Anxiety about the remoteness of our location and cloudy feelings about the Dani opened our watchful eyes. My vulnerabilities became clear to me within this strange culture, yet my ability to transform myself into a resourceful and rugged woman came from my temporary travel mask. Through foresight, I kept my insecurities from presenting an obstruction that blocked Katherine's path to achievement. The primitiveness of our trip peeled away the false layers we were wearing, as we shed our weaknesses and revealed our strengths. Each new encounter with the differences between our native hosts and us developed our character, helping us remove the masks we were expected to wear back home.

***

Dust, still damp from the morning dew, clung to our new boots as the sojourn into the New Guinea rainforest continued, away from our cat and all the conveniences of home. Stripping away the cushions of our existence--air conditioning, cars, hot showers, and such--gave us the potential to reawaken the mysteries of our inner souls.

Our destination, the Baliem Valley, snug and cozy in the earth's lap, allowed our escape from self-imposed boundaries. Julius whistled a tune. Panus, our cook, carried a rice sack full of cooking supplies. Amir, DenDee, and Coughin, the porters, shared the twenty pounds of rice and our two twenty-five pound packs, essential for our trek into the jungle. The clothed men, aged past twenty, carried no luggage of their own. Coughin, the exception, wore only the penis gourd and didn't know his age. The men thought of themselves as entrepreneurs, living in the "city." We wished that Coughin could share his life's tales with us. Our clues were his grey hair and withering naked body, sporting only the traditional penis gourd worn by all Dani villagers. Julius, with Papuan features, spoke enough English to offer a translation of villages' lifestyles. Unlike the other porters and cook, a mop of frizzy curls covered Julius's head; his face featured bushy eyebrows, a flattened forehead, broad nostrils, and thick, swollen-looking lips.

As dawn hovered above the leafy clouds, the moody silence changed, awakened by our footsteps on the fractured earth, bare of earlier tracks. Traces of previous movement ahead showed in broken branches, not in footprints on the ground. Like new-mown grass, the uncurling growth of giant tree ferns supplied nature's scent of freshness. Silvery half-lights penetrated faint grey-blue shadows. Plant life illustrated the kindly influence of light and air. In a winterless land of impenetrable vegetation, drenched in shrouds of mist, I conjured images of unfamiliar and dangerous beasts hiding, unseen. Relentless creepers coiled around the elephantine trunks, sending their young tendrils up high to seek smaller branches for quiet destruction.

Camouflaging themselves, snakes, hanging like vines, added a vertical dimension to fear. Bulging gray muscles of the ironwood tree accentuated the emerald, tree-monitor lizard, motionless from the fear of strange activity. Wanting to examine every detail,

I reached for a fuzzy, heart-shaped leaf, but before I touched it, Panus's hand grabbed mine.

Julius shrieked, "The stinging tree has hundreds of poisonous needles under the leaves!"

I jerked my hand back as the threatening magnitude of the jungle towered over me with its awesome beauty, held in balance between powerful evils.

Feeling small and inexperienced, I felt my independent nature threatened. It would require deliberate thought on my part to learn from Julius's knowledge and hesitate before becoming inquisitive.

I looked at the mass of foliage around me with a renewed sense of awe and trepidation.

Interlocked tree crowns, a hundred feet high, offered flashes of reds and greens from fruit pigeons. Wings flashed and fought in the tree crowns for the same opening in a tree. Tiny feathers sprinkled downward like raindrops on a summer day.

With each step, Katherine and I cleared our legs of foliage, sprinkling water droplets in every direction.

Moisture burned the open cuts and scratches that crisscrossed our bare arms and legs.

Sticky, sweltering heat seemed the perfect weather for shorts and short sleeves, but these articles of clothing were the ignorant selections of a suburban housewife and her teenage daughter, not accustomed to the untamed wilderness.

I guess Katherine thought it was funny.

Choking from laughing hard, she said, "Why did we even bring shorts and short-sleeve shirts on this trip?"

*Author jungle walking*

"Mothers are practical but not always heroic," I said. Better common sense would come into play as we learned of the harsh realities of our surroundings.

Beetles and cockroaches scrambled across our path knocking their leafy safety helmets from side to side. Ahead of Julius, dead branches crashed toward their final resting place.

A huge fig tree (everything here belonged in a giant's garden) quivered as several hornbills showed off their brilliant red-orange necks and protruding beaks.

Startled by the machete chopping new paths, they took flight, creating a whirlpool of frenzy, stirring their gray bodies, larger than those of hawks.

As they began their glide path, they seemed to turn into white tail feathers. In an instant, a brushstroke of sunshine painted our path with an invitation to springtime. Tangles of rattan, bamboo, and ferns, all covered by silver, velvet lichens and mosses, exploded from the undergrowth with each step of our heavy hiking boots.

Liana, woody vines that climb trees, wound from the exhausted soils, giving rattan canes a place to grasp and climb.

Memories of the scent of orchids from my mother's sun porch helped me deal with the mildewed air.

Suddenly, Katherine shouted, "Look!" Clusters of orchids festooned the broad base of a nearby tree "Why haven't we seen more flowers?"

"Nutrient poor soils are created from heavy rainfall, which leaches minerals and carbon from the soil. With the additional warm temperature, decomposition happens very quickly in rainforests.

The red color of the soil reflects the presence of iron oxide due to chemical weathering. Orchids known as air plants absorb water and nutrients from the air, so they grow freely without needing soil for growth.

Decaying material like dead wood and leaves are recycled so fast that they never reach the soil due to the abundance of decomposers like fungi and termites," I said.

Nature's extravagant adaptations thrived in this place. After questioning Julius about the plant life, I saw him point to several pitcher plants, explaining how their leaves form cups of rich liquid, attracting and drowning insects. The liquid actively dissolves the bodies forming nourishment for the plant.

We became living witnesses to a thousand shades of perfection in a world singing with color. Walking greater distances from Wamena would offer a multitude of little pockets of tribes, each with its own traits and characteristics. Welcoming our presence as a gift, not an intrusion, the villagers would, we hoped, allow us to stay long enough to grow roots, not just pass through like sightseers.

The experience with the tribal men and their arrows flying over our heads was foremost in our thoughts as we walked toward a village.

Paul Theroux's words came to mind, "Travel is flight and pursuit in equal parts."

The arrow adventure left us with the ambivalence of wanting to turn around and go home, yet going forward to see what we could see. Did the strangeness of our afternoon meeting with the painted warriors make sense? Research led us to believe New Guinea was a land of human treasures that would be revealed to us if we chose to move onward.

*Mothers gathering children for festival*

One day of trekking, and already we were ahead of our plans for integrating with the indigenous tribes.

The jarring truck ride before sunrise, initiation into long walks, and seeing tribal men in action gave us more distance from the city life of Wamena.

*Children of Waga Waga*

    Under the shade of a tree, a group of children painted to look like birthday presents called to us with their smiles. I loved the name of their village, Waga Waga. Thatch-like golden umbrellas draped over little huts and glistened in the background. Women, possibly looking for the scattered children, saw us. Apprehensive at the sight of light skin and hair, they slowed their stomping and clapping.
    Girls with white polka-dotted faces encouraged the women to line up single file. With deliberate steps, they circled us, freezing now and then, long enough to holler "ieee!" As the tempo increased with their shouts, they added a few dance steps.

*Dani villagers dancing*

Flexing their knees, they slapped their hands against the earth in unison. With Katherine and me in the middle, the group danced past an opening in the fence. Their withered-from-the-sun faces lacked smiles.

Pregnant-looking bellies toppled over four-inch-long sago fiber skirts, covering private parts below. Diets low in calories and protein but high in starch cause a condition known as kwashiorkor.

The most obvious symptom is distended stomachs seen in women and children who are not allowed to eat pork.

With their shaved heads, the women looked like men except for their saggy breasts, tired of nursing for five years.

Somehow, through the dust and confusion, my wrinkled brow and tight squeeze on Katherine's hand relaxed. I looked at the women in the circle and hoped that they would see, before the differences, the things that were the same.

Although we wore strange body coverings and had physical differences, we smiled and acted friendly. Katherine gave me a curious look, raising her shoulders and eyebrows with a silent question of, what next?

*Carrying spears for hunting*

A procession of four warriors appeared, their gentle attitude concealed by their fierce features and bodies painted for war games. More warriors joined as the four danced past the group of women, creating a rhythm with their feet and loud cries.

*Curious looks given to our surprise arrival*

*Katherine watching the activities*

A little compassion, although frail, trickled through the group when a couple of children guided Katherine and me to the middle of the half circle of huts and log chairs.

*Our arrival gave reason to continue the dancing*

Every couple of minutes, the men jumped up and down, extending their arms as if to shoot their bows, keeping the spirits at a safe distance. Women seesawed and changed places with younger boys, shouting stories to the elders.

*Was this really happening?*

The dancing and chanting kept the spirits happy, and the make-believe shooting of arrows protected villagers from interference by those spirits, lingering around and trying to cause bad luck.

Teenage boys joined the dance, their deep rhythmic sounds increasing as they moved toward us and then fading after they passed the other women.

Arms reached for us to join in with the beat of the songs. Within minutes, we joined the group, dancing as generations have before, smiling and clapping.

I felt like I was in a trance with all my senses on fire. Were the music's vibrations the villagers' heartbeats?

Our surprise arrival gave the village a reason to celebrate all day, well into the night. The women swayed back and forth in the same spot and never seemed to tire.

The men stopped dancing to chase a pig that wove in and out of their legs. The pig darted about, looking for an escape.

A boy spread his arms and legs like wings and leapt upon the pig long enough for two men to grab it by its tail and snout.

"Julius, why are they trying to capture that pig?" I said.

"Quick! Turn your camera on!" he said.

*Killing a pig with bow and arrow*

The village chief, with his bow and arrow, shot directly into the pig's heart. As the two Dani dropped the dying pig to the ground, its squeals faded and its wiggling limbs grew still.

Katherine, stunned by the suddenness of this event, looked at me, her mouth open in shock. My head filled with questions for the Dani. Words could not describe our reactions to the scenes surrounding us.

Overwhelmed and somewhat anxious about our safety, again I wondered about the wisdom of bringing my daughter into this wildness.

I wanted to photograph every detail, and while I concentrated on the camera, it was all I could do to capture the activity around me.

I hated to admit that my craving for photography related to greed. A sensitive documentarian dwelling on transitory things in a culture that becomes lost with time might best describe me. Instead of using the words "create" or "borrow," camera brochures use the words, "take more photographs."

There I was stealing, from this complex society, memories that I wanted to own, not forget, during my rocking-chair days.

The other half of my addiction had to do with sharing rare images with anyone wanting a better understanding of who shares their world.

The bewitching details of this peculiar sight, impossible to absorb, would come back to me night after night in the following days.

*Women wearing noken*

*Author trying to absorb the entire scene*

Several hours passed as we watched the village prepare for the feast. We chose to sit on a log out of the way of activity.

For a moment, I embraced Katherine, wanting to share my excitement, and maybe just to let her know that I felt at ease with this situation.

*Forked stick for carrying rocks*

*Building a fire in Waga Waga*

Everyone had a job. The strange tranquility, along with the villagers' legacy of rituals including their invitation for spiritual ancestors to participate, felt puzzling but genuine. No music played in the background, only the rustle of bamboo canes, fighting with the wind. A siren of cicadas announced the coming of dusk. The scene reminded me of previous family camping trips with everyone pitching in to help set up camp before dark, with the only sounds coming from nature. Katherine and I had completed Chapter One of our adventure. Feelings of satisfaction began as I lost my initial fear of the unknown.

*Individuals design their own penis gourds*

With his splayed toes, an elder held a piece of bamboo cut into a V shape. From years of barefoot walking over rocks and vines, the Dani's huge feet developed calloused bottoms, ragged toenails, and flat, wide toes.

He forced a second piece of bamboo through the forked end, rubbing the sticks against each other to create friction. Bent at the waist, he blew on the sticks.

Within seconds, sparks, smoke, and then flames erupted. He lit the bamboo and grass with those flames.

Two children placed the entire pig on the fire, turning it over as its hair singed. Tiny particles of pig hair polluted the air, along with a sickening, unfamiliar smell.

Thirty minutes later, the chief and two elders sharpened their bamboo knives with their teeth.

They stripped tiny pieces of bamboo at an angle to create the sharp point. Two muscled men lifted the pig by its stiff legs, the animal still smoking from the fire. They carried it to a blanket of banana leaves.

A teenage boy scraped the leftover hair off the pig using the edge of a piece of bamboo.

Katherine and I wrinkled our noses at the smell of the singed hair and moved away. Not for a second did we take our eyes off the pig.

*Chopping the raw pork*

According to precedent from myth, the elder who started the fire also made the first cut into the pig.

The three grinning tribal men then made the customary incisions, their voices lost in the sound made by the stone adze, chopping the bones. The stone adze has a short wooden handle attached by a laced bark string.

The stones came from a natural quarry fifty miles to the northwest, but local villagers made the handles.

Adzes could cut down trees, much like an ax, and sharpen digging sticks for farming.

*Women check pork under the steaming grass and rocks*

One man motioned for us to come closer to watch. The whole mess nauseated me.

I take for granted my organized and spotless grocery store. Reminding myself I came to observe how tribal cultures live, I quieted my queasy stomach and, gracious about the invitation, moved in for a better look.

Bloody hands wrapped the dissected parts of the pig in banana leaves.

I realized I had not spent a lot of time teaching Katherine how to cook. Preparing raw beef, chicken and pork gave me some experience in dealing with blood and other organs.

"Does this make you want to become a vegetarian?" I asked.

"No way am I trying this pork even after it's well-cooked!" she said.

Whether some parts of the organs had a spiritual or other meaning, we could not guess, but a few pieces lay beside the wrapped pieces.

The chief stretched the intestines, pointed to the sun, and ran his fingers down the string of his bow, indicating that little would go to waste and that the intestines made perfect bowstrings. He picked up lacey, green ferns to clean his hands.

*Females don't shave their heads until they marry*

Young, naked children straddled the fence, waving pinwheels made of fine palm leaves, waiting for a breath of air to blow and make the pinwheels spin.

A boy, his body painted white, ran past chasing a blue butterfly while swinging a forked stick from side to side.

The forked end, which had passed through many webs of the large bird spider, created a net for catching butterflies.

Bird spiders reverse the order of prey by building strong webs and capturing birds to eat.

Julius explained to me that the children sometimes place strands of fire grass securely around the live butterflies to let them fly alongside them while running.

The play activity of children in our society contrasts sharply with that of the Dani children.

The children appeared as happy, if not happier, than those at home, yet the Dani children knew nothing of battery-operated toys, video games, or bright plastic playthings.

As we watched, they ran, jumped, and giggled, their happiness and energetic ingenuity revealing their childlike spirits.

*Children baby sit siblings while parents work in the fields*

Another compelling contrast between American children and the Dani children was evident in their behavior when the choice came to either compete or share. While American children would most decidedly compete to see who could catch the largest butterfly, the Dani adopted the sharing spirit of playing for fun.

They actively moved to help each other get the biggest butterfly. I also noted that their storehouse of activities did not include dominating types of games, but instead encouraged development of those skills which would strengthen their proficiency in living off the land while developing the dependencies upon each other needed to survive in such primitive surroundings.

A young man sat watching the children, his legs stretched out in the dirt. As they continued to catch butterflies, kicking up dust in the process, the man mumbled something. He smiled and pointed with the look of a father. I asked Julius if he had heard what the man said.

Julius replied, "The elder talks about the good etai-eken his child had."

He explained the meaning of the etai-eken, or "seeds of singing." Seeds located in the lower back of a newborn baby represented all the characteristics of his heart and soul. By the age of one, the baby's seeds move under the arch of the rib cage, where they beat under the skin.

Strong ties within family groups keep the spirits of the seeds from neglect that might cause death. Elders place importance on the happiness and health of individuals. The Dani believe these seeds, or etai-eken, control their lives and have supernatural powers. The seeds of singing provide a continuous influence on the development of every individual's fate.

Spirits of the seeds support good health, but also encourage suffering. Unhealthy villagers cover their bodies and stay home, so that spirits won't see them and cause their etai-eken any harm. People fear the loss of seeds in their sick or wounded family and friends. They do not want to see their loved ones lose their etai-eken.

A wesarun, or curer, will have to try to call the seeds back into place by blowing rapid breaths on wounds or in the ears of sick individuals. He asks the seeds to return to their normal place while waving a feather wand toward the ribs of his patients.

Friends and relatives believe that the death of a Dani weakens their own etai-eken. The fact that someone else's etai-eken can affect the etai-eken of others helps individuals support and strengthen each other.

Members of a village encourage cleanliness for better health, and they help each other with farming and rebuilding of homes, so that all the community has enough to eat and is guaranteed shelter from the elements.

Leaving Julius, Katherine motioned for my attention. "Where is your camera?" she asked.

"Sitting on that log," I replied. "I'll get it and you can take a picture."

"Julius, why are those men removing hair from their bodies?" I said.

*Watching a celebration*

*Teenager helps with the forked bamboo pole*

Some of the men sat in pairs, plucking hair from the shoulders of their partners with tweezers made from the bark of the araucaria tree.

"This is a local custom for the Dani men. They try to remove most of their body hair unless they are in mourning or sick," he said.

In every direction, we could see a frenzy of activity.

Katherine and I positioned ourselves out of the way, but close enough to feel involvement in the excitement.

A crimson sun mimicked the stunning hues of hanging vines nearby. I took my sunglasses off while standing in the middle of a group of children.

They took turns screaming with delight at their reflections in the lenses. A boy about ten years old offered me a hand-rolled cigarette he had lit.

Young girl helping

The festival continued for more than an hour, as women used long, pronged sticks to turn rocks they had laid in the twelve-foot fire pit. Men added firewood they had split with a stone adze. From outside the compound, young girls walked with perfect posture, balancing heavy bundles of fresh-cut grasses for the fire pit.

The women used the pronged sticks to move the rocks to the baking hole. The deep four-foot-square opening held layers of wet grass, sweet potatoes, hot rocks, and more grass.

Smells of steaming pork create excitement

Coils of bark rope are wrapped around the oven

An old woman's stubby little hand sprinkled water over the pile with a gourd, once yellow, but blackened with soot. Men piled the wrapped pork high on top of the banana-leaf oven, followed by more hot rocks sprinkled with river water. Spear grass extended outside the hole, and the people worked together to fold it over the pork, wrapping a thin piece of rattan around the bundle. It would take a few hours for the hot rocks and wet grass to steam the pork.

Hungry mouths delighted at the thought of a special dinner. Mesmerized by the air, carrying its own invigorating spell, we sat watching. Our measure of contentment had little to do with time. The roast pork blew a delicious smell our way as shadows fell gently around us.

*Moving hot rocks from the fire pit over to the oven*

Women went about their unhurried tasks, manipulating long, pronged sticks to pick up the cooled stones, covering the pork and potatoes.

They dropped the stones into the bright tongues of flames in the fire pit, wanting to reheat them. Hummed melodies of haunting fascination came from men's and women's dusk-darkened faces.

The magic of that moment held me there.

Darkness settled in the valley, with the sun melting into the tops of trees.

*Separating the cooked pig into serving pieces*

Two men cradled bundles of banana fronds and brought them over to the chief. Children scrambled for drippings of grease as the chief unwrapped the pork. Men positioned themselves around the banana leaves using the standard eating utensils in the village: their fingers.

*Females eat sweet potatoes as it is taboo to eat pork*

Women uncovered the sweet potatoes and passed one to each adult male before sitting in a separate circle to enjoy their own portions of the meal. Females, forbidden to eat pork, missed the protein-rich meat. Julius did not have the answer as to why when he told us facts like this one. I suspected the harvest from the peanut fields supplemented the women's diet, along with roots, plants, and insects.

The women had sharpened their survival skills to a razor's edge. The elders treated us like guests of honor, with privileges the tribal women did not have, almost as if inventing a third sex. Men and women worked and played with members of their own gender. Women slept in their own huts with children and the pigs.

I said to Julius, "I wonder why the women stay so far away from their husbands and even sleep in a separate hut."

Julius stepped close and explained, "Tribal men shoot a bow and arrow at a woman entering a man's hut without permission."

I said, "You mean they would harm their own wife?"

He replied, "It's just how they live."

I said to Katherine, "We're being honored as special guests."

She responded, "This is a bigger treat than I ever expected to see when we planned this trip."

*Should he dance?*

*Exotic headdress of fur*

*Anxious for a rare treat*

Men invited us to dance with them and handed Katherine a hand-rolled tobacco cigarette.

Pig's teeth attached through the nasal septum looked uncomfortable as we moved in close to squat next to a man. I could see light passing through that opening as another man came close to offer more cigarettes.

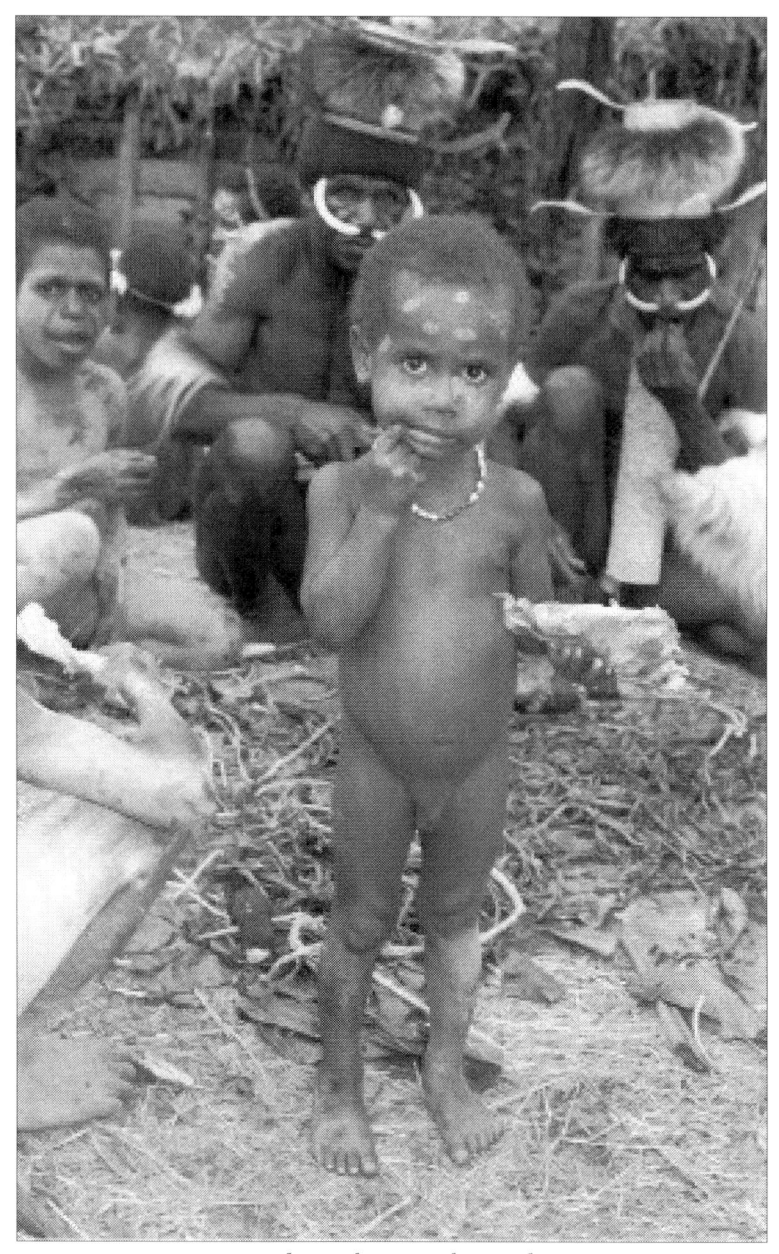

*Only males eat the pork*

"Why do you think some men wear the pig's teeth in their noses, and others don't?" Katherine asked.

"I don't know what it signifies. Maybe it means they recently killed a boar."

The chief motioned for us to join him. His hands dripped juice to his elbows when he lifted two chunks of pork toward us but not the other women.

With butterflies still dancing in our stomachs from the circle of events surrounding the pig, we, with hesitation, declined the roasted pork.

To offend the chief by refusing his gift of food might cause unforeseen problems. We took that chance to upset the chief as we were not willing to take the chance of getting sick from eating undercooked pork.

Before the trip began, we had decided that undercooked, non-refrigerated meat created potential health concerns.

Neither Julius nor the chief understood the idea of a vegetarian diet but honored our wish to concentrate on potatoes.

*Inserting pig's teeth*

The pig bones, licked clean by the male members of the tribe, looked as if they had gone through the laundry.

The owner of the pig inserted the tusks through a hole in his nose to please the spirits.

Julius explained that if men respected the bones of killed pigs and kept them holy, the happy spirits would allow living pigs to grow fat.

Strength, he said, came from eating the pork, and the leftover bones represented the symbol of life in the spiritual world and the material world.

*Eating a sweet potato*

My previous hours of research about the history of the Dani never gave me the answers to many questions such as why the females did not eat the protein of the pork.

If the pork gave strength, then maybe the males did not want to tolerate an increase in female strength.

The ceremony concluded with smiles all around. What began in me as a gripping fear had transformed into gratitude for the position of honor that Katherine and I enjoyed. Reviewing our full day of activity, my mind pondered the possibility of various reversals. For example, had a few Dani, half-naked and with pork bones pierced through their nostrils, walked into a neighborhood barbecue in our country, would we receive them with open arms? Would we have rolled out a carpet of hospitality and sharing, making them the guests of honor?

My immersion into their primitive way of life happened fast. I didn't notice any discomfort from the lack of fresh salads or normal routines.

Instead, I felt the environment heighten my awareness, similar to the ways of the Dani people. My managed life at home directed my responsibilities and influenced my thoughts, leaving little time for living in the moment.

I live in an age of distraction. The simplistic lifestyle of the wilderness pushed aside that chaotic rhythm of life, allowing me to refocus.

Two women alone adjusted to a darkening jungle. The presence of friends back home would tend to alter my reactions. Here friends didn't trespass on my thoughts. I could invite life in.

Unknowingly, the villagers of Waga Waga revived my mental state with a freedom for accepting me and others.

*The chief gives Katherine a set of pig's teeth*

The technological and material differences between the Dani culture and ours made us aware of every moment. More important, the traits of human nature in the Dani culture compared to our own. Our search to satisfy our curiosity about how another culture lives had begun. Ours seemed quite different. How would our observations influence our lives?

*"I have no special talents. I am only passionately curious.* **Albert Einstein**

# Chapter 4: The Mysterious Spear

**Mountains of Baliem Valley**

The morning's white rice served in red plastic bowls tasted bland with the brown river-water tea. Excitement glistened in Katherine's eyes.

"Can you believe we left home a week ago, but this is only our second day in the jungle? That celebration in Waga Waga was incredible," she said.

"We are in the infancy of our adventure, and if I were to go home today, I would feel fulfilled after all the events of yesterday," I said.

Porters chattering away in their native dialect packed and prepared for the day ahead. Occasional laughter pierced the morning of bird voices.

Gazing at the tree's reflections in the muddy brown river, I could hear the sounds of the ripples, lapping the side of our boat dock back home. My mind drifted to the morning this remote-travel idea came to mind. I wondered how the rest of the family was progressing back home, but the fascination of New Guinea held me tight. Recalling the craving for such an adventure, I realized an ambitious dream had awakened me to the real world.

I strive to teach my children that the differences between dreams and fantasy live in the words "determination" and "perseverance." Dreams precede goals and ideas brought to reality. Whimsical or creative entertainment for the mind describes fantasy.

Noticing I had stopped eating my rice, Coughin reached for my bowl to finish it off before washing the cooking pot and the red bowls in the wet sand of the river. His mild intrusion into my recollections returned me to reality, beginning a new day of discovery. Out of habit, he poked his mouth harp through a hole in his earlobe. He tied the harp with handmade bark string. The string had red berries tied to the end that swayed back and forth as he moved his head. As Coughin washed the bowls in the river, pieces of rice fell on the sand. Swallows fought for the precious rice, their voices lost in the rush of the water.

On to the village of Dugum we traveled, still farther north into the Baliem Valley. The tangled, prison-like labyrinth of plants and sun shafts walled in our group and slowed our progress. Fat or skinny, hundreds of vines sucked the life from tree trunks in a race to reach the sky.

Every direction looked like a mural, painted with endless detail; I found myself pausing far too often. Seasons here paid no attention to the laws of other-world winters. Parts of Brazil on the same latitude as New Guinea experienced low fifties temperatures while sunshine soaked our low eighty-degree world. Panus shared the Dani version of a sunscreen paste made from rice. A mysterious presence of spirits whirled about me so out of breath that their message evaporated as it touched my sunburned skin.

Maybe it was just the cooling wind, but I found it more interesting to think that there were spirits almost like guardian angels, sending us that refreshing breeze.

*Julius keeping Katherine's boots dry*

When I had first interviewed Julius for the job as our guide, I had not believed him when he promised he would pick me up and carry me up hills while we trekked.

Nevertheless, here we were, trekking through the wild, and here was Julius, lifting Katherine to his back and carrying her across a swift, turgid river. Not only did he make it across the current, rolling over on itself, but he also never flinched as he walked back to get me, his bare feet sure and strong on the slippery rocks.

Katherine yelled across the water, "Hang on to his shoulders tight, or you will slip off his skinny back!"

"Are your boots wet?" I yelled back

"No, but if he slips and falls, let go. The current is fast but the water is shallow," she said.

He explained with his baby steps on the rocks, "The Dani carry heavy packs on their heads or backs, so this is nothing for me. This way your hiking boots will stay dry."

*Julius carrying Jackie across river*

On many occasions, I had to suppress the words, "I can do it myself." Imagining the discomfort of wet boots or the possibility of slithering surprises lurking beneath the water, I gratefully accepted his offer. Katherine and I eventually got used to the idea that Julius would also carry us over patches of pig droppings. His simple acts of consideration confirmed for us that it was right to hire Julius as our guide. He charted our course with sensitivity to our tender-foot capabilities and limitations, and he did it without a sign of inconvenience on his part.

While walking, we came upon a man with a beautifully hand-carved spear. We stopped to admire it, startling him and bringing attention from his friends. While we talked together the fragile little man, his chin dusted with a gray shadow, whispered to Panus.

"Would he sell the spear?" I asked Julius, who was standing back and watching the scene. Panus, while studying the man from head to toe, might have said, "He is looking for cowry shells," because Julius turned back to me again.

"He owes money or shells for a pig he bought for a festival," Julius said.

"Do you have any I can buy from you to give the man?" I asked.

Julius said something to Panus, who then pulled a six-inch string out of his pocket with fewer than a dozen cowry shells attached. The man's eyes danced with excitement. At the same time the man reached for the string of shells, he extended the spear to me.

"I will pay him for the spear," I said to Julius.

Julius shook his head and said, "The old man is very happy for the trade of shells."

Cowry shells originate along the coasts, moving inland along trade routes. Generations ago, each clan maintained its own portable banking system with shells used as a mode of currency. Mother-of-pearl shells called gold lips took the prize as the largest and most valuable shells. Cowry shells still exist in smaller villages to serve as small change and to decorate the body. The wider the animal-skin neckpiece of cowry shells, the wealthier the man.

*Using my new spear for a walking stick*

I began to understand that these people possessed extraordinary generosity but cared little for the material world. The Dani would share a day's work or food with those in need in order to bring help to the homes of those struck down with illness. They often lifted each other's spirits with laughter and song. Their goodness and generosity made all the work I had done to get there more rewarding.

We could not say we were traveling in a paradise without problems or that all the Dani were angels in disguise. For instance, not long after we had traded the shells for the spear, we stopped for lunch. The cook had prepared fried rice, or what he called nasi goring. The distraction of finding a shaded area for lunch kept us all too busy to realize someone had stolen the spear.

"Julius, help find my spear," I said after noticing it missing from the bushy area where I had left it.

*Wearing headdress made by tribal friends*

I noticed Katherine's eyes closed a few minutes earlier but my whining probably startled her. She must have nodded off only to awaken to the loud noise and quick movement of the porters.

"Mom, what's wrong? Are you hurt?" she said

"No, my spear was leaning against that prickly bush and now it's gone. I loved that spear. The look on that man's face when he touched those shells will haunt me for years. His expression of appreciation when I handed him those shells just sank deep in my heart," I said.

DenDee, one of the younger porters, panting hard, ran up to me with the spear.

Julius said, "DenDee said a man was hiding behind a tree holding the spear so tight that DenDee had to step on his foot to cause a distraction for him to let go of the spear."

Villagers coveted the fine dark wood that came from the mountains. The six-foot long spear was more than an inch thick, carved silky smooth to touch. One end came to a sharp point and the other rounded smooth. Many offered to buy it from me later that day.

Earlier, when the old man had handed me the spear, he said what sounded like, "Abarek, abarek." Later Julius translated his words, "Spear that has killed a man."

Frustration. I wanted so desperately to ask the owner of the spear to share some of his stories of the spear.

I knew that Julius could interpret the stories for me, but I wished I could ask questions myself and understand without having to rely on an interpreter.

I still felt like an invader, digging and probing into the lives and secrets of the people around me, knowing that some of their stories should remain hidden from the rest of humankind.

Although a curious woman at heart, I did not want to impose on, or pry into, the lives of others; but if given an opportunity, I would listen and learn.

As a week had passed, the strangeness of our environment evaporated.

Various traits and customs, foreign at first, became the norm. As certain as life exists, this new environment lived through us, pulsing through our veins.

No longer strangers, we felt free to jump, without inhibitions, into this exhilarating experience. Our masks of protection no longer hid our insecurities.

We managed to weave our lives into the lives of a primitive society on the brink of absorption by a world of materialism.

I hated the feeling of recognizing the potential fate Dani culture might endure, for these people could have no concept or idea of our world.

Although we held the keys to advances in a modern society, they held the keys to life itself.

*Handmade musical instrument*

Sounds of handmade musical instruments signaled our arrival into Dugum. Young men played crudely carved guitars, while older men hummed ancient tunes. The mystery of the name Dugum had evoked images in my mind of huts, overgrown with fallen debris and with quiet people peering through the cracks of bamboo-slatted walls. Those images quickly changed as the entire male population came to life with hearty greetings of laughter. Men raised their arms signaling us to enter. Children darted about chasing a dog while an old man, humming on his mouth harp, squatted in a doorway. Dugum appeared welcoming with pink flowering landscapes sweetening the air. Clean, peaceful and content.

In the middle of a grove of the tallest trees of the jungle, the araucarias stretched a hundred feet straight up with perpendicular branches providing room under nature's shelter for the village below. Like sunlight on a Hollywood set, the everyday mid-spring-like weather perfected the scene. "Katherine, pinch me so I know this is not a dream. The people are so inviting," I said.

"The same with the first village of Waga Waga. Is it because we are strangers, and they want to learn something from us?" she said.

"Julius told me earlier that visitors--whether family or not--always give a village a reason for a celebration," I said.

*Chief Kusaw ready for mock warfare games*

The chief appeared like an illusion. A fan of white egret feathers haloed the red garland of parrot feathers, encircling his head. A fierce, white mask of paint could not hide the ripples of smiles from his forehead down to his chin. Perhaps he thought we came to his village, courtesy of the spirits, to bring eternal prosperity and blessings to his community. His muscles stiffened with apprehension when he realized we were two women, traveling alone.

I asked Katherine, "Where's Julius? I don't know what to do, and the chief looks pretty serious."

She replied, "I noticed he was looking for his sunglasses a while back, and the others must have gone with him to help with the search."

"What should we do?" I asked.

"I don't know. Maybe just keep smiling and try to shake his hand," she said.

The chief followed our every movement, and his lean body stood erect like a soldier, waiting for some sign of communication from us. We had no way of expressing the inexpressible. We exchanged smiles with "Halo and selamat petang, or good afternoon."

Those words signaled an invitation as the chief said, "Selamat datang, welcome."

"Nama saya Jackie," I said and then pointed to Katherine and said, "Katherine."

*Tree-branch ladder into Dani hut*

Time had forgotten this village. Life slowed long enough for us to participate. No longer speculating, we now experienced the magnitude of our journey. This mysterious place forced me to feel the chasm between my existence and theirs. Change awakens fear, a barrier that sets boundaries. My quest for understanding turned my fear into bold risk taking.

Chief Kusaw showed us his compound: a hut for his three wives, five children, and many pigs, and his private two-story hut. As in the village where the Dani people first welcomed Katherine and me, the women in Chief Kusaw's compound kept the hard-packed dirt floors mattressed with dried grass. Taboos prohibit sexual relations after a woman becomes pregnant and until the child reaches about age four. This hiatus frees the woman to spend more time in the fields, taking away the burden of having several young children close in age. Breast feeding acts as a natural method of birth control, and it continues until a child is five or older. The Dani believe sex weakens individuals, and this belief created the need for separate housing for men and women. Briefly, I wondered if the women knew the concept of jealousy, since their husbands could have as many wives as they could afford to buy with pigs.

*Walking home after a day of field work*

Farther down the path we could see the rest of the village compound surrounded by a wood fence, nine bamboo huts, a cooking hut, and the village headquarters.

Katherine and I stood alone in the center of this strange, but inviting, village. The villagers had invited us with welcoming cheers but now had disappeared. We didn't know where to go, whether we were staying the night, or waiting for villagers to return all dressed in feathers and painted skin to begin some type of dancing ritual.

"Where is Julius when we need him?" Katherine asked.

"I'm surprised he let us move forward into this new village without him," I said.

Several gray-haired men wearing penis gourds motioned for us to join them in the village "office."

A feeling of drowning engulfed me as the men encircled us and motioned toward the hut. I was suddenly fearful. Thoughts of unwanted sexual advances alerted all my senses as I felt that now familiar flow of adrenaline.

I looked at Katherine and said, "Should we try to run or just wait and see what happens and fight them off if we need to?"

Katherine looked uncertain. "I don't think we have a choice."

I looked in vain for Julius and the porters. I clutched Katherine's hand and felt the weight of responsibility for her safety. Did Katherine sense my fear? We realized that we had a welcome invitation when entering the village. Now alone, without our support team, had we lost control of our safety? We knew how the Dani felt about females, which intensified the situation.

I released the tension on Katherine's crushed hand. Six men, Katherine, and I squatted to enter the four-foot-tall woven-grass doorway of the bamboo-slatted hut, the very hut where men prohibited women. Why did they force Katherine and me to go here? Every bone in my body trembled with uneasiness. Sweat poured from me. Why was Julius taking so long to return to us? If I ever needed him to explain our situation, it was that moment with the six men. Katherine patted my hand, and I marveled at her self-assurance, although I told myself a young girl might not fear rape because she sees a smiling man as harmless and does not necessarily understand what he wants.

Trying to be calm, I reached for the courage of a teen. I did not want to alarm my daughter, so I gave no indication that I was searching the hut for some sort of weapon to defend us, in the event the men had bad intentions. I saw nothing I could use to thwart an attack, and again I thought of Julius. Where could he be?

Our eyes started to adjust to the strangeness of the hut interior. Bundles of bows and arrows tied with bark strands hung from the rafters. Nails of slivered bamboo held net bags heavy with extra bowstrings, wrapped in straw, along with irregular stones and fetishes. Matted with pig grease and sweat, brown furry armbands hung under a headdress of rare cassowary feathers. Odd-shaped spare penis gourds circled the uprights of the fire pit.

Below near the fire pit, the focal point of the hut, a six-inch-round gourd held boar tusks for a man's nostrils which I remembered from Waga Waga.

"What are those things over there?" Katherine asked.

"You mean those two knives made from bamboo resting on top of the pile of beech and lisanika leaves?" I said.

"Yes, and are they going to use them on us?" she said.

I said, "Of course not. Just try to be calm and keep smiling."

On the floor, scraps of food and tobacco spilled from a curved piece of bark. The air, dense and hot, made breathing difficult, especially from the musty smells of drying animal skins. Sometimes goose bumps have nothing to do with the weather.

We found ourselves in an indefensible situation. To relax and to try to understand the meaning of the predicament with this group of mysterious Dani men would test all levels of our confidence or, should I say, my confidence. Our shared inquisitiveness brought silence. A dismal odor of anxiety seasoned every breath. Even the men stopped their chattering once everyone formed a circle around the fire pit.

The Dani women sleep with the pigs. They care for and feed them. Men sleep in their own huts, threatening to kill with a bow and arrow any women entering their huts, including any of their wives.

Because of the Dani view of women, I was concerned about these men, and Katherine's safety weighed heavy on my mind.

A woman among the Dani tribes receives less compassion than the cherished pigs, owned by the men.

Katherine and I could not depend on these same men to show us much more respect than they did their own pigs.

Julius never could explain why the Dani treated us with such respect, even though we didn't eat their offerings of pork or smoke their cigarettes. Curiosity, the common language of people, may contain the answer.

Chief Kusaw's piercing look showed his keen interest in our arrival. I scanned the details of his face, wondering what happened to his earlier welcoming smile.

We appraised his cold, black eyes. Embarrassed and with questions, but no level of comprehension, we stretched our lips sideways, hoping to appear smiling.

Many people have asked us, "How do you get along with people when you don't know their language and you have no interpreter?"

Our travels have taught us that although languages can vary within a mere few miles, facial expressions and body language speak a universal language understood by all.

When you connect your body and its motions to your thoughts, the importance of speaking the local language diminishes.

The most important factors in communication lie in what your body expresses.

Katherine, much younger than I and with fewer apprehensions and experiences, had the edge in communicating her thoughts.

*Trying out a fresh rolled tobacco leaf*

    The elaborately painted faces of the Dani tribesmen glistened in the darkness as occasional rays of sunlight tunneled through gaps in the thatched roof. Their requests to smoke hand-rolled tobacco leaves and their offers to share the knowledge from generations past in a traditional men-only hut gave me a feeling of trust. I sat cross-legged with the elders of the village.
    "How do we tell them we don't smoke?" Katherine asked me.
    "Both of us will just say, 'No terima kasih,'" I said, "the Dani way to say, 'No thank you.'"
    Chief Kusaw, indifferent to my uneasiness, motioned for me to move my hiking boots. Under my legs in the deep grass lay a child-sized bow and arrow. With slow formality, he placed the arrow tip on my lower leg and pulled back the bow as if to shoot.
    We experienced sensory overload with the smell of singed pig skulls hanging inches above our heads and the prickly grass under us. Sounds floated skyward from the harmonious voices of brown faces, heavily lined with a wealth of experiences. One of the men blew his nose, shaking his snot to the dead grass beside him. He ran his fingers through his jet-black, matted hair to clean them.

I felt apprehension while I tried to understand the meaning of the arrow Chief Kusaw had pointed at my lower leg. Restless curiosity kept me from flinching as the men surrounding us relaxed and chattered together as they smoked. While trying to interpret their conversation, I saw images in my mind of bows and arrows flashing by, and I remained watchful.

I remembered reading about some African countries using the technique of bloodletting to cure malaria in the late 1800s. Maybe the chief wanted to show us that method. Laughter took the place of our suspicions as Chief Kusaw placed the bow and arrow in my hand as a gift.

Breathing more easily, I realized my heartbeat could slow down from 150 now that we crossed those first hurdles. They returned our smiles with blank words. A mutual connection developed between East and West.

*Men's huts of Dugum Village*

Questions consumed me about this idea of the bow and arrow aimed at my leg, so after the chief adjourned his strange meeting, I searched for Julius.

Instead of trying to find us, he had gone to the cooking hut, thinking about dinner. I helped cut veggies, hoping I could talk with little distraction. He agreed that this method of puncturing the skin and allowing some blood to escape might cure malaria, but he did not know why.

For the Dani, blood has immeasurable meaning. It carries magical powers that hold the secrets of life. They understand that their lives depend on it. A break in the skin exposes the blood to the world, therefore turning the blood impure. They assume that sickness or injury contaminates all blood, and this situation creates the need to extract a small amount of polluted blood through incisions in the skin by shooting small arrows into the veins.

I tried to explain to Julius the little I knew about malaria, and I asked him to share it with the chief. I explained that the parasite lives in the blood in the beginning of the illness and much later moves to the liver, causing lifelong symptoms and often death.

By removing blood, they are removing some of the parasites. The dignity of their struggle with malaria inspired me.

The Dani believe spirits cause all trouble, including diseases. Western societies' doubts about the effectiveness of folk medicines are not as strong as the Dani's deep fear of doctors and hospitals.

Based on my urban experiences, I wanted to label this place as poverty-stricken. Chief Kusaw unfolded the Dani's lifestyle. He showed the beauty in their simple ways, a pure and natural life, unhampered by possessions.

The Dani heritage of caring for each other dominated their lives. Their naked bodies and the lack of material wealth had no effect on their sense of pride. The lifestyle of the Dani revealed their passion for a timeless existence.

Katherine and I felt proud contentment to travel where invisible spirits prevailed, preventing a region from moving forward in time.

Outside, women came home from the fields, as duty- bound as the closing buds of nearby flowers.

Men conceived the creative ideas. Women listened and carried out the drudgery of boring tasks.

*Some Dugum men dress like this, every day*

Work for males consisted of occasional hut repair, clearing a field, fashioning a new spear, repairing arrows, or maintaining the irrigation network around gardens and fences. To fill idle time, they also knit ceremonial skirts for women, wove arm bracelets from bark, and trained gourds to grow in the shape of the penis sheath. The men made all the important decisions about the pigs, such as which pigs to fatten for ceremonies or to use for breeding. A man's wealth, determined by the number of pigs he owned, could buy numerous wives to take care of the pigs and fields.

Horizontal strands of gray severed the skyline, signaling the dinner hour. A sweet potato baked with the juice from the red pandanus fruit for flavor rewarded a day's work well done. Tobacco smoking followed. The vein that gave the Dani the richness of their day-to-day lives came from the satisfaction of their accomplishments.

*Julius cooking dinner*

Julius continued to busy himself after our long conversation about malaria, cutting vegetables for our mie goreng, or fried noodles. The brown river-water tea sat steeped in solitude. Flames under the wok filled the hut with a soft glow. Bubbling oil from pig fat mixed with the unfamiliar smells of bones, teeth, and skins drying in the corner. In a circle, three men sat weaving bracelets with a bone awl, using pandanus tree fibers, rolled into string on their ash-whitened thighs.

One man reached for my arm and measured above my elbow.

"Julius, what is he doing?" I asked.

"He make you arm band."

The men finished the narrow bark string bands and laid them on the dirt floor.

"The wide yellow armbands made of pig scrotums are worn tight above the elbow and help scare evil spirits away," Julius explained.

Julius supplemented information not perceived by our eyes and our ears, as appearances often hide interesting details. Our hosts' unguarded simplicity started to push away the clutter of my life back home. Neither Katherine nor I believed in spirits; however, certain changes developed in our visualization of a culture that at first glance had appeared savage and uncivilized. In doing our best to tap into the important facts of tribal life, we began to adjust our vision. Perhaps spirits do exist.

They did not inflict evils upon us, but what else could have opened our eyes to the beauty of the relationships among these people? We filled our bowls with noodles soaked in dripping, unrecognizable green stuff. Soon we adapted to the oily taste. After the three men had finished our red bowls of leftovers, they fitted each of us with bark armbands to keep us safe on our journey.

*Large cowry shell neckband and neck feathers symbolize wealth*

Chief Kusaw came in to talk with us. Through hand motions he asked, "How many days until you return to my village? I want to make you a gift."

I shook my head and motioned we would travel north for many days and not return this way.

He wanted to weave a special bracelet that chiefs wear. He pointed to the yellow three-inch-wide bracelet on his arm, and he wrapped his hands around my wrist for a measurement of the width of my arm.

The Dani watched everything we did. After dinner, inquiring eyes focused on how we used jackets and boots. A bond between our worlds took shape with their approval of our curiosities.

Life's simpler pleasures, such as listening to a song, pulled me deeper into their world. The significance lay in the bond of two worlds, rather than the words or music of a particular song.

Echoic shrills of sawdas, or cicadas, choked the chief's compound where a young boy opened a door of a sleeping hut for us.

He picked up the grass to fluff it while beetles and cockroaches raced with centipedes for cracks in the walls.

Connecting the rafters to the vertical bamboo slats, webs of magic were spun with freedom by black spots with green eyes.

We had flashlights for our quick trip to the dark outdoor bathroom.

Back in the hut, grass mats made a nice covering over the itchy grass under our sleeping bags, which had mosquito-netting, attached by Velcro.

The children, their eyes wide with curiosity, filled the doorway, watching every move we made. Our rituals appeared as strange to them as theirs to us.

Outside, two huge, fruit-eating bats, called flying foxes because of their long snouts, brushed the underside of a beech tree with their five-foot wingspread

Katherine and I liked to fill our journals with memories of the day.

We both sat on the sleeping bags hoping for a little more light in the day for writing.

When she pulled out several colored markers, young eyes outside our door grew wide with interest.

Katherine said, "I was going to draw in my journal. Maybe those kids would want to watch?"

"Ukeemay!" I said. Enter.

*Kids coloring with Katherine in Dugum*

Language issues did not limit our contact with the children. We learned the Dani words for sweet potato, or ipomoea, mouse, or keecus, pigeon, or goura, mosquito, or naa mowk, house built of wood and straw, or honai, large boat, or prahu, blue butterfly, or kupu kupu, snake and insect, or waro, and an armband worn by men, or tekan. Each child drew his or her interpretation of different animals or birds. They did not understand the concept of Katherine needing the markers for the rest of our trip, though. The young boys and girls of the village wanted markers of their very own.

In the beginning of our trip, I thought feelings about people such as Chief Kusaw would fade. With determination, I hoped to recall my new friends through the new phase of my life. I knew before I left Dugum that its visions would pulsate through my veins like a stampede of wild horses, rushing to nowhere, but controlling everything in their way. This village showed me both the security of cultural identity and the dark side of human nature, in its depiction of ritual warfare. From lopping off two fingers on small girls after the death of a relative to jumping out of the way from barbed arrows to fear of attack at night by ghosts, life among the Dugum Dani is not easy, but there is a strong sense of security in living in a close-knit community.

Suddenly something caused the children to run away. Chief Kusaw appeared at the door of the hut, his hands inviting us to follow him.

Katherine said, "I thought we were staying in the hut for the night?"

"I guess the chief wants to show us something," I said.

We walked outside the hut, adjusting our eyes to the extreme darkness unlike our hut with the soft glow our flashlights gave the room. The chief stopped at a large rock above the compound, which gave us a bird's-eye view of the dancing below.

Flames from a fire highlighted villagers, moving their bodies like sensual ripples on the water, knees moving up and down. Women jumped with abandon, chanting.

Their jellylike breasts followed. Coiled fiber skirts and net bags flew higher and higher, exposing bare bodies. The live music was such an awakening. The uncensored layered depths of sounds gave life to the surrounding stillness of the village.

*Dani man from Dugum*

While the dancers stopped to catch their breath, the chants increased in sound, and the men began their circles again.

The sound of plucked guitar strings, fingers pattering on handmade drums, and low chants encompassed our space as we said goodnight to our friends.

*Resting after dancing*

Splashing tonight's canvas with the afternoon colors of Chief Kusaw's world involved little conversation. We returned to our hut in silence.

A compelling impulse after contact with Dugum is to want to give that experience weight in my life. Remote travel separates me from the familiar.

I become more conscientious about the little things in life: from the children drawing simple animal drawings, to the details of men weaving armbands, to the smells lingering in tribal huts.

The village people of Dugum gave me access to those pearls of life. Only seven days into the sojourn and already I sensed a change in how I viewed the world.

*"I'm not going to limit myself just because people won't accept the fact that I can do something else."* **Dolly Parton**

## Chapter 5: Women Fully Clothed

My preferred kind of adventure includes awakening to the melodic sounds of villagers yelling across mist-covered valley fields. Those moments sink deep. Each new day brings dynamic possibilities from the singing that greeted our arrival to the handshakes during goodbyes.

As I walked past the last hut, one of the men from the cooking hut, waiting to say goodbye, stopped me. After he scraped a tooth with his jagged fingernail, he offered me his wesa, a religious rock, decorated in feathers and used in religious ceremonies.

My hand curled inside my waist pack for some rupiahs. His ringlets of gray curls shook back and forth as the seasoned man clasped my hand. A tear slid down my cheek. I knew that years later this day would come back to me, and this time of leaving would return to me.

I memorized his hand over mine, an essential aspect of this passage. Saying goodbye to this village of Dugum made me realize how far I'd strayed from the role of wife, mother, chauffeur, and cook, and how much closer we had come to our initial goal's discovery.

As I walked away, my feet felt heavy. Did we need one more day in Dugum? Our brief visit gave meaning to my comment about life, living through us as we travel, for with every exciting hello, we endure a sad goodbye.

The enchantment of nature's balance touched us in many ways. One might think of the muted brightness of the stars in the city, compared to the natural brilliance of stars and moon in the darkness of the jungle, where city lights and pollution do not exist.

When you leave the city, the twinkling returns. Even the dimly lit becomes bright.

*Crossing raging river on scary bridge*

The children of the village ran behind us, laughing and waving goodbye, and as we continued on our way, they slowed and began to turn back, still laughing. I turned before crossing the rattan suspension bridge for a final view of a lost culture in all its majestic simplicity.

Pausing in this solemn place, I felt envy for the villagers of Dugum, where we had felt contentment.

The pig ceremony in Waga Waga opened our eyes to the Dani world, but Chief Kusaw opened our hearts, not through trying to take or claim the bit of modern civilization we brought with us, but through his gracious giving in allowing us to share the substance of their values.

They had no materialism to buy, sell, or hold in their hands. The gold, owned by these people, lay in their hearts, enriched by their lives harmoniously balanced with nature.

*Leaving Dugum Village*

*Sweet potato fields on the way to Muliamo*

A clearing in the impenetrable wall of green revealed a mural of gardens, each separated by a maze of irrigation canals. Men used long, fire-hardened paddles to scoop out the canals or ditches, throwing the weeds into the gardens for compost. The canals had sloped banks, plastered with mud, for a look of tidiness and protection from erosion.

Between the ditches, women and girls planted sweet potatoes in mounds two feet apart, using cuttings from mature vines.

Rain washing away dirt around the cuttings gave the women extra work until they pruned and weeded. For three more months, they would keep the mounds covered with foliage, to encourage stronger roots.

The advantage of the lack of change of seasons meant planting all year.

These fields of green contained a conspicuous sight, the movement of clothed women, travelers from afar. Katherine and I looked like yellow roses cast against the dark green leaves of a rose bush.

We could not compete with the porters' quick pace and skilled balance across algae and mud-covered poles bridging the ditches.

My eyes focused on toe tracks in the soggy mud. My body moaned as I thought about how heavy my feet had grown. The leftover smell of burning brush smothered each breath. Log bridges floated in the rain-filled ditches. Amir pulled a log toward him and stepped across with ease.

Boots or no boots? I thought it was too much trouble to remove them, but by my second step, the log disappeared under water. Amir reached for my hand, but caught my arm instead, and we fell into two feet of muck. Everyone laughed but me.

Wet boots take days to dry. I stumbled and wobbled to the higher mounds of weeds, while the moody sky, tinged with the darkest of grays, threatened our day.

The moss forest ahead turned into a blur, as walking required all my attention. Parts of the days sometimes seemed empty, like the simple steeping of brown river-water tea. Later I discovered that these moments cemented the experiences and lessons I had learned. Much like the covering over sweet potatoes, they buried the roots of my lessons.

The lush green carpet of moss invited rest for our feet, which were tired of squishing in the mud with boots. Katherine stepped into a hole, masked by saturated cushions of dead leaves. My legs gave way, while I reached for her hand. I felt relief when I fell back on my pack, taking the weight off my legs. The pack cushioned my fall but did not keep my hands from sinking into the moist ground.

Thank goodness, I offered to carry the larger pack instead of my camera pack that day.

A bustling mass of insects ran up my arms and quarreled with my fingers, while I slapped at the bugs. Katherine slipped out of her boot, held tight by the rotten banks of the hole. Hyperactive ants, unhappy with her microfiber socks disrupting their morning, fought back, biting.

Unpacking a corner of the heavy pack on Coughin's back, we found the anti-itch cream for the red welts on my wrists and Katherine's ankle. The items we packed helped make our trip safe and enjoyable for our tender-foot tendencies.

Each of the men wanted to try the cream on various bites on their legs and arms. They passed unfamiliar words, mixed with English, back and forth, along with the cream. I hoped the modern conveniences we shared with the men never overshadowed the importance of their traditions.

Unpredictability. I liked that word and maybe even those ants. Both represented the astonishing diversity of a place and its people.

Our group stayed together almost brushing each other with each step.

Tangible moisture draped the air, diffusing the sunlight, leaving behind a fungus of wood decay. After crashing through the beds of moss, the supine, red trunks of beeches waited their turn to enter the villages as firewood.

With his machete, Julius cut canes of bamboo, opening a path. Elastic streamers of new growth sprang back if bent out of the way. Vines hung like the rigging of a sailboat, trapping sticky lianas.

Trees wore clothing of thorned rattan, sometimes painting red streaks on bare arms. Ferns stretched upwards on tree trunks, while orchids, gulping air for life, hid underneath.

Our arms and feet fought the entanglement of tripping roots. Distorted branches caught us off guard. The bamboo groves hid the spongy, lichen-covered bogs that, when stepped on, turned thick as oatmeal.

Smells of the rotten jungle permeated my frayed river- and sweat-soaked clothing. Each day's labor added to the aches and pains of the day before. The day, half-gone, claimed my strength. Intuition spoke silent words of courage, assuring me the situation would improve. Recognizing earlier that nature always retains balance, we looked forward to some easy going.

With perseverance as my guide, determination kept my boots moving forward. Black shadows hid patterns of white light from the sun. It seemed like an enchanted forest: dark, forbidding, and unwelcoming, except to its neighbors, the bats. It struck me as a place where I might expect to meet a dragon or witch at any moment. With a tangible sense of anticipation, I thought we would soon surface from the depths of this unforgiving forest of dampness. Finally, we emerged from the thickest part of the vegetation, and the going got easier.

The hard, yellow light dried us out during the remainder of the afternoon and the remaining easy walk to Muliamo. In the distance, groups of tribal men, carrying spears, walked in the same direction as our group. Two men quickly came up from behind and slowed long enough to explain in a language Julius understood that Muliamo would host a large festival for three days.

*Rainbow over Muliamo*

*Village men ready to start tribal battle games*

Ahead, chestnut fences, outlined with dried palm-leaf thatch threatened to conquer the overgrown jungle. A rainbow showed like a halo over Muliamo.

The waning and welcomed sun's warmth sank deep into my skin. Nature, like a waterwheel, spilled out life in increments, dumping different shapes, colors, and smells into our consciousness.

The village of Muliamo greeted us with afternoon shadows, hiding blossoms scenting the air like candy. Flowering purples bordered the dirt paths, meandering to each two-level, round hut, outlining the compound.

The rotation stayed the same. Each day nature treated us with surprises of different types of blooming plants, smelling like a florist's shop versus gloomy streamers hanging to the ground. I now felt comfortable taking responsibility for the risks this trip might uncover.

The fear of the unknown had diminished as we had come to know the Dani, and I had a much better understanding of nature's interface with humanity.

The villagers of Dugum helped me understand how they integrated nature into their lifestyle.

Bundles of information, defining every individual, hid deep down inside us.

Here in this unknown place, I could begin to sense the strands unraveling. With nothing to push against me, I welcomed my acquaintance with my inner world, breaking away from boundaries and accepting our new lessons of life.

*"Adapt to the pace of nature; her secret is patience."*
**Ralph Waldo Emerson**

## Chapter 6: Goose Bumps

Perhaps they smelled our one-hundred-percent DEET mosquito-repellent-covered bodies, mixed with the smell of the chocolate bars in the emergency first aid kit. From several neighboring villages, they gathered in our grass hut to celebrate. As they jumped from the bamboo ceiling, they seemed to laugh with delight as the darkness offered a cover for their playtime.

Realizing they could not expect gourmet food service, these little mouse-like creatures of Muliamo, which Julius called keecus, decided to play hopscotch over our sleeping bags with all their friends. Scurrying up and around the thatched roof with the tribal drums and soft chanting as a backdrop, the little guys sought our hut for their party. Their dwarf-sized clawed feet did handsprings on my body. My muscles tensed with each landing. The sleeping bag covered my head, but when a couple of keecus plopped from my shoulder up to my head, I shuddered. How could a person weighing 115 pounds fear a few skinny little mice?

The empty foil energy-bar wrapper must have made its way around the hut and back again from keecus fighting for its ownership. As they came close, they smelled of oatmeal mixed with vegetable oil from the wrapper.

My fingers flipped the unfailing flashlight on at the slightest movement on my body. I caught a glance at those beady black eyes, sitting on top of a cone of a nose, when I tried to scare one away with the light. The fat keecus crawling up my leg didn't notice the slow movement of my pulling back the layers of mosquito netting. Mice have a keen sense of hearing and smell but not seeing, I remember. My kids raised every kind of mouse, gerbil, and hamster, so they taught me some lessons about the small rodents. I swatted my hand at the little guy, hoping to scare him into convincing his friends to find another place to forage for food. His scaly tail longer than his body got caught for a second under my hand. The idea of touching it scared me back into the safety of my bag and tightly closing the netting around my head. The keecus allowed me to doze off, and then they started in with their games of chase. Whispered words in a foreign tongue distracted me from thinking about the different smells filtering through the cracks of the bamboo walls. Morning seemed more like days than hours away.

Our "beds" were no more than grass on dirt, and the discomfort of such an arrangement changed my sleeping patterns. Not wanting to waste the smallest moment of this once-in-a-lifetime opportunity, I took advantage of sleepless nights, to rediscover myself. The conceptual images of housewife after two decades became real.

I didn't realize I was lost in maintaining a chaos-free household. Would taking time to nurture the nurturer help me find out all over again my deepest passions? Throwing myself into the unknown allows me to experiment with new ways of living by acting more freely.

Family expectations and daily pressures are left behind, allowing a freedom for being truly aware and awake. I loved opening my eyes in an unfamiliar place. It gave me a sensation of mystery.

My senses achieved a new intensity. Neither coffee nor cooked rice gave me the urge to untangle myself from my sleeping bag/blanket/mosquito-netting mess. The scent of the Dani intrigues us and lingers with one at night. They doused their shoulders with pig fat for warmth. For decoration, they covered themselves with unrecognizable leaves and tied grasses with feathers and bark string about their arms. Cowry shells stitched on animal-skin necklaces covered their chests.

Morning called for shaking our way free of itchy, dried grass. We changed clothing despite the challenge of our temporary home's low ceiling, which hovered only four feet off the grass floor. There was an opening in the center of this two-level shelter, but even that didn't help me, a five-foot-eight tall woman.

Fires in the middle of the hut kept us warm at night, sending their leftover smoke up through the hole at the center of the second level and out the roof of woven, rainproof grass.

We hadn't seen any communal women-children huts when we entered the village.

I had asked Julius, "At what age do boys go and live with their fathers?" Julius shrugged his shoulders, held up five fingers, and then raised his eyebrows as if to change his mind and held up ten fingers.

The blinding first light of our day-nine morning made it difficult to see the silhouettes of familiar shapes. How peculiar to think about all the mystery and strangeness of those simple forms walking toward us, each carrying a bow and arrow or spear.

Katherine's nonstop itching called for a closer inspection. I saw hundreds of tiny bites, swollen and itching for a scratch, as we moved outside to better light.

"Where did these come from? I don't have any bites," I said.

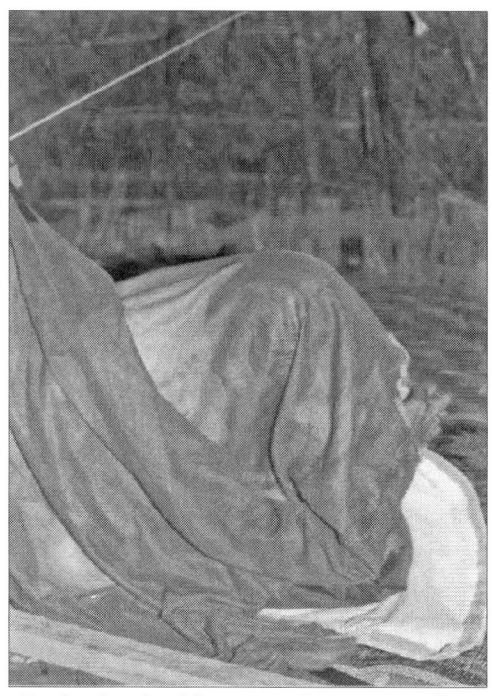

*Katherine inside mosquito net reading*

She looked down at the ground, thinking about last night. "I remember crawling into the bedroll, but I didn't close the mosquito netting over my head. I lay on my stomach and used the flashlight to read for a long time. There were all these teeny black spots on the pages, but I thought they were specks of dust from the grass," she said.

"I'm so sorry. I never dreamed there might be insects in the grass," I said. "I haven't been sleeping well. The soft grass under my bedroll felt so good that I fell asleep before reminding you to close your netting to keep bugs out."

As she revealed this information to me, I felt guilty for not being more watchful, especially after she had remarked that she could see tiny black dots all over her book. Checking the grass for insects. Another checkpoint before bed.

This time we did not have to contend with the naa mowk, or mosquitoes, but the red dots covering her entire body. She counted more than 300 bites on one arm. Katherine never complained, but did ask to carry the anti-itch cream in her waist pack. We never did figure out what those bites were. They looked like fleabites but without animals around, I doubted that. Our hut sat close to a small pond of water attracting insects like midges or no-see-ums.

"Katherine, show your arms to Julius. We need to know if these were insect bites or a poisonous rash from something you touched," I said.

"Where is he?" she said.

"I would guess he is in the hut next door, helping Panus cook the rice for breakfast," I said.

*Julius eating dinner*

Her wrinkled brow told all as she walked toward me from the other hut. "He said a word but I couldn't understand, and he went back to talking with Panus," she said.

"Okay, must not be a big deal. We'll just try to treat the itching with Cortisone," I said.

I wondered out loud, "Could Julius's lack of attention mean he thought we were spoiled and weak for complaining about a normal everyday occurrence for the local people?"

Concerned about the safety of two white-skinned women, one with yellow hair and blue eyes, our friend Julius asked some local villagers about the increased activity. Julius's heart opened wide to people, absorbing everyone into his life without barriers or questions. The Muliamo villagers liked Julius and explained that about two thousand tribal people would gather to celebrate Independence Day, socializing through mock war-games and dancing.

*Muliamo village*

While some might refer to this as blind chance, I believed that--with enough anticipation, organization, and determination--people could enhance their luck. Our serendipity included seeing 2,000 tribal people in the middle of an open field. Our lives slowed down in Muliamo. We left behind the dense weave of the canopy that had plunged us into the haunt of poisonous snakes and monstrous insects. Muliamo had no trees, just open fields of silver spear grass and a lovely breeze.

*Group from a distant village ready to start war games*

"Listen," Katherine said. "It sounds like singing in the far distance. Almost like chanting."

The people looked like they could be the subjects of picture postcards, except alive and full of movement.

With the wandering villagers came bananas and biscuits, bland vanilla-flavored cookies.

The festival started in the afternoon, but we felt it had already started. Hours seemed minutes, as we watched various Dani and Yali compete in pig races, dance contests, or warfare games.

Their curiosity about us matched ours about them. Walking past us, the tribal men looked at us; and then, as if they had seen ghosts, they turned and looked again. They pointed to the strange hiking boots hiding our feet.

*Pretend war games call for incredible body decorations*

After I'd photographed an older man, he walked toward me, rubbed my shirt fabric between his fingers, and slid two fingers inside one of my pockets. His eyes asked unanswerable questions. I looked around to see what Katherine was doing.

"The fact that nylon fabric dries quickly when wet is of no concern to this curious man, is it?" I said.

"No, and look that man next to me just untied my boot lace," Katherine said.

"Their curiosity is equal to ours. I'll never forget how lightweight the first penis gourd felt when Julius handed me one to hold," I said.

The unique afternoon had no chance of ever happening again. The temptation I had to stare turned into a burden for me.

If we protect their environment, tribal people will thank us by their presence. For example, Katherine and I traveled to Ecuador to meet the Huarani tribes the year before this New Guinea trip.

A huge oil spill a week before our arrival coated the rivers for miles, killing animals and people. The following year, through shared letters in the mail from our guide Luis Garcia, we found out that the oil company had savaged the forests, depleting wildlife and natural food the Huarani hunted.

Hundreds of tribal people moved to the outskirts of big cities, looking for ways to survive. Luis said the only Huarani left were hidden so deeply in the jungle that it would take days to find them.

Dani, well known for their friendliness to the first explorers, did not mind two white-skins wandering about. None of them ever asked for money, but on occasion, a few asked for a cigarette in exchange for our taking their photograph. They smoked hand-rolled tobacco but valued our gifts of market-bought cigarettes. Somewhat addictive, the clove flavoring smelled sweet coming from our shirt pockets.

*Fierce looking warriors simply interested in store-bought cigarettes*

We relied on others to do and make things necessary for our survival. Trading goods or services meant bartering. Often, we exchanged rice for vegetables or offered leftover dinner for a hut for the night. When we offered villagers cigarettes as a trade, we showed them that we cared about trading something they valued. Immediate bonding took place with the gift of a cigarette from us. Julius provided language skills, provisions, a positive attitude, and an awareness of potential sensitivity for keeping us on the right track; however, it took patience to learn the balance.

Julius, along with Panus's intuition, had a remarkable way of figuring out how to overcome difficult situations, such as meeting with villagers who spoke an unfamiliar language. Dealing with snakes or building a fire in the rain never seemed to disrupt their positive spirits.

Julius kept us aware of inappropriate behavior on our part, such as entering a man's hut without an invitation. An awareness of potential sensitivity, along with keeping a positive attitude, helped maintain the patience we needed for balance in this new culture. We tested and strengthened our level of harmony by our willingness to endure the hardships we faced.

With dusk came a light wind: perhaps spirits had awakened for the evening festivities. Silhouettes started taking shape in the sunset. We walked around and around the different groups of tribes who came from as far away as a three-day walk.

*Helping a friend*

Earlier we had watched villagers smash an assortment of rocks. They used the powder to paint patterns on each other's bodies to distinguish each one's village. Those patterns tried to tell us a story in the dim left-over light of the day.

Tribesmen and women reached out to us, trying to communicate. Anything imaginable could have happened to us. A tribe, having checked us out earlier in the day, may have decided to carry us off in the jungle. Nobody in the universe, including Julius, knew our location. Katherine and I were just two white spots, wandering in the middle of a concert of painted black bodies.

*Jale tribe wearing rattan hoops over their penis gourds*

Outfits, consisting of rattan hoops around the waist and penis gourds, sticking out from underneath distinguished the Yali or Jale people from the Dani. Shared qualities sometimes hid behind barriers of language or appearance. Daylight smiles erased apprehensions. Nighttime caused those smiles to become one with the black sky.

Once darkness had fallen, we received the invitation to dance, and it felt welcome. A song, repeated for hours, accompanied the vertical jumping of some individual tribes as others swayed side to side.

Katherine said, "The dancing looks like something computer-generated. Somehow, while dancing, they all reach down and slap the ground in unison."

"I know. Every direction I look I see groups with their own songs and dances," I said.

*Proud of his rare sea shell necklace*

*Some villagers walked three days to attend festival*

Hundreds of tribal people dotted the grassy fields, singing and jumping, each village dancing to a different song. We joined, clapping, entranced in an ancient rhythm to celebrate life. Tribal people danced in the center of activity, showing us new steps.

The persistent rhythm of the drums had a magnetic, alluring affect within my soul. Spellbound by the repetitive dance steps and the nakedness of the night and the men, I felt as if I had swallowed an anesthetic.

Found energy from watching others kept stirring at my feet. I was treading in deep water; continuous dancing kept me gasping for air. I felt numb except for the vibration when my feet touched the ground.

Loud music provided a language for us to communicate with each other, the spirits, and our inner selves. Our frenzy and passion ended with Julius's appearance and news of dinner.

I said to Julius, "All day I have not seen anyone eat or drink?"

Julius said, "Men bring no food. Spirits keep them happy without food."

The best meal of the trip awaited our fingers. The games, dancing, and laughter entertained our minds while our stomachs ran on empty. Now we realized our hunger pains needed attention. Julius had scrounged around the villagers throughout the day, trading rice for fresh vegetables and fruit. Julius called us to a private dinner. Our feast would have summoned the entire village, if we ate near other villagers. Julius wanted to protect us from the begging stares.

After Panus finished cooking the rice, he brought overflowing pots inside the hut, where he and the three porters slept next to our hut. Nasi goreng, or rice with cabbage, green beans, and carrots on the side, mie goreng, or fried ramen-style noodles, corned beef from the can warmed in a wok with an egg/sugar batter, and soup made with cabbage and a few potatoes greeted our palates.

The cabbage soup with the canned corned beef satisfied a one-week-long hunger. The prior week had included a few vegetables, but mostly a bowl of rice a day and as much tea made from brown river-water as we could drink. Katherine and I, like selfish children, kept the beans and carrots for ourselves.

We finished every vegetable, knowing there might not be any again. The rice sat alone and untouched.

Our two spoons and two red, plastic bowls from the first day's market received constant use, making them a good investment. We failed to make a major dent in the noodles and rice feast that our gracious guide had acquired and prepared.

That night, the three porters, Amir, DenDee, and Coughin, finished the leftovers. I noticed they never used the spoons. They needed no sand that night to scrape the bowls clean. Panus rinsed them with river water and balanced our dishes on a bush to dry.

No soap wrappers or trash to dispose of, and no leftover vegetable scrapings for the pigs' favorite part of the day. Eating utensils, chairs, and tables mystified the Dani. Gourds carried liquids.

Maybe squatting, which replaced sitting in a chair to relax, gave the Dani the perfect posture needed for carrying heavy loads on their heads or backs. Good posture prevented back problems.

The groups attending the festival came empty-handed, except for their spears, bows, and arrows.

We never understood if villagers preferred an intentional fast or observed a tradition to avoid eating during festivals of this type

*Pig fat darkens skin but help keeps the night chill away*

Families in home villages stuck to their usual pattern and ate sweet potatoes. During a gathering, villagers often traded a variety of foods cooked in a communal pot and enjoyed with fingers. Villagers did not mind that we needed utensils, but the language barrier prevented us from knowing how they felt about our desires for a more complicated existence. Dani lives did not include beds, blankets, clothing, or metal cooking utensils.

Twilight's golden rays had faded into a whirlwind of nighttime colors. Before every inch of sky lit up with stars, we prepared for total darkness. Minor details taken for granted back home evolved into major challenges. Back home, light switches simplify the tasks of changing clothes and finding a toothbrush.

I put the flashlight, our guide for the night, in its net bag, pinned with care to the top of the sleeping bag. Buried in the backpack, we kept Ziploc bags, in case it rained, full of extra batteries. While reflecting on the day's discoveries, I positioned the flashlight for extensive use every night by my journal.

Knowing my daughter and I functioned on a balanced playing field helped us both feel more confident, and it strengthened the mother-daughter bond. We learned to listen more intently, which brought a deeper respect for each other. I thought that brainstorming with a parent for the best strategies adds a level of maturity, unknown to most teens.

"I'm stuffed. We had more variety in our dinner tonight than all the previous weeks' dinners combined. Do you think you learned anything new today?" I said.

Katherine flattened her sleeping bag after shaking it free of potential thieves, looking for a warm home for the night. Snakes, spiders, or even a small cuscus might find a rolled-up bag a comfy resting place.

Content that her bag was safe, she said as she crawled inside, "The best thing I've learned is resourcefulness."

"Sand for scrubbing and the river for rinsing. Think our friends will believe that?" I said.

After curling up in a bedroll, I liked to ask a few questions each night. Reflecting on the day's activities gave food for thought.

"Do I listen to your ideas and thoughts of how to do things?" I said.

"Well, since we have a guide, I never thought it was an issue. The worst thing that has happened to me was when that man tried to grab my boobs while I was bathing in the river."

"Yes, a mischievous prank from someone just curious about whether we look like their women under all our clothing."

"I know that I could have wondered why you weren't a better lookout for me. I don't remember having that feeling ever. Maybe I felt I was more of an equal and smart enough to take care of myself. After that I wanted to leave my clothing on while bathing and you never pushed me to do otherwise," she said.

We had made a variety of decisions together, Katherine and I, and we both thought doing so worked out much better than if I, as the mom, simply dictated every move we made. Often a mere glance at the other sufficed to communicate a response or a question. We couldn't have developed that kind of relationship through a conventional mother-daughter planning a holiday meal together. The process of dealing with unusual circumstances and mutually overcoming obstacles developed a permanent closeness in spirit.

Magic began as I tossed and turned in my sleeping bag, nestled in the dried grass, hearing Dani songs in the distance. Something pulled me from the safety of my grass hut to go wandering.

Of course, I was aware that the jungle never sleeps. Nocturnal life included poisonous snakes like the death adder. Disregarding potential dangers, I opened the door of my grass hut. Someone had switched off all the world's lights. Crawling into the savage night, looking up at the clearest sky, I realized the rich sounds beckoned me toward the music. The high altitude deep within the New Guinea forests made me aware of every breath I took.

In particular, I watched for the nocturnal creatures with their strange lures capturing victims like the strong-as-steel web of the rampaging, predator spider. Locals say the spider can move faster than lightning and torture its victim for a year. Slithering soundlessly as a shadow, the death adder snake, with its triangular-shaped head, looked no different from the tree branches catching my heavy boots. Two children, hiding in bushes, startled my walk. My flashlight found a container full of red, baby, carpet pythons, a favorite pet.

My footsteps ended outside a music-filled grass hut with smoke emerging from the roof.

I crouched near the door, hoping to remain invisible. In and out through the three-foot-tall woven grass door, their naked bodies, black as the night itself, gently brushed by me. Some on hands and knees crawling. Others just crouched. But they all stared as they moved past me into the hut. Dressed in feathers, paint, animal skins, and no clothing other than the habitual horim, tribal men crawled past me to join the festival inside. Did I look at danger in the face? Unable to interpret their whispers, I shivered with goose bumps covering my sweaty but chilled body.

A village elder crawled back out the dusty opening of the hut and reached for my hand.

No hesitation. These fierce-looking warriors had given me permission to enter the men-only festival. Thoughts of Katherine asleep back in our hut caused me to hesitate, just as I glimpsed inside the smoke-filled room. What if something happened to me? Did Katherine have the fortitude to figure out the next step? My adventurous attitude pulled me inside, not worrying about the consequences.

The execution of a trip deep in the heart of a jungle requires a strong self-trust.

I had crawled into a book about a forgotten people. I felt hypnotized by the chanting of century-old songs. The bewitching music encouraged a few to stand and jump around like some type of dance. Two men would sing one part, and another would solo, with groups joining in, each a living note in a triumphant song of life. The intensity vibrated through my soul, provocative and frightening.

In this primitive setting, the fire illuminated the whites circling their eyes. The secrets, the dangers, the power of the jungle had followed me into that hut. As I sat in the grass, my knees locked tight to my chest, I tried to make my legs disappear. Maybe they would not ask me to dance. The men sang louder and louder, encouraging a Dani chief to stand up and dance for me.

His flat feet, pounding up and down around the fire, revived memories of sitting around a fire with my daughter Carrie. She watched Maasai warriors in the same style of dance in the bush country of Africa. The Dani's forty-nine smiles sank deep inside me. Somehow, they knew I desired, as a traveler from a faraway land, to understand their story.

Through tears caused by thick smoke, I watched a wrinkled hand reach for me and felt it touch my arm.

An old man hoped to share with me his last smoke of tobacco rolled in a lisanika leaf. His long fingernails dug into my skin.

The pinching pain brought me back to reality. I smiled as I waved the tobacco away.

I pointed to him, hoping he understood I didn't smoke and wanted him to enjoy it. Physically the night would end, but the ceremony had carved out a place deep inside me.

Hours later, back in my home-away-from-home grass hut and restless from my connection, I snuggled deep into my security blanket. The rewards--from giving in to the temptations of that music that called my name--teased my thoughts.

I relaxed, content that the tiny mouse-like creatures limited their game playing to the outside of the mosquito netting, encompassing my sleeping bag. Unable to run between my toes, the hungry scavengers found revenge by controlling my no-sleep night with using my sleeping bag like a trampoline.

Deep, harmonizing voices with no musical instruments echoed from around every corner throughout the night.

Nighttime did not attach itself as an appendage to the afternoon. It developed into a separate world with its own spirits, light, noise, and movement.

*"There's fear that keeps you alive. And there's fear that keeps you from living. Wisdom is knowing the difference."* **David Swenson**

# Chapter 7: Arrow Aimed at My Heart

I thought about how the village's waking in the morning was like a Christmas present, opening before us. The revitalizing, fresh, morning air made the loss of sleep unimportant.

The dense humidity within the hut gave me a comfortable feeling. I slept in my long pants and long sleeved shirt from my "roaming in the darkness" walk the night before. New experiences lay in wait each time I crawled out of a hut.

**Surrounded by friendly spirits**

Wandering at dawn gave me time for thoughts of home and family left behind. Breakfast contained carbohydrates: white rice, homemade white bread, bananas, and, yes, Julius's brown river-water tea. A cloud, visiting the valley floor, submerged the meticulous fields in glimmering, morning dew. A few women, children, and pigs walked toward the fields, their songs rolling toward the mountains.

Before brushing my teeth, I needed to check the water situation. If we had already consumed the previous day's purified water, a normal situation, I had three choices: brush without water, walk to the river about a half a mile away with my water purifier and purify some water, or use boiled leftover brown river water tea.

I decided to take a walk to the river. Finding a private place after I made my choice took skill, as villagers wanted to watch my every move. Once I'd reached my destination, I brushed my teeth but realized too late that I'd forgotten to bring the purifier, water bottle, and some of those little packages of tissue with me. I walked back to the hut with my mouth and brush covered with toothpaste. If I found myself quite alone on my walk, I might look for a jungle toilet, a place protected on all sides by bushes.

To achieve privacy and rid myself of followers sometimes required walking two miles. One village had holes in the ground for a toilet. Grass mats leaned against poles on three sides. The missionaries or government groups that came in had taught the people how to build outhouses, but they forgot to teach them how to use them or what to do when they were filled.

*Visiting Muliamo from far away*

In centuries past, explorers, missionaries, and governments knocked on the door of the Dani culture, while making an effort to deliver civilization to an uncivilized lifestyle. Did these previous emissaries of goodwill see the beauty of the Dani lifestyle or did their modern technology blind them?

Meandering meant time for morning greetings and candid photos. Passing various huts, I heard a Dani group weaving a melody that rose and fell with elastic repetition. Everyone had a part. Alone, it sounded like nothing, but together the harmony came from the heart. Dreams of translating their words interrupted my patient listening skills. Maybe tribal music of the spirits had no translation.

About ten huts bordered a pocket-sized lake.

I took care to avoid any pre-made paths while watching the people at their chores and memorizing every detail in a focused effort to suspend time. Brief thoughts of returning home melted as I absorbed each moment and activity. Every part of me wanted to understand all the elements about this world of times past.

How can one even begin to grasp the simple yet complex evolution of tribal society that exists much the same today as it did thousands of years ago? Why did the spirits inhibit the development of these people, while other cultures worked to harness the powers of nature? Katherine and I had many questions and few answers; but determined, we tried to grasp every concept blown our way.

I spied a woman working quickly, readying fresh cut grass for the hot sun to dry so that she could use it later for a bed. The Dani prefer sleeping on thick piles of dried grass versus hard-packed dirt. Her humming never slowed when her eyes caught mine. Not sure if she would permit my intrusion, I pointed to my camera and used hand motions to ask if I could take a photo. She quickly gathered her baby pig, her four-inch-long hipiri tege, or sweet-potato spear, used for digging or a weapon, and her noken, or string bag, and hurried away into the forest.

I was disappointed, but I had heard that the presence of whites in the community might upset some of the women. Julius could not explain why the women were afraid of two strangers in their village.

As she rushed away, I marveled at all the things she carried with her and was disappointed that she wouldn't allow me to take a picture of her in her traditional Dani coverings. The noken the women carry, acts a bit like a shopping bag and remains an ever-present part of the female's apparel.

The women fashion the bags by rolling bark fibers on their legs until they make them into string.

The dye for fibers comes from brown ferns, clay, and the outer skin from orchid tubers of yellow, white, and orange. Handles of the bags wrap around the forehead and hang over the back, after the women fill sections with firewood, babies, pigs, and/or sweet potatoes. The bag helps ward off the morning chill while the women walk toward the fields at dawn.

A spear, polished from frequent use, along with the noken, make up a key part of a woman's normal dress.

Aware that Katherine might wonder about me, I started back to our hut.

Katherine and I often went for our own quiet walks among the villagers. Traveling separately but together strengthened us as individuals.

It enabled each of us to search for our own personal answers and experiences, while simultaneously building the bond between us.

We would look at each other on one of our returns with words unspoken. Any event observed by the other could later reignite shared memories between us.

Across the lake, a young teenage Dani girl of black skin and black hair shaved close to her scalp stared at her reflection in the lake. She wore nothing but a grass skirt. On the opposite side of the lake sat Katherine with her blond hair and blue eyes.

She wore a wild purple frog print on a shirt, spilling over her many-pocketed shorts. Her feet, dangling in the water, sent ripples across the small pond.

What went on in their minds? Our whole trip crystallized in that one scene. More than symbolic, the meeting of those two cultures shared the qualities of one basic human spirit.

The two opposites couldn't ask each other, "What are you thinking?" Neither could reply; however, they looked up at the same moment and smiled at each other, recognizing the true bond within humanity.

Spirit winds carried soft chanting in our direction, reminding me of the Independence Day festival for Muliamo on the other side of the wood fence.

I called to Katherine, she ran to me, and when we reached the hut together, we loaded our pockets with cameras and granola bars. We started out to join the celebration.

The concept of mingling in this context stretches reality, like oil mingling with water. We tried to blend in as unobtrusive observers, despite our foreign appearance.

I was curious about the variety of gourds, so I asked Julius, "Tell me about the shapes of these gourds and if they have any meaning."

He pointed out that, "Men wore straight, twisted, or curled penis gourds, some of which reached their chins."

I asked, "Where do these come from?"

*Participating in Muliamo celebration*

"The gourds come from vines trailing over rooftops. The men grow the gourds, and if they desired an extra-large, curled, or long gourd, the men attached rocks to the vegetable to guide its shape while it grew on the vine," he explained.

Then as I looked around, I began to notice the variety of body decoration among the people and wanted to know more. I asked Julius, "Where does all the color come from?"

He said, "The men wrapped colorful feathers, grasses tied in knots, woven bark, and strips of animal fur around their upper arms. Feathers from the large, flightless cassowary completed the headdresses of cowry shells woven onto the men's headbands."

*Spears or arrows, a personal choice*

"But what about the caps," I asked.

He said. "Children collect large spiders from the forest, encouraging them to spin their webs on prepared frames. Villagers then weave webs into a fabric for men's caps or strips of 'magic' to wear about the neck. Neck strips provide protection from spirits that attack the throat."

Katherine walked so fast I lost track of her for a few minutes. I wanted to capture with my camera as much of these men, scattered in every direction as far as the horizon as I could.

"Slow down," I said as I finally caught up with her.

"Look at that group staring at us like we are aliens," she said.

*As surprised to see me as I was them*

Maybe a hundred men sat cross-legged in the grass. An unfamiliar tribe wore gourds, stuffed with fetishes, covered by red cloth. A younger man stood up from the group and walked up to me. He touched the camera and just looked at me without expression. I pulled a photo of my family from my back pocket and showed him. I then pointed to the camera and to him and then the photo. He smiled at the photo as if maybe he understood this was my family. Explaining that the camera took that photo was beyond my ability.

*Some men wear the pig's teeth pointing up*

White teeth, whites of eyes, and the white boars' teeth worn through the nose made a blinding contrast against the blackness of the groups of men. While using my mind as a camera to capture the details before me, I challenged myself to avoid the villagers' stares. With inquiring looks, they murmured behind my back. Color seemed to speak of individualism, framed against their athletic torsos.

I had more questions about color. "Julius, there is such a variety. Where do they get the pigments?"

He responded, "Crushed rocks mixed with water will create a readily available white paint for those with artistic talents. Nature supplies all the other colors."

"Don't you wish you could see what some of these men have seen?" Katherine said.

"I wish Julius had a better understanding of the different languages," I said.

"I see him talking with people in each village we visit," Katherine said.

"I don't know if he is trying to communicate our need for a place to sleep and prepare meals or if he is having a real conversation," I said.

"He always disappears after dinner, doesn't he?" Katherine said.

"Yes, and that is the time he should share stories from the village we are visiting. He might prefer to spend his evenings alone with the porters and cook, rather than entertain us," I said.

Tribal warfare games had started. While I drifted among the natives, Katherine strayed. Leaving to find Katherine might mean missing the war games. Sometimes overwhelmed by the intensity of it all, she would go to our hut and read for a few hours.

The government, along with missionaries, had taken years to convince the tribes to stop killing. Pretend war games took the place of killing and villagers re-enacted scenes from ancestors' stories. Worried about Katherine and not paying much attention to what happened around me, I found myself in the middle of a tribe, crawling through the grass toward me, with bows and arrows clacking above their heads in one hand. One man carried a clawed foot of the cassowary to suppress enemies.

At my back, another tribe crouched low with bows and arrows pointed at me.

Embarrassed to stand in the crossfire in the middle of the ceremony, I wondered what they thought. Did they wish they could use their arrows on me? Did their passivity exhibit a sign of their character or just tolerance of the intruder?

Inching closer to the outskirts of their game, I faded from view, and their attention turned again to each other.

*Pig's teeth hang from a hole in the nose*

*Running to challenge another tribe in warfare games*

I could understand that in our world, a re-enactment would call for use of blanks instead of live ammunition. But arrows? I asked Julius, "Do people get hurt in the war games?"

He replied, "Their precision and skill with bows ensured that once released, the arrows landed in front of the enemy, rather than in him."

I asked, "But are they satisfied just to play a game where no one got hurt?"

He said, "These scary-looking men fulfill their destiny as warriors when they crawl through that field."

I believe any National Geographic photographer would envy my rare opportunity.

*The men stay in great physical shape all their lives*

Laughter caught my attention. Crowds gathered in a line not too far away. Above the line of black heads, one blond head and two arms waved back and forth: Katherine.

The fifty feet separating us contained racing pigs encouraged by the women, who tried by yelling, to get them to run faster.

I was confused, so I asked Julius, "What is the purpose of all this running around?"

He explained, "The woman who chased the first pig, crossing the finish line, won a gift provided by the government."

"Who supplied the pigs?" I asked.

"Women brought their own pigs and came from a nearby village to participate in the race."

A huge container of water on a truck offered a welcome fluid relief to those who had walked all day the day before and who had danced all night last night.

*Government official at Muliamo*

*Several local officials wanted their photo taken*

Some government employees who had come to encourage the celebration of Independence Day asked me to photograph them with Katherine. Earlier my questions about the facts on Independence Day were totally ignored by Julius. I guessed he didn't know the exact meaning of the holiday. My photo-taking caused some excitement, and soon other men, most of them from the Jale tribe, wanted the privilege of standing beside Katherine for a photo.

I said to Katherine, "Does the sexual connotation bother you, seeing these men with extensions tied on to their penises?"

Answering potentially embarrassing questions takes a lot of time for a teenager. I remembered this fact from my own youthful days. Katherine hesitated a moment, looking a little embarrassed, and said with a smile, "This is funny."

*Happy with his gift of a clove cigarette*

Her smiles reminded me of her youthful attitude and lack of interest in talking about sex. I felt relieved. Thousands of naked tribal men surrounded us, probably not the most comfortable place to have an uninterrupted conversation. I needed Katherine to feel safe in confiding about her emotions. What an honor for me to see village men, wanting to pose with my daughter, while sharing laughter and respect for us both.

Katherine, needing a break, noticed something. "Look mom, there are some women selling tangerines."

I said, "Let's find out if we can get some."

"They are three for about five cents," she said.

I said, "What a treat! You know that because of potential bacteria, we have been careful to eat only fruit that we could peel, so we deserve a treat as we have not had much fruit on our trip."

We delighted in the heavenly nectar. Those tangerines added fuel to our general excitement of the day.

Although the day had grown its hottest, we took little notice. Sun had devoured the yellow fields, compelling the tribes to break up their games and begin the long journey into the coolness offered by the dense forests. With the mountains in the background, they looked like trails of ants, marching in line through the haze of the midday heat.

I asked Katherine, "What would you think about hiking to the river?" The anticipation of an ice-cold river bath convinced me to leave the friendship of the tropical sun as the tribal people had done.

She said, "That sure sounds good. Our hut tried to lure me inside with its dark, cool atmosphere. My sweat-saturated clothes needed more than a cooling off."

Then I remarked, "These people dress in practical ways."

"Let's go," she said.

"Not so fast. Let's make sure we get all our stuff together."

I never thought of laundry time as one of those ready, set, go times. A nearby river or a bucket of water called for an entire list of to-dos.

"What do you want me to do?" she said.

"Gather all the dirty clothes, the water purifier, a bar of soap for bathing and laundry, shampoo, a towel or sarong, a toothbrush, toothpaste, a bag to carry wet clothes, and our clean clothes. We can do this together," I said.

Getting to the river required constant attention to our legs. Previous paths cut with machetes left sharp-pronged branches that cut like knives. Salty sweat irritated scrapes from thorny bushes.

More than once, my shouting, "Thank you for hiking boots!" disturbed the hornbills resting in the crests of the trees.

Thorns on wiry branches wanted to attach themselves to our long pants. Smells from tramping down the musty, moldy deadness that fell from above us reminded me of visits to my grandmother's cellar, another brief flashback from our world.

The village of Muliamo offered a shallow stream that, even through sunglasses, looked clear. We wanted to cool off, but curiosity brought crowds to watch the strangers from a faraway land.

Julius left us at the river, remembering Katherine's modesty. Despite the heat, the onlookers, and the possibility of waterborne diseases, I knew I would welcome feeling clean again.

I cautioned Katherine, "Look out for the ants!" Army ants carried loads twice their size, crisscrossing the water's edge and their mounded homes.

"I know I need to run through them quickly," she responded.

We learned this elementary jungle lesson in the Amazon. The river's edge bore no resemblance to the beach at Mazatlán. Wooded debris choked the edges. Tiny-clawed creatures scrambled from under dead leaves threatening bare toes.

The promise of squishy leeches between her toes kept Katherine's feet high and dry inside her safe, smelly hiking boots. The thought of my bare toes plunging into the tingling wetness far outweighed the bother of pesky leeches or clawing crabs.

For Katherine, a few splashes of icy water felt refreshing, but the possibility of changing clothes and bathing escaped the agenda that day for her. Peering from behind every vertical object, the whites of wide-open eyes glistened and waited. We needed to bathe, a necessary evil of trekking in the tropics, and it never bothered me as long as those eyes kept their distance.

After all, we looked at their naked bodies all day, and they wondered if we looked the same, physically, as their women. There were times when safety became less of an issue for me and hiding my femininity for protection against rape was a lesser evil compared to the choking humidity.

We ignored the constant sounds of screeching in the overhead canopy and rustling in the undergrowth around us. Just as Katherine completed lathering her head, a wild boar darted from the thick brush. It began blowing a warning snort for its friends--or was it for us? Katherine froze, bent over at the waist with dripping, soapy hair. The boar used the river for a toilet, taking what felt like forever.

Chills took possession of me. Standing still in my unclothed body, I whispered to Katherine, "Don't move."

Boars attack with their heads up so they can slash your legs with their sharp tusks. Fear flashed through me. My brain raced with thoughts of how to protect Katherine, as the boar kept moving closer.

Gradually, stepping backwards, my body shook uncontrollably. Trying not to disturb the wild boar, my feet stumbled over river rocks or roots. Slowly, slowly, I reached for my camera, hanging on a tree branch at the river's edge.

The thought of a wild pig charging my naked body passed as I concentrated on keeping my camera from dropping into the water. The camera was my only weapon for swinging wildly at the animal. The movement could distract him while Katherine could move back and run for her life. Screaming would bring the men hiding in the bushes out in the open. That and the motion might scare the boar away.

*Wild pig interrupting bath time*

The sharp stones hurt my tender feet. My splashing and jumping from stepping on sharp rocks and roots caused no reaction from the boar. Naked and scared, I stood there with the camera in my hands. Waiting for the boar's next move, I took a picture of him in front of Katherine. The boar kept its head down and began drinking water. Katherine looked at me and I at her, and laughing at our ridiculous situation, we scared the boar right into a pocket of thorn bushes.

Katherine said, "I was so scared; I didn't know what to do."

"All I could think about was how to keep you safe. Meeting with a wild boar was a risk I didn't think about when considering our jungle adventure," I said.

After a quick wash of clothes, I dressed again, and we started on our way to find Julius for our return to the seclusion of our Muliamo "home." The fading sun watched over the wet clothing we hung on the bushes, but it could not act as a policeman.

Scheming hands stole a few pieces, as we paid attention to the villagers, sweeping the paths with handmade brooms of branches tied together with bark string.

My special travel towel made of quick-drying, lightweight polyester was still hanging on the bush when I came back for it, though, and I was thankful.

That evening, the three of us inhaled the fried noodles with fried bananas, not quite appreciating the artistic arrangement of the banana fronds Panus had laid under the two red bowls as placemats.

Sometimes Julius, acting as guide, assumed the privilege of eating with us. He used his hands--never dropping a strand of noodle. Panus kept busy, preparing rice for the rest of the group since the noodles were gone. The full moon lingered, not caring what caused time to stop in its tracks in this valley. With each passing day, our self-perceptions began to merge with the lives of the Dani.

*"If you surrendered to the air, you could ride it."* **Toni Morrison**

## Chapter 8: What Is a Ghost Story?

Darkness carpeted the village as Julius fluffed a new bundle of dried grass under his sleeping area on the lower level of our hut. Because our hut was a two-level, we climbed into a two-foot opening, using a branch ladder with steps worn smooth from time. The level above had dried grass, covering the uncomfortable round, bamboo poles used as a floor.

Every night Julius slept close to us for our protection. His presence soothed away thoughts of harm. After shaking the woven grass mats and lighting several mosquito coils, he motioned for us to return to the first level and sit, while at the same time, Panus entered with some hot, brown river-water tea.

Drinking liquids in the evening for me meant finding a private jungle privy with light from an intimidating starlit sky. While unknown creatures, scurrying over my feet, were enough to keep me, full bladder and all, hiding in my sleeping bag, getting caught with my pants half down dampened my enthusiasm for the visit even more. The feeling only intensified on those occasions when I had dropped my flashlight while wondering about the white eyes behind the trees.

Wrapped in the warmth of the fire's glow, Katherine asked if anyone knew a ghost story.

Julius replied, "What's a ghost story?"

Using hand motions to define a ghost made no sense, but asking about spirits might lead to an explanation. Julius began a story passed down from his ancestors. The Dani believe the souls of the dead return to haunt the living, whether enemies or friends. The spirit worlds mirror the material world. As Julius began to speak, the jungle songs playing outside set the mood.

"One night while Wosi sat inside his hut by the fire with his son, he shivered as a movement of air passed through him. His son's story-telling continued without interruption, but he shook with fright. The next night, while he was walking back from visiting his pregnant wife in the women's and young children's hut, leaves started to rustle in every direction.

"How could the sound come from everywhere around him? With each quickened step, the sound followed him home. On the third night, he awakened to the smell of smoke, filtering into his hut through bamboo slats, but saw no sign of the fire outside. Soon his crops deteriorated and his wife, children, and other women fell ill, as unusual plagues frightened the village.

"Wosi asked, 'Soul-healer, please ask the dead ancestors to explain.' They replied, 'Wosi's father, while running from warriors, felt a shot in the back with two arrows and died a coward, so he could not enter the land of the ancestors. To retaliate, he turned into an evil spirit to seek revenge on families and friends.'

"The soul-healer told Wosi he would have to take care of his father's spirit. Wosi built and decorated a beautiful house for the spirit and sacrificed many animals, but the spirit continued to torment the community. Wosi decided to try to scare away the spirit.

"On a moonlit night, Wosi waited at the edge of the forest with bows and arrows. A heavy shadow appeared with two holes in its chest. Screaming and shooting arrows, Wosi chased the spirit as it floated through trees and under logs in panic. As a spirit, he could move through the air and pass through things.

"Relentlessly, Wosi had the courage and determination to win. The illuminated holes in the spirit's chest began to absorb the shadow. Seized by panic, the spirit melted away. From that night, Wosi's tribe never walked in darkness. They no longer believed one soul too many continued to occupy the village."

I shivered, thinking about Wosi's father's spirit still out there, flying about, angry. I could almost hear the swirling spirit battling for my attention.

Ancestral beliefs remain strong. I asked, "Julius could you give us some facts about your family?" I never understood what tribal ancestors Julius had. I had difficulty interpreting his words. He said, "Dani religion involves pacifying the spirits by living a good, prosperous life."

"Please give us an example."

He said, "Far from the huts, the villagers build wooden enclosures called sili or mokat ai, or spirit habitats, using dried grass bundles, representing the deceased. After a body burns, the spirit lives with other spirits in this structure."

"What are these made of?"

He said, "The wood sides surround compartments and have a tiny doorway for the spirits to enter. Spirits wander into villages and gardens, so the villagers must build several sili. Ceremonial animal sacrifices appease the spirits. Ganekke, or sacred objects like stones, confront the spirits."

"Do the Dani have funerals?"

"Funerals, an important Dani rite, lasted many years. Cremation offered freedom to the new spirit that turned to the living relatives for satisfaction, including some mutilation rites no longer practiced."

"What kind of mutilation?"

*Missing fingers*

"Supplementing cremation, some tribes removed fingers from a young female relative's hand to make the spirits happy. A string tied off the finger a half-hour before the ceremony. Just before the crude stone adze fell, the people slapped the girl hard in the upper arm to dull the sensation. They placed her hand on a piece of wood and severed the finger. They used tightly bound grass to stop the flow of blood. They dried the finger for a few days in the cooking hut, burned it, and laid it to rest in one of many secret burial places."

"That must have been horrible."

He continued, "The girls, four to five years old, carried their hands in the air to show their bravery, which also helped control the flow of blood. If a girl ran away crying, refusing the cut, she avoided punishment. Her shame completed her penalty. Tribes no longer practice this mutilation, but many middle-aged women have four to six missing fingers."

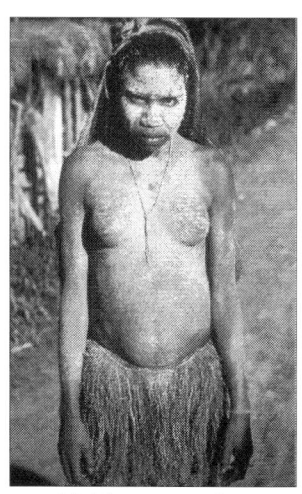

*Girl in mourning*

Julius's talk of girls made Katherine remember one we'd seen on the road that morning. Katherine asked Julius, "What happened to the young girl covered in mud?"

He said, "She was mourning for a deceased family member. For about a week, it's important to cover yourself in clay to become unattractive. When the spirit comes to take the deceased's soul, he might look for a beautiful living soul to take with him, if he's unhappy."

"So did she have a finger missing?" Katherine asked Julius.

"Yes, that's the tradition of these villagers," he said.

The Dani had passed along the story told in Julius's words for hundreds of years, and his heirs would pass them on as surely as he might pass on to future children his curled black hair, tall body with narrow shoulders and hips, or flat stomach. The Dani lived the life of their ancestors, unrehearsed and with pride. Summoning that incomprehensible ageless knowledge heightened my sense of wonder.

Stone Age men have the same drive and need as modern man to search outside themselves for a greater power. No matter how educated or remote, they have a universal need to find direction or purpose.

The spooky stories, the darkness, and the rafter-to-rafter acrobatics of the little guys in their gray suits meant another sleepless night. When traveling, I change my sleep routine to a couple of nights awake, sensing a motherly need to guard the physical and material parts of us. By the third night, though, my exhaustion wins with the reward of a deep sleep, and I am ready for another few nights as night watchman.

Entering the black playground of the night creatures and wandering souls caused two white-skinned women to put on a coat of extra confidence in locating a jungle toilet. The mystery of my surroundings penetrated my consciousness, as each footstep grasped for solid ground. The labyrinth of the vines intertwined with pandanus, or bamboo, resisted penetration, so even the flashlight beam could not help us find spaces for our feet.

Secure after our return from the jungle maze, we pulled and tugged at our sleeping bag arrangement. Getting inside took patience. Arranging the folds of mosquito netting over our heads and enclosing ourselves using Velcro meant I dealt with claustrophobia every night. I had found some tightly woven mosquito netting at an Army surplus store and cut it up into two pieces, each several yards long. I sewed Velcro around the edges of the netting and the outer edges of the sleeping bags. I should have practiced getting in and out a few times. Way too time-consuming for an easy exit. On the positive side the security of that bag and extra netting Velcroed around our bodies kept the night mysteries at a distance.

Katherine and I reflected on the mysterious scenes we witnessed. We preserved some in memory and left others discarded with the wilted vegetation of the machete's blade.

We talked about the culture. Katherine said, "I really envy everyone here just because they are so content with what they have. Remember the woman who touched my hair and then wanted to shake my hand? She only had two fingers and no clothing except a four-inch long bark skirt but just wouldn't let go of my hand."

I thought about the idea of where you are born. I said, "What if we were born here in this village? Villagers may have shunned a woman with a strong sense of independence who required alone time. I find it hard to give anyone the key to come inside my heart, but yet I don't think the materialistic things in my life are important."

My eyelids were heavy with tiredness from the meeting of the wild boar and Wosi. The day we ran into the light rain causing leeches to escape the thick underbrush to find our healthy legs for feasting came to mind. Fraught with worry about how Katherine would handle the blood-thirsty parasites, I constantly wanted to stop and have Julius help remove them. Katherine never flinched as he pinched them off.

After a while she said, "Can leeches swim? We could walk in that shallow river and view the jungle looking in from the outside."

"Yes, leeches are in the river. Walking in the water wouldn't protect us from them," Julius said.

The natural flow of one's personal life comes easier than the effort to reverse the currents. At home, we find it comfortable to play roles, making ourselves into different people. The routine of responsibilities, bills, and telephones gets scrambled. Katherine's acceptance of our new circumstances helped with my own transition. She wasn't concerned about the blood running down her leg from the de-leeching.

Katherine showed me vacant areas, which led to the discovery of new insights. Almost asleep, she said, "I have smiled at over 200 people, and a naked man tried to sell me a carrot."

"He disappeared before Julius could buy the carrots," I said.

Hmm, a cold salad to refresh my taste buds. However, it wasn't the salad I needed most. The discovery of being content without it made me smile. My heart sensed Katherine reaching out to me, taking me into her life, teaching me how to take my mask off, and daring me to reach inward to myself. Despite our age differences, we understood each other.

Lion-hearted Katherine. Tackling every opportunity without regret is a great asset for a travel partner, along with the ability to see beauty in all kinds of moments. Katherine always loved butterflies so the excitement in her eyes didn't surprise me the morning she focused on a black spot causing a yellow flower to move the branches on its bush. The butterfly, a female of the birdwing family, opened her wings to a full six inches. Katherine noticed the fuzzy white hair sticking straight up from the birdwing's long cylinder back. "The lime green stripes make it more beautiful than the blue morpho butterfly we saw in the Amazon," she said.

I had never asked Katherine if she wanted to know more about the jungle's flora and fauna. At this point in our trip, I didn't know what we had accomplished by experiencing the intricacies of the jungle. Learning about nature was a great way to start the process of demystifying oneself.

When I think of my life back home, I feel like Georgia O'Keefe when she said to her lover, "I'm glad I'm gone, but I miss you terribly."

I think Katherine and I perceived in each other a need to change our view of the world.

I knew that travel takes you away from familiar circumstances. The community framework kept us both tethered tightly, not allowing us to confront our true selves.

Having a lot of alone time on jungle walks and during dark nights in huts, unlike the many distractions of home life, offered the opportunity to tend to our own needs.

Family and friends had no idea why we needed this type of journey. An anonymous writer said, "The worst regrets in life are the risks not taken."

Not developing our potential might cause the biggest regrets in our lives. I wanted this trip to help my friends and family understand that getting away was not an abandonment of them but an unmasking of me.

Neither Katherine nor I had any regrets about leaving our cocoon of ordinary life behind. Courage had found a place in our hearts. After many days of travel, leaving the reality we knew behind, we mastered primitive ways well.

In our world back home, a mother's and teenager's togetherness might involve a few hours a day. Here, with no microwaves for pizzas, no brewing morning coffee, and no hot showers to freshen up after a long day of hiking, we learned to cope, and we learned how much we truly enjoyed our new and deep companionship.

I developed inconsistent reactions to this uncluttered lifestyle. After a sleepless night on a dirt floor, with guides snoring on the bottom level of the hut, drums in the distance, and creatures crawling up and over my sleeping bag, I found myself cranky and wanting strong black coffee, a condition that often led to poor decisions.

The nights I slept from pure exhaustion, I awoke ready to face a hundred complications. A bowl of rice three times a day left me lifeless, but then Panus would surprise us with a couple of bananas for breakfast or a bowl of cooked vegetables for lunch.

*Sharing smiles our only form of communication*

Sometimes instincts about safety dictated our choices. Other times, with no rhyme or reason, risk controlled the situation. Organizational skills, common sense, patience to deal with the unknown, and an unending trust for all humanity carried us over the tough spots. When I needed space to sort out the next step, I often left the group to find a quiet spot to review my hand-drawn map, check my calendar for the time remaining, and read any notes I might have made from home on the choices facing us.

Katherine deserved all the credit for putting up with my indecisive domain of influence. Everyone looked to me for advice on where to go and how long to stay. Fresh vegetables and comfortable surroundings encouraged my wanting to stay an extra night but then, there was always that unknown opportunity ahead.

My spirit, with the tender spots unveiled, opened doors seldom unlocked. The previous morning Katherine and Julius had decided to take a shortcut, using a dirt path against my idea of staying inside the jungle. By taking that path we met the young girl in mourning, which opened the explanation later about the removal of fingers. Our environment influenced us. Societies we encountered had common traits, though often different customs.

Dependence upon each other dominated the villages touching our lives so far. They balanced their lives with nature for happiness, fulfillment, and survival. In contrast, our society values individualism, and we do not always approach issues with the same spirit.

Preliminary planning helped in making the decision to live the tribal life, rather than limiting ourselves to observation. This journey would mean living with the people, attempting to eat what the people ate, and doing our best at blending and participating with those our paths crossed. The level of comfort my soul received in accepting dependence surprised me. Trust, the basis for that dependence, fell into place as the locals shared unconditionally. Katherine, while drifting off, asked, "Mom, do you think we have found what we were looking for?"

Instead of answering her question, I undid the bag and reached over and patted her shoulder. My thoughts led back to when Brennan, her eleven-year-old brother, asked why he couldn't go on this trip with us.

I listed miserable things: possibilities included breaking a leg while still having several weeks of walking to do, coming down with malaria or other diseases with no doctors for weeks, getting bitten by a snake or tarantula, eating no food except rice for days at a time, walking for six to eight hours a day in intense sun, and maybe seeing one tribal person the entire trip.

He asked, "What's the fun part?"

I replied, "That is the fun part. It's the risk, the respect, the building of self-confidence, the self-assurance, and the challenge of not knowing how to read a map or menu, and the satisfaction of experiencing the journey."

Someone once said, "It is part of the nature of exploration that you seldom find what you are looking for. The quest keeps going, allowing the human mind to feel it is earning its keep."

In the morning, we tumbled out of our sleeping bag mess without hesitation, knowing a whole new day of explorations waited outside. The first few days in a new village I change into my policeman mode, surveying every little detail around us.

We walked among staring tribal men and tried to guess their next move. We adapted ourselves to each new situation.

Slowly, a safe feeling brought us comfort. Apprehensive women and children hid behind trees until they felt we were safe, and then they exchanged with us timid greetings of "Lauk, lauk, or hello."

*"I am doing what a woman can hardly ever do--leading a life fit for a man."*
**Isabella Bird**

# Chapter 9: A Gathering of Pigs

The sound of rain splattering off foliage in the distance moved in our direction. The short, beating droplets danced on the bamboo slats of the hut, giving the air a fresh, clean smell. Villagers, ignoring the sudden shower, busied themselves with cutting long lengths of dried grass to repair a roof. Upward lines of smoke, encircling the valley, hid their villages from the morning mist. Forty thousand feet above, a thin white line caught my attention. The simple pleasures of the jungle blurred all thoughts of technology or people with appointments.

"Those passengers are probably tearing off the plastic wrap of their stuffed chicken breasts right now," Katherine envisioned. "Remember the flight when they ran out of chicken dinners, and you had to eat a smelly fish and rice meal? Don't you miss steaming hot coffee in a Styrofoam cup?"

"I guess coffee is the last thing on my mind," I said. The distance of time rather than miles permeated my heart. Today we would penetrate more deeply within the jungles of northern New Guinea.

*Beautiful hut with grass roof*

The comfort of Muliamo had produced a magnetic pull as our adventure moved into the end of its second week. After saying "Sawma, sawma" or thank you we walked away from the villagers and chief with sadness. The journey, like the river, had to keep flowing. To me, life could not exist without travel, and the rise of the bend ahead pulled us forward. The thought of a road existing in this remote place beckoned us. We occupied a space in time, with many past moments preparing us for this one. Whether we followed a track laid for us or immersed ourselves into virgin exploration made no difference. As witnesses to more years than the human mind can grasp, we found a magnetic pull towards our own capabilities.

As we journeyed out of the village, Chief Kusaw, with about ten men, passed us on the road. I wanted to leave with the chief the same feelings of respect he had given to me.

*Sharing cigarettes with friends from Dugum*

He had a sense of belonging with the whole universe. All parts of creation relate to one another, and this shared belief meant satisfaction of desires for everyone because of their commitment to be together, much like the theory that giving invites giving.

The energy of giving offers a meaningful direction to how we view the world.

Helping--without expectation of reward--expands our personal awareness of those around us.

Generosity and grace build on each other.

*Waiting for the games to begin*

We recognized every individual with Narak, narak, a greeting of touching hands with no English translation. Hugs didn't seem appropriate with naked men wearing penis gourds, bird feathers, armbands of leaves over painted bodies, and pig tusks protruding from their nostrils. We almost exhausted our reserve of clove-flavored cigarettes, used as a thank you, so we said our goodbyes with a few photographs and many smiles.

Chief Kusaw and his group changed course toward the two-day walk to Duyum. Some carried black palm bows and arrows. Others toted eight-foot-long spears. The Dani walked long distances, plowing or cutting down trees with hand tools and attending three-day dancing festivals like Muliamo. This activity created athletic bodies with narrow shoulders and flat stomachs.

My eyes traced every muscle as they walked. Part of a day for a Dani man includes moving heavy logs for bridge building and traveling on foot to cut those logs down.

His physique matches the intended function of his body, as the "form follows function" idea suggests. Consumed with the beauty of these people, Katherine and I stared in every direction.

Ready to run with the day, my body wanted to lead all the way. Indonesians take life slowly, which lowered my enthusiasm, as the hardest part of our trip greeted us early that morning.

After three hours of climbing up and over rocks and loose dirt, I talked with breathless difficulty.

Coughin, playing his mouth harp, harmonized with the rest of the group, humming their favorite song. The music felt like a rope wrapped around my waist lifting me with each forward step. Breathing hurt.

I used both hands and pushed hard on my spear and bow, which made perfect walking sticks. The real struggle settled in my knees. I dug into the rocks for help. Looking up, I at last saw sky instead of more boat-sized boulders.

The spiritual ambiance at the top of Pyramid Mountain revitalized us as we soaked up the beauty of the valley floor. Clouds floating atop nearby mountains looked like Marshmallow Fluff on a chocolate sundae.

*Contributing a pig to a celebration*

While the sun provided us shadows that were the color of our friends, we brushed the hands of villagers with luak luak and narak, and continued our trek. Men on their way home from morning markets carried bundles of firewood and squealing pigs hanging upside down from long sticks.

Women and children ran past on the opposite side, their smiles faint but their hands always extended flat, to brush over a passing stranger. A sky filled with cumulus clouds looked like the never-ending dunes of the Sahara.

A schoolteacher named Edmond with two young boys stopped to talk. One boy carried an old-fashioned black typewriter in a plastic bag, the other a small backpack. Edmond, a Madura islander, transferred to this area in the government resettlement program that paid $200 a month to people who would move from packed-like-sardine islands to work in the remote isolated islands.

Edmond told us, "We believe in teaching the young people the ways of their tribe; but to survive, we need to teach the ways of others."

Edmond, the first person who spoke any English at all besides Julius, invited us to stay at his schoolhouse overnight, if we wished.

We thanked him for his offer. It would be a wonderful and unexpected side trip. Julius sweetened the suggestion by saying, "The schoolteacher heard of another festival in Gondura several hours from here."

*Katherine walking through peanut fields*

We said, terima kasih, and started on our way. While we trekked over dirt paths through peanut and sweet potato fields and around rice paddies, women bent at the waist busied themselves with pulling, planting, or digging.

Pigs and children, free to explore while the women worked the fields, peered with cautious curiosity around tree stumps at the heavy boots we wore as we dodged the ruts of hoof prints left by pigs. Fences encircling village compounds marked property lines and kept the pigs corralled.

"Wait," I called out.

I steadied myself as I tried to pull my pants loose. The cutout steps on the tree branch ladder were designed for small bare feet, not clumsy hiking boots. My right foot slipped off a step. Slivers caught my pant leg. My left foot had already stepped over the top of the fence line.

"Katherine, this fence is cutting me in half!" I said.

Katherine grabbed Panus's arm, turned him around and said to me, "Don't move. We'll help."

*Crossing over a fence*

The tree-branch fences last years because of the mounds of grass slung over them by villagers for protection from water. The tribal people, according to Julius, owned property in the Baliem Valley. One could buy land from the Dani, paying the annual tax to the government.

"Did I hear Edmond say he paid twenty dollars to own his house and property?" I said to Julius after Panus jumped back over the fence and freed the wood slivers from my pant leg.

"Some villages owned property as community groups," Julius answered.

Time, an element ignored by the locals, let our stomachs dictate when to complain. We smiled at the sight of the nearby creek. Within minutes, the porters had mats in the grass for resting and a small fire ready for cooking rice. We dipped our bare feet in the ice-cold creek, planting them on smooth rocks. Loose, floating debris irritated the scratches left from crossing the ladder. The deep water made the creek feel more like a river.

I whispered to Katherine, "What if the world truly is flat and here we sit at the edge?"

Katherine laughed, and then observed, "We haven't seen any fish in the rivers or streams. Isn't that strange?"

"Good thing or we might have fish every night with our rice," I said.

I reached over as if to hug her and instead tickled her side. Catching her off guard almost caused her to fall forward in the water.

A cold drink sounded terrific, but the purifier, which generated iodine-flavored water, rested in some locked bag. If Katherine or I had forgotten to put the keys back in our waist pouches, we would have to remember where we put the extra set, either pinned in our bras or stuck in some pocket by mistake. Each bag had its own key, and all the keys looked alike. The bags always stayed locked. Just when we locked the bag and put the key away, we would remember one other little thing, and we'd start the process all over again.

Unfortunately, isolation spells locked bags, ensuring that curious hands keep out and potential thieves stay clear. Stealing the entire bag was an option but not likely. Too many people might question a naked tribal man, carrying a canvas backpack. Every article we packed contributed to our survival, from the first aid kit for our body to our music, which linked our minds back to reality. Any item misplaced could make our lives less comfortable. Passports, money, and return tickets had uses later, but the first aid kit, flashlights, protein bars, malaria pills, and mosquito repellent were all needed now. Without them, we could easily die in this place.

Steamed rice melted in our mouth after our long, strenuous walk. Dishes washed with gritty sand made us realize the wastefulness of plastic bottles of liquid soap.

*Katherine taking a drink from the water container*

Taking advantage of some rest time, we removed the bottom section of our nylon travel pants which unzipped at the knee. Our backpacks grew heavier as the day half passed. The full backpacks felt like rocks against our backs, both while we were walking and while on the ground used as pillows.

Katherine said, "We have huge backpacks full of stuff we need to survive. These people have nothing of material value, yet, who are the ones who smile all the time?"

She continued, "Our possessions don't determine who we are."

"Most of the things we have with us improve our quality of living, like the water purifier," I said.

*Wearing gifts from missionaries*

"Yes, and like the clothing we chose for this trip. These people live simply on the land. These people don't get into wars or colonize and are just happy to live with their sweet potatoes and pigs.

Missionaries come and go, telling them that they have to wear clothing. One group of women we saw wore bras and grass skirts and didn't know any better," she said.

"Is that why it's not important that you spend several hundred dollars for one outfit like your friends?" I said.

"Things themselves can't harm us or force us to do what we don't want to do. When possessions turn us into something else, we stop developing who we are, and those things can be an obstacle to future happiness," she said.

Katherine's level of maturity often surprised me. There were few situations back home when we had conversations like this.

I had time to sit down and listen, and she could expound on personal feelings about life.

"Mom, did Julius really wear a Liz Claiborne sweatshirt the other day?"

"Yes, and notice how his personality changes when he wears those headphones and huge sunglasses? He acts more important than the other men."

We finished our rice and packed up our mats as the sun cast shadows along the tangled mass of creepers, matting the jungle floor.

We were tired, but we slipped our backpacks onto our shoulders and followed Julius and the porters toward the next village.

It took strength to step with determination until, squinting, we caught a glimpse of Gondura after leaving a pocket of bamboo trees, snarled with vines, thin branches, and a harmless, green, tree python, marked with painted jewelry.

The spirits passed over the tenacious kunia, or silver spear grass, to warn the villagers of our arrival.

"Look! It's a lake. I'm beginning to love this place," Katherine said, flashing me the first smile I'd seen in a few hours.

*Plowing up silver kunia grass*

Surrounded by the silvery ripples, a man stood leaning on a pole. I stared at him, soon realizing that the brilliant rays of sunlight created silver mirrors on the blades of grass.

Slash-and-burn farm techniques, still used in some areas, result in kunia grass, covering the blackened terrain.

A shadow traversed the grass as a black-capped lory glided by, expending little effort. His orange and red body landed on some dead limbs in the bamboo thicket, and I admired his blue tail and black mask. Rows of rhododendron defined the dirt path. The pink blossoms, broader than my hand, crossed over a fresh-cut yellow log bridge.

***Archway into Gondura***

*Well maintained village*

Two monitor lizards, oblivious to their shared heritage with the famous Komodo dragon, basked in the warmth of the rocks lining the creek. Crossing another new log bridge, we entered Gondura through a pink-and-burgundy-flowered vine archway.

The village boasted immaculate grounds, with not a dead leaf or limb in sight. Julius walked toward a few round huts.

Plants and flowering bushes entwined the bases of the huts and a twisted trickle of a stream encircled them.

"How will we answer the call to nature in the middle of the night if we stay in that hut?" I said.

"What do you mean?" Katherine said.

"The height of the door is just above my waist and look at the stream of water circling the hut. We will have to remember while crawling through the door to immediately manipulate the wobbly log bridge over the water," I said.

I thought that squatting to move through the door and then immediately stepping over the stream tested mental awareness and physical dexterity.

Not something on my mind when half asleep.

*Gondura fish hatchery*

Two rectangular ponds, each a fish hatchery, bordered the huts on two sides. Inside a fifteen-foot diameter hut, families gathered gourds, a black cooking pot, and an overstuffed animal-skin bag. The family accepted Julius's thanks for allowing us to sleep in their home. With their special possessions, the family squatted to leave.

Inside, carpets of woven-grass mats hid the hard-packed dirt floor. Sunlight streaming through cracks in the ceiling revealed a huge hut with glowing embers in the center.

"Are we all staying inside this hut?" I said to the group.

Julius only spoke broken English. But, along with hand motions and eye contact, I translated his words to mean this hut is far superior to the smaller huts of the village. Plus, I can watch over you and Katherine, staying here close by.

Our group found enough room to fit inside. Because Dani men sleep apart from women, convincing Julius to allow the porters and cook to sleep inside with us required skill with words. Julius did not often comprehend our messages. He may have considered sleeping inside a privilege reserved for him because he acted as our official guide. After all, he earned two dollars a day, while the others received only fifty cents. I knew DenDee, Coughin, Panus, and Amir appreciated one night less of sleeping outside the hut in the grass.

Twenty, handmade palm-fiber mats circled the fire pit. Four poles created a barrier for the pit, preventing people from rolling into the fire and providing support for the roof. Fires smoldered throughout the day in village huts to ward off the Indonesian chill of the 6000-foot altitude.

The warmth of the days called for short pants and short sleeves, but the night chill called for heavy clothing. I wondered how any of the men could feel comfortable at night, wearing only horim. Outside, women cleared dirt paths with tree branch brooms. Katherine and I followed fifteen teenage boys--single file--to the river, and the clear water beckoned to us.

"We could take our boots off and jump in?" I said to Katherine.

"Yes, I remember the times we used to do that. Hardly a day went by without dipping in the lake behind our house back in the States," she said.

"Don't you think the time has come for us to wash the dust from our hair and scrape the dirt from under our fingernails in the cool water?" I said.

The boys, carrying large river rocks to the fire-pit, returned to the village.

"What are those sounds?" I asked.

"Are those kids singing? It has a pleasant but mysterious melody," Katherine said.

"Let's find out," I said.

The sounds were so haunting that I wished my tape player had been a recorder.

As we approached our hut to gather clean clothing, towels and soap, we saw the boys arranging a circle of rocks around the mounds of firewood. The singing faded to that of only a couple of boys, paying close attention to their duties, as the others wondered if the young blond girl in their presence was a dream.

Newcomers to the village brought attention like a presidential arrival, and Katherine and I were no exception. Village curiosity compelled young men to run past, trying to touch me, half-naked, as I prepared to bathe. The running men scared Katherine, and she was thankful she had not yet undressed. The inquisitive boys kept watch behind trees and bushes as I wrapped a sarong around my body and slipped my pants and socks off. I washed my shirt, pants, and undies and rinsed the sarong after slipping into dry, clean clothes. Katherine did the best she could in washing her body with her clothes still on. She carried her clean clothes back to the hut for changing.

At least the laundry smelled river-water clean before we retreated to the hut to read and watch our clothing while it dried, draped over bushes. Silk undies and nylon shirts and pants take an hour to dry. Socks take one to two days to dry, because of the humidity.

If we left the area of the hut, we hung the wet items inside. If we were leaving, and something was still wet, we safety-pinned it to the outside of a backpack.

Hunger for solitude afflicted Katherine and me at different times. Well-being requires healthy portions of alone and together time. In solitude, I came to know myself and to appreciate the many nuances that distinguished me from others. Writing down reactions and perceptions in my notebook helped me remember the lessons involving my senses. I kept going back to the question Katherine had asked earlier about whether this trip had satisfied our curiosity.

We created physical and emotional demands on our bodies by diving into an almost prehistoric land. Subtle, calming, natural, and much more fulfilling rewards fed our hearts and minds.

We recovered from the physical demands after food, sleep, or even a quick rest after lunch.

The pain in my knees after walking rocky paths for six hours went away after an hour of watching Panus cook lunch. The more lasting rewards were those left over after questioning our own preconceived ideas about a fourth-world culture. That deliberate introspection, as our bodies recovered during visual moments of pristine beauty or while mesmerized by tribal rhythms and customs, made us less narrow-minded and more accepting of a culture so different from us.

Venturing into uncharted territories, I collected new information that I would later sift and file for a lifetime of memories. The challenges of keeping warm without wearing clothing helped me understand how the Dani live their lives. They use the tools of their environment for their homes, food, and health such as covering their bodies with pig grease and ash for warmth on cold mountainous nights.

Young women headed into the village, carrying tall plants that they had dug from the jungle floor, adding the final additions to the temporary rectangular homes they built for visiting tribes to sell their goods.

Stubby logs formed a line for seating and established a border around a visitors' area.

Sunday afternoon peacefulness soon turned into rush-hour traffic as visitors from other tribes began descending upon the tiny village of Gondura. Drifts of tribal groups outlined the ditches along the main dirt path through the village, which consisted of only twenty or so grass huts. A modern cement building served as headquarters for the local government chief who was to be honored by the next day's festival.

*Selling carrots at the Gondura Festival*

As an observer, I learned to merge with a tree or bush. These hide-and-seek games required patience. As long as I remained unnoticed, the Dani or Lani people, filling the air with laughter, went about spreading carrots, potatoes, leafy greens, and stacks of gourds. From my secret hiding places, I watched them working in their temporary lean-tos, exchanging vegetables and ideas. I was part of their lives in a way they would never allow had I walked directly into their midst. Overcome with reverence, fear, and anticipation, I wanted to grasp the whole picture, but photography seemed out of the question. Rather than invade their privacy, I felt more comfortable tail-boned to a dead branch, watching with respect and wide-eyed wonder. I can make a mechanical record of images through photography, particularly in new situations of beauty; however, doing so often results in missing the moment. Adjusting for exposure and framing a subject might cause me to miss something.

A predominant spirit, a feeling like a whisper of wind, lingered. I took a deep breath while my mind and my body gathered itself. Once the Dani felt my presence, their activity changed to low mumblings. Two older women, taking a short cut to get to the road, interrupted my hiding. It seemed as if a zipper on the tree had opened and out stepped a spirit from the future. They watched even the blinking of my eyes.

Contemplating how to take in this situation and make it part of my life, I decided to move out into the open by walking up and down the hard-packed road. Rice sacks, so full of vegetables they could stand on their own except for a slump at the opening, separated families. The families must have spent days filling their sacks with food to trade for salt, foods they could not grow, or handmade tools. Several groups kneeled next to a small pond off the road, scrubbing potatoes or carrots until I came into sight. Their astonished looks surprised me. Seeing me for the first time, they stood motionless and stared.

After days of living with the Dani in Indonesia, I felt accustomed to walking among strangers. Adapting to their language, their lack of clothing, and their primitive way of living took time and patience. Each new village felt comfortable after a few hours of talking and meeting with locals. That triggered a question. "Katherine, can you imagine what it might be like if these villagers showed up on our street at home and what we might say or do?" I said.

She said, "We need to remind ourselves that we look mysterious and unique to these people when they see us for the first time."

"Yes, in all of our travels, we need to constantly remind ourselves of the golden rule," I said.

She said, "They take the time to allow us to be a part of their lives and let us wander around as we please, greeting us with their smiles."

*Beads signify a particular village*

At dinnertime hundreds of festival guests blanketed the grounds, some seeking shelter in makeshift huts with the majority making themselves at home inside the local villagers' compound. My brow wrinkled, witnessing discourteous actions. People sat in flowerbeds, urinated in the innocent little stream that wound around the permanent huts, broke huge pieces of bushes for sleeping pads, and dug holes for fire pits in the yards of their hosts.

Women would unload their net bags full of carrots, spreading them on top of beautiful yellow flowerbeds. If plants got in their way, they pulled them out by the roots to make room to sit. Inquiries over the price of vegetables opened squabbling matches among the women of the village and the visiting women. The lack of respect surprised me; yet the locals and guests showed contentment with the circumstances.

We explained to Julius during dinner that in Western society, a stranger could not sell his goods on private property without asking permission of the owner. If he did so, the owner could call the police. Julius did not understand the concept. No one here knew about courtrooms or lawyers, as the Dani do not know about ownership, jealousy, competition, and dishonesty, things that we take for granted in Western society.

For Gondura, the honor of selection from government officials as the site for a festival gave the local people something to anticipate and an opportunity to demonstrate pride in their community. Gratified with a memorable festival, the villagers did not mind the visitors' destruction of the landscape.

Our brown, river-water tea and peanut-butter-covered biscuits gave us a once-a-day protein boost. Peanut butter came in individual foil packets, and the biscuits were what we call cookies in America. Loughin came into our hut with his bamboo mouth harp. His penis gourd poked him in his nose as he sat on the dirt floor.

I laughed out loud but immediately tried to hide my embarrassment with words.

"How uncomfortable to have to deal with that gourd all day and night," I said to Katherine.

"I wonder how he keeps it from breaking," she said.

He sometimes shivered as he played the same tune repeatedly. With age comes poor circulation, meaning chills, and he obviously showed signs of not dealing with nudity very well. His body bulged with the muscles of a twenty-year-old, but the wrinkles on his face showed evidence of bewitching stories that we knew we would never hear. Three inches of tight black curls streaked with grey sat on top of his head like a hat. Soft trails of sunlight highlighted the whites of his eyes, and the twelve-inch long cowry shell necklace carried decades of secrets in its tiny little crevices. He had a cross-looking face due to sagging laugh lines--until we put our headphones on him! We could not tell whom he liked better, Sade, Phil Collins, or Paul Hardcastle, but he started to smile as soon as the headphones were over his ears. Coughin's attitude reminded me of a quote by Joseph Campbell: "People say that what we're all seeking is a meaning for life. I don't think that's what we're really seeking. I think that what we're seeking is an experience of being alive."

Knowing what interested the Dani about me would enable me to explain myself better. I had limited capabilities, from where they stood. I could not find my way on a jungle path, fix my own food, build a fire in the middle of a damp forest, expose my skin to the sun without chemicals, weave a string from bark, or handle a machete without dropping it. I couldn't catch a cuscus for dinner, enjoy a beetle for a snack, or even walk fifty feet without boots. The barriers of language and comprehension gave me the feeling I could never answer their questions.

Julius presented us with a double-wide smile left over from the first day we met. Prior to leaving the hotel, he begged for money for shoes. Funny, that situation vanished from my mind until now, as I looked down at his feet. His shoes had holes in the toes, with soles worn thin. After hiring him, he led me to believe he needed money for shoes to wear on the trek. Being naïve and feeling sorry for him, I gave him an extra twenty dollars to buy some new shoes, which he never bought. Julius wanted to talk, and a guilty look crossed his face as he said, "My brother's girlfriend left him for another man after my brother had given her parents ten pigs toward a marriage contract more than three years ago."

I said, "That sounds horrible."

He continued, "When the girl married the other man, her parents never returned the pigs to my brother."

"That's not right."

"I plan to offer the local policeman 50,000 rupiahs, [twenty-five dollars], to have him talk to her parents in order to get the pigs back, so I need to get my guide money now to do this."

Katherine and I laughed and shook our heads. He could not comprehend the idea that his borrowing so much money from us to pay the bribe meant that when we returned, instead of our paying him for guide services, he would have to pay us for loans. We didn't have a written contract other than a few scribbled notes in my journal.

"I don't really want to do this because you won't have your guide money at the end of our trip, but if that is what you want, we will do that for you."

Late that night, he came to me with that same double smile and said, "The in-laws agreed to return the ten pigs, and they added two more as an interest payment for the problem, so I thank you for helping me."

Interesting gossip passes from village to village like wild fire.

Coughin had fallen asleep with the headphones on, which convinced Julius to allow him to stay inside the warm hut. Time to push back the night. By removing the tops of the flashlights, I found the bulbs gave us better ambient light. Katherine and I propped the flashlights upright between piles of mats which made the room bright enough for us to write for hours about our day.

We had limited concentration because of the two snoring men. An animal skin, hanging directly above the flames of the fire, gave off a putrid smell. Didn't the family living in this hut full-time notice the odor? Leaving the safety of the hut, we headed out to find a jungle toilet, a risky undertaking. Holding hands with Katherine seemed a more reassuring alternative than exploring at midnight alone. We walked a good quarter-mile, passing visitors sleeping in ditches. We tried to find smooth roots or rocks to walk on, our loose flip-flops creating friction with the brush.

I tried to imagine the companionship of a guardian angel, encircling us as we walked, though this pleasant thought battled with a much more negative one: meeting with a warrior, painted and ready for a kill.

We stood watch for each other with flashlights, circling in opposite directions, to help keep our space private. We shivered with uncertainty during that dark walk, but after a while, we started to relax. It seemed that if the Dani held any malice toward us, they would have shown it earlier.

A mother-and-daughter walk through the shopping mall would never match our jungle walks, scoping out the dangers in the dark. Katherine read my heart when she reached for my hand, more than a daughter supporting me on my journey. With even small events such as sharing the only egg in the village, closeness developed between us like that of best friends.

A mutual desire had surfaced as we spent hours exchanging ideas about plans or whatever came to mind. I think Katherine was beginning to see her personality as an appendage to mine. Alikeness creates attachment. I measured my closeness with my mother by how much we had in common.

Eleanor Roosevelt said, "It is not fair to ask of others what you are not willing to do yourself." This quote served as a good reminder to me when Katherine and I returned to the hut and found Julius had not cleared the dinner dishes but had, instead, drifted off to sleep.

The village was meticulous for a reason. The women understood, even if Julius didn't, that keeping huts clean and food put away kept pests at bay. The gray creatures found a gourmet heaven with the leftover rice and biscuit crumbs in our hut. I knew if I didn't clean up, the rodents would jump with joy all night as they snacked on our leftovers, not caring if we slept in their way or not, even scampering over our faces and landing on our heads. I had no way to find water for washing dishes in the dark, meaning I could look forward to little to no sleep.

The only break from the incessant snoring came when something knocked at the door. The sound disturbed everyone's sleeping. Within minutes, a deep sleep returned to everyone but me. I heard movement near me. The manifestation made me aware of every movement my own body made. My mind wanted one of my senses to communicate to me. My arms, glued inside my sleeping bag, failed to reach out to find my flashlight. Probably a bad dream? Nights like this never had answers.

At the first sounds of the village waking, my fidgeting with bags began to wake up the group in my hut. Preparations for the festival began outside as the dark shades of the woods lightened, forcing the night's eeriness to retreat.

During my quarter-mile walk to find some privacy, Julius was exploring and located a treasure.

"How would you like to bite into a bunch of three-inch bananas?" he asked. "Couldn't wait to show these to you."

My mind smelled bacon and whole-wheat toast with marmalade served with an over-easy egg on the side, so my smile of gratitude was not quite as genuine; but I said, "That will taste good to us. It's a nice change in our food options."

Outside, men worked energetically, hanging a wooden sign with the village name, Gondura, printed on it.

"Why is Gondura having a festival?" I asked Julius. "Gondura is

*Pig, brought to Gondura for festival sacrifice*

centrally located and represents the government. So officials chose a Dani man to be the policeman," he said.

"What does the policeman do?" I asked.

"He tries to keep the people from fighting with each other and with surrounding villages. The villagers are very happy with the choice of a Dani to represent them. They feared a stranger from another island with a strict and unfair presence," he said. Julius continued, "The second reason, and the key reason for this once-every-four-year gathering, was that an important man would initiate the Ebe Akho, or ceremony given to please the spirits. Hundreds of marriages and initiations, along with a huge pig killing and feast will take place. The host of the ceremony will receive gifts of many pigs. Villages measured time by full moons and events like this ceremony. The people celebrate life daily instead of the anniversary of a birth." Even Julius could only estimate his age. The group of twenty-year-old men carried more rocks from the river, still singing. In America, community service of this type would generate laughter by neighborhood boys who would much prefer a payment of money, rather than appreciation. Their group effort symbolized personal commitment to families and community.

*Babysitting little brother*

As more and more people tied pigs to stakes in the clearing, more people also brought piles of vegetables, sweet potatoes, rabbits, and chickens. These gifts for the chief of Gondura honored the government official, coming later that day. Huts arranged in a U-shape gave way to an open grassy area. The fire pit, close to the open end, measured ten feet by four feet and was full of twelve-inch rocks, carried by the singing, young men.

Our hut stood at the mouth of the compound, central to the spectacle of activity. Boisterous foreign chatter lured us from the quietness of our bamboo refuge. The sun had gone to work, separating the clouds. A myriad of indigenous peoples gathered in small groups, chattering loudly until we entered the area.

Some wore clothing brought by missionaries who must have scolded them with words like, "Such a disgrace to walk around in full view, wearing nothing but a penis gourd." Important village chiefs and elders wore civilian clothing or uniforms, but most villagers maintained their normal dress code of penis gourds or fiber skirts.

*Unusual penis gourd*

Like a Dani warrior stalking his quarry, trying not to disturb events as they unfolded, I ended my walk in front of a candy-cane-shaped little man. The curls in his hair matched the curly stitches of his hat. Pushing hard on his walking stick, he quivered as he gathered the strength to lift his eyes to look up at mine. Years of pigs' teeth passing through his nose had left a gaping hole which allowed light to pass through as he turned his head.

Holes in his ear lobes and nose framed the broadest smile, bordered by the wrinkles of time. The size and shape of a man's horim are a very personal choice.

Just like some of us choose tight over loose fitting clothing. Some men stuff fetishes, tobacco and other magic objects inside the horim and cover with a piece of red fabric.

Void of apprehension, the little man uncurled a finger to point at my flip-flops. Flip-flops came in handy for rocky, river bottoms while I bathed. They provided relief from heavy hiking boots in villages with short, soft grass, free of pig or human droppings. My heart longed to offer him my flip-flops just so I could enjoy his welcome smile. Years of barefooting over rocks and vines had made his duck-like feet take on a webbed shape, with the toes spread flat like a Chinese fan.

Passed from generation to generation, the ritual of the singing boys and the rubbing of sticks together to start the fire marked the beginning of the deserving ceremony. Red with flames, the sticks lit several chunks of wood, resting under the heavy rocks in the pit.

Crossing a path a child, pulling a bark string with a purple flower attached to it, played the game called wam-wam, or pig-pig, a favorite childhood amusement in Indonesia. Julius was not familiar with the language of this village and often had problems understanding explanations like the rules of the game.

From his rocky promontory, the Gondura chief ran toward the group of several hundred men, some dressed in military khaki. His red and blue print shirt clashed with his 1960s-style orange gym shorts, bearing white stripes on either side.

*Gondura chief killing pig*

Waving a bow and a single arrow, the chief ran past me, whooping and hollering. Just as loud, but screeching and squealing, came a blimp of a pig intent on seeking escape. Not until they cornered the pig between two huts and a fence did the chief even try to shoot. His precision marksmanship struck a fatal blow, though it seemed a bit like shooting fish in a barrel.

One by one, the men untied smaller pigs, removing the bark-string from around the animals' mouths and hooves. As each of the pigs escaped, the men stepped back to allow each of the visiting chiefs the honor of the kill. Dead pigs sprawled on the manicured, unblemished grass.

The pungent smell of singed hair grew stronger as men picked up the pig carcasses by the ears and tails and laid them on steaming rocks. Once singed, each pig was skinned and butchered, and the cut pieces were wrapped in palm leaves.

"Let's go for a cooling walk in the river," Katherine said. "The icy water will numb the burning blisters on our feet."

The sun was only three-fourths of the way toward sunset, which meant we still had time to wash clothes. Yesterday's bathing scene remained fresh in our minds, so we opted out. Besides, we could still stand to smell each other which was more than I could say for Julius, who probably had not bathed the entire trip.

The two of us sat balanced on a log over the shallow water, our legs swinging, and talked. Katherine had wisdom beyond her years. She always gave me a sense of importance during our conversations, emphasizing how much she valued my opinions. On the other hand, perhaps I grew younger and wiser. Either way, we found it easy to share lessons of the journey.

Sometimes the words a mother speaks to her daughter appear meaningless at the time, but Katherine had the maturity to understand, tucking them under lock and key into the treasure chest of her mind. Before her teenage years, Katherine wanted to learn to sail. Katherine was an excellent swimmer, having grown up on a lake and swimming every day. By the time she was twelve, she was teaching lifesaving to older kids on the lake. The number one rule when taking the sailboat out was to wear a lifejacket.

"Why, when I'm such a great swimmer?" she would say.

I was watching from the porch as the wind filled her sail as she tried to tack before hitting the nearby shore. The boat went over--capsized! My heart sank as I searched for that orange lifejacket to come up out of the water with her head bobbing up and down. Never again did I hear any complaints about wearing that jacket.

Windblown and disappointed, she finally righted the boat and made it back to our home dock.

"I know a hug is all you need. My job has always been to teach and protect you. But after watching you handle that boat all alone, I can see you have grown into a smart, competent young woman, who no longer needs much help. You handled that boat tipping over so well. Each time you fell off the keel while trying to rock the boat upright, I cheered for you."

"I hate sailing," she said.

"I knew that if you learned to deal with the trying and the doing that you would succeed," I said. "Come on, let's get a Popsicle."

"Okay, but next week if it's real windy, would you ask Allie or Brennan to go with me so I don't capsize again?" she said.

Like in a dance I think that experience changed Katherine's steps toward carving out a unique identity. The dance would inevitably change again and again.

Of course, I hoped that when she was older and became a mother herself, she would remember these conversations during which we grew closer and bonded, deepening our relationship.

I found it difficult to dispose of negative thoughts and my reactions to the curiosity of tribal men; however, I did not have the authority to make changes in the ways of living deep in the mountains of New Guinea. The elements that go into making each day special vary as widely as the trees we passed.

Suddenly two monitor lizards, disturbed from their afternoon tanning, spattered us with cold droplets of water. We kicked sprinkles back and forth, almost falling off the log, trying to reach deeper water.

The sounds of screams and crying fractured our reflective mood. "Grab your wet clothes and let's leave now," I said.

I slid my flip-flops on and started to move away from the river as the sounds became louder. I could see a woman run across a distance of open ground. Her youngal, or skirt, woven of strong fern fibers by a woman's nearest male relative and worn by married women, hung low around her hips, restricting her escape. Behind her several men had given chase with tree branches clutched in their hands.

As they grew nearer, they swatted her back again and again. Red lines crisscrossed her back. I felt fear creeping into me. What if they see us and change their direction toward us? I start to run but realized I couldn't hear Katherine behind me.

"Katherine, where are you?" I hollered.

"Mom, come help me!" she yelled back.

Adrenaline kicked in. If ever I felt like flying, then that was the time to begin. Was there something ahead of me that I didn't want to see? Were the two men part of a group of men out looking for women to attack?

A labyrinth of vines and sharp bushes were not there before, but now they were blocking my view of the river and Katherine. Vines caught a shoe and caused me to fall. While I was down I could see Katherine's shoulders like she was crawling.

All of a sudden I was sliding down a muddy slope into the river. The current was fast, and I couldn't right myself, but I could see Katherine safe in the distance splashing in the water, herself.

"What happened to you?" I yelled.

"I got my footing and stood on the slippery rocks with one shoe on and one shoe left behind.

I dropped one of my flip-flops in the river and tried to chase it. I caught up with it, but when I reached for it, I fell in," she said.

"Thank God, you're okay. I had visions of your being captured by angry tribal men," I said.

"I was so scared when I saw those men chasing that woman. Ouch! The rocks are so sharp and I keep losing my balance," she said.

We finally got close enough to help balance the other and make it to shore.

"Let's get out of here," she said.

We took a different path toward Gondura, wanting to go in the opposite direction of the women running.

We found a tin-roof shack with villagers, selling cigarettes, biscuits, and warm soda pop in glass bottles. We rested with Cokes and bought all of the vanilla English tea-biscuits they had, as well as additional cigarettes for thank-you gifts. Sitting on the ground, we took deep breaths, and I put my arms around Katherine. With teary eyes and dripping clothing, we both shivered. I knew that the scene of that terrified woman, crying and running from the men with their wicked tree branches, had shaken Katherine, just as it had shaken me. I explained to her that we had no control over the events of the day, but I could see that my words provided little consolation. I could only hope that Julius would be able to help us understand what might have transpired between the woman and the men chasing her.

Our yearning for experiences with tribal living did not change even though we faced unpleasant real-life situations. A better understanding of the Dani strengthened my commitment for traveling in that valley and understanding the bad as well as the good; this insight kept me focused on the purpose of our month there.

"Life here feels inseparable from magic," Katherine said.

"Villagers told Julius that the spirits rewarded one of their men by allowing him to catch a cuscus for the festival feast. The spirits chose him for their magic, not because he was a good hunter," I said.

"Do you think the spirits considered that woman running today evil and would let her die from her attackers?" Katherine said. "We can talk to Julius about what happened after dinner," I said.

Maybe confused or wanting to seek out the forgotten smell of vegetables cooking, Katherine said, "Let's find our way back to the hut."

Panus procured carrots and cabbage. He must have traded some rice for the vegetables. He understood by then that Katherine and I didn't eat much rice, or at least he should have. By that point on our trip, we should have eaten half of the rice he carried in the sack on his back, yet the twenty-five-pound sack was almost full. Panus prepared the mie goreng, and we all sat down and ate our fill. We had eaten only baby bowls of rice and bananas for breakfast.

We invited Panus and Coughin to listen as Julius interpreted. They soaked up my stories of my grandparents coming across the vast ocean as children and growing up in the Midwest. My grandfather remembered living in deep caves in the ground, covered by four feet of snow above. At one time, a horrible fire destroyed their cornfields. Grasshoppers killed their corn crop another year, forcing them to dig new caves in another area. The Dani men understood this battle with nature, but they could not comprehend our lifestyle today with computers, automobiles, and vaccines. We asked Julius to explain the scene with the woman. He said, "The woman you saw chased and beaten earlier might have cheated on her husband. Some tribes punish this act with death, but in her case, they imposed the shame of banishment from the village."

I asked, "What will happen to her now?"

"I don't really know, but this is a severe punishment and will change her life," he said.

He continued, "In ancient times, Indonesians had a custom of fire-walking which Dutch rulers outlawed. During traditional Indonesian events like weddings and feasts, men accused of adultery or of seducing young unmarried girls could walk over red-hot stones to prove their innocence. They laid coral rocks over kindling until the coral reddened with heat. With long sticks cut at the end to create forks, the villagers removed the smoldering wood to expose glowing hot rocks. Wearing a red loincloth and rubbing saliva over his feet, a man prayed to the spirits for protection. Burned feet indicated his guilt of adultery. Juice from the betel nut relieved the burns." Julius didn't know what kind of punishment the guilty received.

As Katherine's mentor and role model of cultural values, I didn't want her to feel any antagonism toward males after the episode involving the woman earlier in the day. The Danis believed in their socially constructed ways of living without needing proof or reasoning behind them. Parents and grandparents taught children to hold on to their beliefs in spite of pain to individuals. The language barrier prevented us from communicating with the Danis about intercultural emotional issues. At least we had each other. Katherine and I talked a little about significant values in our lives. This was a seminal moment in the growth of my daughter. Katherine showed me her strength to handle this difficult situation without her mother's coaching. That day offered a chance for bonding to let Katherine know that I trusted her to handle life's issues. Somehow, I managed to resist the common tendency of a parent to wait too long to recognize that she had the right to make mistakes of her own and trust her as an adult thinker on social issues. It was time for me to let go.

I wanted nothing more than to share a nonjudgmental relationship with Katherine, giving her the freedom to develop into the woman of her dreams. She had to work out her views of male and female relationships in her own culture without protective parental coaching based on this single incident.

Darkness encouraged Katherine to return to our hut with Coughin, ahead of the others, to ward off the keecus with her flashlight. Keecus showed their black, glassy eyes in the cracks of the walls. Usually nocturnal mammals, mice offset their weak eyesight with a sharp sense of smelling and hearing. Any crumbs of food summoned dozens of mice, which is why Julius decided to serve dinner in the hut next door to ours.

Everyone helped carry the dishes back to the cooking hut, leaving Panus to clean them.

Chilled with the thought of the three men waiting at the village edge for the unfaithful wife to return, I passed up my usual walk into the jungle. It required my best powers of persuasion to convince Katherine to crawl out of the safety of her bag and to walk with me past a few huts to "water" a pink flowerbed.

Knowing that the local people made a habit of using the areas right outside their huts as toilets, my not wanting a long walk meant contributing to the problem.

All those visitors lined up on the road and just the idea of spirits of the dead pigs, seeking revenge, convinced us to find a discreet place nearby. Visions of the afternoon's festivities danced in my head.

Our boots felt heavier than normal after such a long day tramping about in them, and even with flashlights we found ourselves stumbling a bit over the log-covered water path.

I sighed in relief as we re-entered our dark little hut; and after my boots came off, I felt safe, tucked inside my bag. I looked at Katherine and, with no words spoken,

I could tell we shared similar feelings and similar thoughts. In the glowing light of the fire, we exchanged loving smiles.

*"The wise man travels to discover himself."* **James Russell Lowell**

# Chapter 10: Walking to Woot

By acting as detectives for each other, Katherine and I changed our method of how to take our morning baths.

After our last episode, with boys rushing past us trying to touch us as we undressed, we felt more comfortable watching for spies.

Never knowing where the next river might greet us, our additional once-a-week morning responsibilities included purifying cold water to take our nasty-tasting malaria pills.

We started malaria pills the week before we left the United States. We would continue to take them for four more weeks after returning home. The parasite can live in your bloodstream that long.

I paused at the edge of the river and stared into nowhere, remembering the day back in Jayapura and the distractions while purifying water to take the pills.

\*\*\*

Two travelers from Norway were on a little porch outside our room laughing like kids at something Katherine had said.

Katherine responded to my call to come back and take her malaria pill, but I did not stay to supervise her taking it when I heard one of the Norwegians call my name.

After leaving Los Angeles thirty-six hours earlier, we stayed in Jayapura for four days, waiting for approval on our travel permits. A group of scientists stayed at our hotel.

Each day they would venture off into the jungle, catching varieties of mosquitoes to take back to their university in Japan in a search to understand malaria.

They invited us to see their display of hundreds of labeled mosquitoes and explained that the absence of mosquito nets over our beds, even in a city, created a hazard.

Our concern focused on the mosquitoes the scientists studied. Guidebooks warned us to use extra protection against mosquitoes in the jungle, but not once did I think about needing protection in the city.

*Research work on malarial mosquitoes*

I let my guard down in Jayapura, feeling safe surrounded by buildings, cement streets and people dressed in Western clothing. Not until the last day of our trek did I realize the importance of malaria protection.

\*\*\*

Startled by two intruders, yellow whistlers, gliding into the nearby araucarias, I reminded myself that every seemingly insignificant detail of life here needs checking and rechecking. The moments immediately following an accident or illness are not the times to open an incomplete first aid kit. Much consideration must go into what might go wrong, as it might be necessary to travel some distance to reach a competent medical facility. New Guinea's tropical jungle terrain causes scratches and blisters that turned into infections within days. Taking care to clean, dry, and bandage my blisters took time twice daily. Doughnut-shaped foam bandages kept my boots from rubbing my toe blisters raw. The threat of bilharzia worms, which live in water, entering through our skin or the soles of our feet encouraged us to get bath time over quickly. Vaccines for yellow fever, typhoid, cholera, hepatitis A, tetanus, and polio gave us some peace of mind.

I also learned some valuable lessons from prior travels. I'd scratched open a mosquito bite in the Amazon a year earlier and developed an oozing, swollen, and infected sore for three weeks. A wise native gave me some dragon's blood, a red liquid excreted from a tree used for medicinal purposes. Two days later the bite had almost cleared. The magical tree sap even cured an itchy rash like poison ivy, covering my stomach, a rash that had been bothering me for two weeks. In the jungle, a cut, a broken bone, or an illness can lead to death. Research and care had gone into stocking our first-aid kit for the New Guinea mission.

Surprisingly, the sarong — of all things -- served as our best friend. A four-foot-by-six-foot piece of fabric, hand batiked or tie-dyed, in my case, served as a pillow, a skirt to wear to dinner in the larger arrival and departure towns, a towel, or a cover-up while bathing. Wrapped around and tucked into itself above my chest, the sarong worked as a shower curtain. We could bathe while wearing our sarongs by reaching under them with a bar of soap, and we could slip on a clean, dry sarong over the wet one, allowing the wet one to slip to the ground without exposing ourselves. Like a dry sponge, the clean sarong blotted us dry as we quickly slid into clean clothes.

*Katherine resting on a foot bridge*

My decision to reach for my boots changed after I heard a sugar glider snooping around in the brown roughness of the leather. Perhaps the boots smelled like one of her favorite plants, or did they look like the bark of her favorite tree? Her baggy pouch camouflaged the baby peering out. She looked like a squirrel but had a black stripe running from her nose to her forehead. Both mother and baby focused on me not with looks of caution, but curiosity. Sitting back on a smooth rock, I let the sun do its work on my feet. My arms moving caused the animal to shift her direction without hesitation.

Beginning the hurry-up-and-wait process that epitomized the trip, I asked Julius, "What time was jam karet?"

Jam karet meant rubber time or island time in the Caribbean, the time you say you plan to leave, but not the time you actually leave. Knowing his answer by then, we replied in unison, "It's okay; it's okay."

We had taken as our password "hakuna matata," which meant "no problem" in Swahili. Chanting "Hakuna matata" back and forth over footpaths worn into the loose dirt seemed more tribal than "No problem, Mon."

*Coughin guarding Katherine while resting*

Into our third week, I could not believe my calendar. Time disappeared in the kaleidoscope of our days. Bath time completed meant on to the next village. We ventured into isolated areas close to the Baliem River. Lifting my feet to find a more or less flat rock to balance on, I drew deeper and deeper breaths. I trailed behind the porters and Katherine by fifty feet, wondering why I took this trip then rather than twenty years earlier.

I hollered at Julius, "Why do we go uphill again? You said no more walking up!"

"I thought you would like to see the view from the top of the mountain," he replied, while waiting for me to join the group. The expression on my face made everyone laugh, as they all guessed I would rather walk along the flat riverbanks than see another panorama. Turning toward the river, I joined in the laughter, hoping to distract the group from going up the hill. The men loved to tease me when I tried to use words in their language. My attempts heightened everyone's sense of humor, a benefit of not speaking the language.

*Children from Pyramid Village*

Hiking along the river felt glorious. Light painted watercolor pictures as the sun woke up the river. "Lauk, lauk," with hands slightly touching gave us the feeling that we shook hands with a spirit, instead of a villager on her way to the peanut field for a day of digging. Ahead, three children stood in some shallow water. The boy ignored us as he continued to dig for treasures. A toddler balanced on the shoulder of his sister. The small child held a stone in her mouth with one hand and held out her free palm filled with fossils, for which we offered a few coins.

I asked, "Why do these children wear clothing?"

Julius raised eyebrows toward Amir and DenDee to query the children.

They responded with the fact that the children spoke a tongue not familiar to anyone, but we heard the names Java and Pyramid.

Julius said, "I assume they belong to the schoolteacher from the village across the river, who transferred from Java."

The road leading north from Wamena forked and ended in Pyramid, bringing missionaries stocking up on market items like chickens, vegetables, fruit, and hot Cokes.

The thought of chicken made my mouth water. Our direction of south and east headed away from Pyramid, so we would eat more rice and noodles for the next week.

*Daytime hut for shade*

We had informed Julius at the beginning that our hiking pace would equal that of an eighty-year-old because we wanted to enjoy the scenery. Miscommunication, or a problem with translation, caused Julius to ignore our request. Women in the Dani culture are not self-sufficient, compared to women of Western societies. Males are the decision-makers. Disgruntled at our air of independence, Julius turned up the Phil Collins volume on our CD player after adjusting our headphones to fit his head. I warned him that the use of our player was limited to the life of the batteries.

He felt incognito in his sunglasses, sent to him from a German friend he had guided years earlier. Singing and swinging, he shocked everyone that we met. His turquoise polyester sweat suit covered a pink knit shirt. His socks, hideous fluorescent pink with royal blue flowers, salvaged from some American teenager, clashed with his clothing as well as the environment. His second outfit, a pair of pants, brown to absorb three weeks of dirt without showing, and a T-shirt, brighter than Muliamo's tangerines, completed his monthly wardrobe.

The discord between noise from disrupted birds and Phil Collins had to change. Julius showed off his level of authority to the porters and cook. For us, he found it easier to turn up the volume. Our perception of Julius began to change. Katherine and I worked hard at learning adaptability. I believed Julius's job as a guide demanded greater flexibility than that of his clients, who came from a faraway land. Maybe the role of decision-maker and interpreter weighed heavily on Julius's shoulders. He was our security blanket. He told us where to walk, what to eat, and even when to pee. Day after day of listening to his ideas that often sounded like orders annoyed us at times. The sweltering heat brought out the worst in everyone.

*Children running to greet Coughin*

No photo opportunities availed themselves on our afternoon walk as I heard only Katherine's crunching footsteps. Blades of grass, brown from the color of time, won the race with locals for height. The thin, sharp blades fought back with red cut-marks on my arms. The photographer's journey presented more challenges than the cultural trip the two of us shared. The camera seemed haunted by problems with light, rain, permits from officials, and people running away as the shutter tripped.

Obstacles defined when and how I would take photos. The extra weight around my neck helped to remind me to shoot. The view over a fence ahead presented a meticulously tailored village.

Coughin sat in the grass, leaning on my twenty-five-pound travel pack. Behind the children, who ran toward us laughing, stood rows of huts. Each had bushes planted neatly, copied from the neighbors. Rows of yellow flowers circled the village.

Clothing spread before us in a line on the inviting green grass, as if an invisible clothesline lay across nature's carpet, waiting for the adjournment of the cloud cover. The children all wore ragged clothing. I wondered if the adults did as well.

"Lauk, lauk," bubbled from every giggling child. The children must have understood Coughin. They tugged at the pack's shoulder straps so hard the kids all fell with a domino effect from the weight.

The children pointed to the ground saying, "Ah Low Nik." We forgot to ask Julius later if they referred to the name of the village.

Coughin rubbed his neck, signaling me to dig for my Tiger Balm, an ointment similar to our deep-heat lotions for sore muscles.

After a few minutes, a burning sensation replaced sore muscles, which for some reason feels terrific. At night, I passed the jar around to everyone. Often, I would fall asleep with burning knees and shoulders.

"Is this the same jar that Luis gave us in the Amazon last year?" Katherine said.

I smiled while remembering the day my knees screamed for relief and said, "Yes."

"I love that burning hot sensation that relaxes the muscles," I said.

Woven mats felt comfortable on the soft grass.

No obligations, nothing to do but kick back, envisage hot showers, and dream of ice-cold mineral water.

The children yelling, "Yoroick, yoroick," or pigeon, muted the growling of my stomach.

Protein bars sounded sooo tasty, but our limit of one per day did not leave us with any to let the children sample, and we needed every bit of protein we had.

*Panus and Coughin crossing fence*

Cockatoos of speckled colors dotted the yoli myrtle trees, fringing the fence. Distracted by the racket in the trees, Katherine and I watched with startled surprise when Julius and the other three climbed over the fence long after the two of us. Amir picked up one of the bows, given to me by the chief of Waga Waga, pointing at the youi myrtle trees with their red wood and then back to my bow, showing a movement of carving wood with a sharp tool.

We had developed a form of communication with random, jumbled hand movements, winks, nods, and eye contact.

Katherine and I spread-eagled on the only two mats, leaving no room for the others. Julius smiled right before rolling a betel nut from one side of his mouth to the other.

His cheeks looked like a squirrel's, storing up for a long day of hiking. Chewing on a part of the green flesh of the nut, mixed with lime powder to reduce the sour taste, has developed into a favorite pastime of indigenous people the world over.

Adding a little mustard plant colors the juice red. Teeth, stained red from betel juice, turn black after years of chewing. In Thailand, many older women had no teeth. Their variety of betel nuts left black stubs for teeth and blackish, purplish gums.

In Borneo, my young guide had said to me, "The older generation believes strongly in spirits. If a spirit likes your pretty teeth, he might take them. To be ignored by the spirit's search, we chew betel nuts to blacken the teeth, which make them look as if they have disappeared."

Julius looked disgusting when he drooled the red-black liquid as he talked or when his mouth dripped of the nasty liquid while he chewed.

Katherine and I looked at each other with a sigh of, "Oh well." He had an air about him of powerful expert, which brought him respect from the natives and others we encountered. Overreacting to minor details would hinder our ability to experience the adventures ahead.

We said, "Sawma, sawma," to all the children and they said, "Terima kasih," after we completed our rest and continued on our trek to our final destination for the night: the Village of Woot.

As the children chased us, yelling, "Sawma sawma," I realized they were all boys.

In a moment of recollection, I remembered all the villages greeted us with male children and/or men.

*Pigs are a prized possession*

While we walked along curling dirt paths in peanut and sweet potato fields, females, pigs, and more pigs busied themselves.

Women play a major role in the ipomoea, or sweet potato, cultivation.

Men clear the fields, build the fencing, and lay out the irrigation canals.

The women take over the planting, weeding, and harvesting, along with taking care of young children and pigs.

The first settlers, some 25,000 years ago, relied on yams and taro for staples and later on sugar cane, bananas, and the sweet potato, introduced in 500 A. D., according to some geneticists.

Sweet potatoes bring high yields even at 5,000 feet above sea level, out of range of the malarial Anopheles mosquito.

A brilliant system of parallel irrigation canals allows for periods of fallow times, when unplanted fields stand next to planted ones.

Primitive slash-and-burn techniques still used elsewhere require ten to twenty years of fallow time between crops, resulting in lower population densities.

*New purchase from market*

Men treat wives as a necessary source for wealth; however, they do not come cheap. Long ago, a wife cost 120 old cowry shells, 120 new cowry shells, 300 glass beads, and a female pig. Today in the larger villages, trade goods serve the same function, and each girl can fetch 300 old cowries, a machete, a steel ax, five large pigs worth $1000, many shirts, blankets, pots, and, for a special girl, a sewing machine or typewriter. Men can have as many wives as they can afford. After explaining this system to me, Julius said that in many small, poor villages a wife costs five pigs.

Often, he would ask, "How many pigs to marry Katherine?"

"Hundreds," I would always reply, pause a few moments, and laugh.

He would interpret my answer, and one by one all faces around me would break into laughter. The sound echoed to children still watching our departure. Nothing in life compares to the sweetness of children's laughter.

Walking under a tree we disturbed a group of lorikeets. They scrambled in all directions, leaving no distinction between leaves or the beating green of their wings. Screeching at our intrusion, they searched for an opening in the sky.

I stepped up my pace to catch up to Katherine. When she slowed, I reached for the glistening green object in her hair. "Do you want to keep this feather?" I asked.

She did one of her sister Allie's "Ohs" where you say the word for several seconds and almost sing the word. After saying "No way to keep it pretty," she held it high, blew on it, and watched it float away.

I heard the call of a lone crow, causing me to wrench my head, looking for him. High in the canopy, reflections of sunlight bounced off something red.

With the zoom lens extended to its highest magnification, my camera enabled me to see a huge nest with shiny red berries and red flames of flowers. The diligent bowerbirds collected objects of like colors.

Capturing the antics of tiny birds, feasting on crayfish in the shallows of the river, awakened my photographic spirit. A whistler flew down to a branch twenty feet away. He cocked his white head as if to show me the black ring around his neck, and looked at all the commotion of my fumbling for a shorter lens. Through the twisted roots of a tree, a single shaft of light struck his eye, and I focused.

He stalked something, and his curiosity and yellow body disappeared. Any hopes of capturing long-lasting memories of the unique bird vanished.

Streamers of moss caught in my hair. I twisted and ducked, and my hands fought the tangles of the spider-web-like mess. My camera flailed about but remained secure around my neck.

The moss felt like a nest of baby snakes had fallen on me. Shivers ran from my shoulders to my toes.

Julius and Panus responded to my ruckus. In their native tongue, the tone of their voices reassured me. Embarrassed at my anxiety, I laughed at myself, thinking my youngest daughter, Allie, would have said, "Mom, chill out!"

The blackish water of the Baliem River reflected the balletic movement of the jungle canopy. The middle-of-the-day sunrays invited play in the shallows. The youngest members of the group splashed, screamed, and raced through the icy water. Panus and DenDee chased Katherine and Amir, while Julius watched. I envied their playfulness.

The young men loved making Katherine laugh. The river gave Katherine a perfect opportunity to get back at them, chasing and splashing.

Singing and laughing offered a pleasurable respite from ordinary life.

*Katherine and porters playing in the river*

*Coughin watches the porters and Katherine splash in the river*

Coughin, closer to my age or maybe older as he did have a few gray hairs, seemed to feel comfortable around me.

The oldest of the porters, he carried the heaviest of packs and did not seem to mind.

He licked his thick and cracked lips often. Tight curls framed his round face. He laughed with enthusiasm at everything said, no matter if he understood or not.

He motioned toward my bar of soap, lying on a rock. He copied my motions of lathering my entire body.

The difference? He remained naked. I left my clothes on, and I washed them at the same time.

His whole body foamed white with bubbles. He smiled at perhaps his first bubble bath.

Neither of us understood what the other spoke, but we knew what we meant. His leather-like face changed from wrinkles of the seasons to wrinkles of laughter.

Round, five-by-five-foot rocks bordered both sides of the river.

Taking giant steps that looked like a game, we continued our walk toward Woot.

If one person fell on the rocks, he or she had to move to the end of the line. Of course, I came in last. I rationalized that my bare feet got wet from dripping clothing.

I envied the freedom the young men had, living as generations had done. No obligations, except a carefree afternoon and trying to forget about baby-snake apparitions.

No one day could illustrate the memories building in my heart. The sun painted pictures, using shadows as paint.

Hundreds of butterflies fluttered around us, unhappy with our invasion of their territory. Their white and yellow spots polka-dotted the gravel-strewn path.

Waves of shimmering warm color boomeranged from treetops to the water's edge, transposing the shapes into a thousand fluorescent ghosts.

*Woman passing us on trek*

    Boots snapped dead leaves underfoot. Silence does have its sounds. The periodic silence of the jungle makes hearing the voice within you more clearly. As we moved toward the village of Woot, new anticipations intoxicated my thoughts. My journal and heart overflowed with every conceivable expectation I had for this trip.
    Light began fading, signaling the harmony of frog choruses. As we emerged into the deepening shades of the forest, a sunset of crimson-tipped clouds changed tones as if a painter tried to find the perfect hue for his canvas. We sang, but not as loudly as the singing coming from the village of Woot. Maneuvering our packs, we climbed the fence up and over a narrow log.

Faces stared from inside doorways. Julius motioned for us to turn around and climb the fence again. We learned that a small wedding ceremony would take place that night. A few relatives and friends had taken all the space for sleeping. The village chief suggested to Julius that we travel on to the next village, two kilometers away. The crusty, runny noses on the children and adults of the village gave me an uncomfortable shiver.

"Mom, a lot of the people there looked sick. What was wrong with them?" Katherine said.

Julius explained, "It's a common respiratory infection."

I said to Katherine, "We have avoided exposure to sickness, disease, or death. Maybe Julius kept us at a safe distance, which also allowed the villagers a security to maintain their privacy. I think if we are careful, we will be all right."

A sense of relief guided my feet up the log, balancing on the fence. My strange feeling toward the questioning looks took time to overcome.

Julius said, "This village has never seen white skinned people before." I felt anxious about the introductory period of entering an unknown place, but often-eager smiles and natives' curiosity about us made the transition easier.

Twenty or more men and male children approached us on the path, surprised by our appearance. They stared straight on, and I felt uneasy.

Apprehension never ceased as we encountered each new village, unable to foretell our arrival. The awkwardness of not speaking a single word of their language increased.

Julius questioned the group with different languages of the valley. They answered him with heads shaking no, but smiling.

Julius said, "We can stay in their village."

We walked less than a kilometer and then climbed over a fence into a small village. Several men spread out grass mats and motioned for Katherine and me to sit. This signal of welcome induced whispers of relief, as we recognized the gesture of friendliness.

Previous encounters with new people had taught us initial passivity would invoke their curiosity. Curiosity, in turn, would lead to exchange, as they realized we would not threaten them.

Fears disappeared as we came to know the people I would need to remind myself that fear and anxiety function as our greatest enemy, our greatest roadblock to new experiences.

We excite the Dani just as they excited us. With time, that strange mutual understanding in curiosity promotes trust. The singing, laughing greeters back in Dugum reminded me of the friendliness of the Dani and of how worthwhile it felt to get to know each village. We made every effort to allow part of their lifestyle to live within us.

*Writing in our journals in the No-Name Village*

While we pretended to write, absorbed in our journals, we attracted stares and attention.

The males of the village circled our mats, as we waited to sense their response to our presence.

Julius asked the name of the village but could not understand the men when they replied.

"They act like they have never seen women traveling alone before." Katherine said.

"I know. I agree. The men keep staring," I said.

"I guess it's possible we are the first they have seen," she said.

Amir carried our heavy packs into a two-story hut nearby, and Julius came from nowhere with carrots, unknown green vegetables, and cooked sweet potatoes.

"Isn't it uncomfortable to prepare all this food with all these men watching? This must look like a feast to them," I said to Julius.

In a soft voice and with a huge betel-nut stained smile, he said, "Yes, but we will have leftovers for them."

*Children watching us inside hut*

    Nobody in our party spoke the language of this village, except a few words here and there. Intimidated after an hour of enduring observation with staring eyes, Katherine and I decided to move inside our home for the night. The round hut had two stories, and I assumed that Katherine and I would sleep in the fresh grass laid on the bamboo planks of the second level. A bamboo ladder with four steps leaned into a small opening above our heads. Outside the door, several children crouched in the dirt and watched, hoping for a glimpse of another lifestyle.

    We would eat dinner in the lower area, which was about four feet tall, so we sat and wrote in our journals. The entire evening, no local village women appeared, only naked men, wearing penis gourds and young boys dressed in ragged shirts and shorts. The early evening arrival gave us little time to meet the villagers before darkness fell.

*Pig grease and soot cover the body*

The previous village of Woot left me guarding my senses. The Woot villagers appeared unwelcoming and almost scary looking, without the normal smiles and welcoming attitudes.

Greater distances from the small village of Wamena with its vehicles and electricity meant we would visit indigenous peoples, not used to seeing many tourists or backpackers.

Katherine and I did not leave the hut the entire evening. Julius brought our food into the lower level and then disappeared.

Cooked vegetables and rice were a nice treat after the many boring meals of plain rice.

As Katherine maneuvered up through the tiny opening into the second floor she said, "The top of my head touches the ceiling up here."

"Does the grass smell fresh cut? Fewer fleas than in old matted grass, where people and animals have slept," I said.

"Would you read some of your notes on the last village they called Woot. I wondered if Julius had found out more information than what he explained as we left the village," she said.

I asked Julius for more information, but he didn't understand my question. He said, "We are far from Wamena."

I said, "How far in miles or kilometers?"

He said, "Maybe many days' walk."

I realized that distance must be measured by time because of rivers, mountains and dense jungle growth, making direct travel impossible.

He misunderstood my question but made me think about how we view distance mathematically, compared to their way of thinking.

My few notes left us both with questions. So far this village felt comfortable after a good meal and the idea of staying in a village where people faced us with sickness and unhappy looks made me shiver.

Many hours of walking gave us reason to crawl into our bags. The cool temperature allowed me to pull the sleeping bag up to my ears. This gave me a sense of security against both big and little creatures.

About midnight, the mystery and silence of the evening changed. During hours of lying awake, I listened to the sounds of the night.

My senses sharpened with a mild flush of adrenaline. Noises unidentifiable. Feeling vulnerable, I feared I knew not what. Maybe we misjudged the friendliness of the villagers. A desolate feeling hung heavy over me.

Whispers, mixed with a sound like chomping on bubble gum, interrupted my introspection. The room had a chill like a desert after dusk, but my hands touching my face dripped with sweat.

Someone came inside the lower level of the hut, further sharpening my apprehension. A blanket of chills swept over me, incapacitating my thoughts and body.

Slowly, as if the movement of my arm might cause a noise heard from down below, I found my flashlight and the pepper spray attached to the waist pack. I prepared for the unexpected.

I whispered Julius's name more casually than I felt. I received no answer except mumbled words. Vulnerable against the control these villagers had over our stay, I repeated his name, hoping that his brain, not tuned into English, might change channels.

Time, a puzzling phenomenon, played tricks on our minds. The longest of days can disappear, but the shortest of minutes can seem to last an eternity.

This night revealed itself as the New Guinea of legend. Mysterious subjects of myth and speculation.

To make matters worse, the urgency of finding a jungle toilet loomed too close for comfort. The hard day's walk had driven me to drinking brown river-water tea, my only choice on any menu.

After gathering flashlight and toilet paper and slipping into boots, I paused and inhaled a deep confidence-building breath, despite my fear. My boots felt like lead weights.

My right foot on the narrow log, I descended with caution into the uncertainty of the lower level, not knowing who or what lingered in the darkness. Shaking nervously, I wanted to get over whatever might happen next. My body almost fell into the bed of dried grass.

While the beam of light shone in his face, Julius smiled a dripping, greasy smile, as did the others.

"Julius, what is going on?"

"In honor of our visit, the chief killed a pig to roast and share with us," Julius mumbled with his mouth full.

"But it's three o'clock in the morning," I said while looking at the gourd bowl, filled with pieces of cooked pig soaked in pig fat.

Around me, the porters' hands dug deep into the liquid, coming out with pieces of meat-covered bone.

Four men squatted and ate. The light of the flashlight caught their grease-smeared chins.

Chewing and sucking like malnourished children, they motioned for me to join them. After all, the feast was the result of our presence. The further we strayed from civilization, the more a village celebrated in our honor.

As with the rest of the journey, we felt an inescapable mixture of pleasure and pain.

*Head garland made from prized red feathers*

*"But to me a dreamer of dreams to whom what is and what seems are often one and the same."* **H. W. Longfellow**

## Chapter 11: Leaving the No-Name Village

We escaped the transition from darkness without consequence. We guessed the teensy black jumping spots on our writing journals from the night before were fleas. We itched everywhere.

Neither of us slept much after Julius awakened us with his three A.M. dinner. Then the roosters started their morning song. After many journeys with sleepless nights, one develops a hatred for roosters with the alarm clock clearing of their throats at four o'clock in the morning.

By the time we could tumble out of the darkness of the hut, the women had gone toward the fields.

We played games with older boys while the elders watched, and we felt our spirits brought closer together.

The lives of these simple people change little from day to day, except for their weather.

*Making friends with Dani children*

We organized races; they tried on our boots, and we almost got the idea across of hide-and-seek. Boys taught us the game of sigogo wasin, or kill the hoop. Two groups separate and take turns as they throw and spear a cane hoop as it sails through the air. With string, two seniors played a game similar to our cat's cradle. As they formed designs, they told stories to the younger children.

A game similar to our building a house called o-o sili, or wood village, started under our feet. Children using flat, pointed araucarias seeds outlined an entire village of fences, huts, and gardens made from leaves, bark, and flower petals. They don't know competition while playing games. Even in kill the hoop, they keep no scores. In their adult world, skill with cooperation outweighs competition.

The villagers' simple activities verified our earlier observations of the significance in building the communal spirit, necessary for life in a hostile environment. The children's sensitivity highlighted our day. They seemed more impressionable than children of other villages. Their openness to our involvement and eagerness to teach us games offered us the chance to fill our morning with a happy diversion.

"Fear makes strangers of people who should be friends," I remembered reading in a book by Shirley MacLaine.

Barriers down, our new acquaintances added new heights to our lives. Completeness echoed in the faces of this sanctuary. Contentment originated and lived there, in the village with no name. People worked hard, played hard, and laughed hard. Julius tried to explain the villagers' obsession with wanting a close connection with us. "Only missionaries have touched their lives. They see no other white-skinned people. They have never seen yellow hair or blue eyes."

The azure sky turned angry, bruised with clouds. Rain ponchos were unpacked and ready for a day of work. We crossed the wood fence, perhaps leaving those people more than a gift: a memory of stories from their light-skinned visitors. Goodbyes were always difficult with villagers whose hearts went into making our visit unforgettable.

"Did playing games with the children make you think of your younger brother and sister back home?" I asked Katherine.

"I do miss swimming with Allie every day and maybe even Brennan, teasing me a little now and then," Katherine replied.

Being rained upon was nothing new to us, so we began our day drenched by a downpour. Few days passed without a short rain, just enough to raise the humidity and grow additional underbrush to slow our travel.

Gravel paths boiled with noonday heat mirages. Rain came down so hard it hurt, and we decided to retreat inside a woman's long hut.

Dozens of children, a few women, and pigs filled the forty-foot-long hut. Araucaria tree branches filled several noken, or string bags, hanging from pegs of bamboo. The women treat infected rodent bites with a potion made from boiled araucaria and then cover them in white ash from the fire pit. Most Dani believe that all creatures, except the smallest of insects and reptiles, have etai-eken, the seeds that control a life. Many of the Dani's superstitious beliefs revolve around their pigs, second in importance to family. Narrow stalls in the huts protect the pigs from drowning in irrigation ditches or from being lost or stolen, especially when women are not watching them. Blood from dead pigs covers sick pigs, or they feed the sick pigs sweet potatoes basted in blood.

*Women's long hut*

Inside the women's hut, my eyes burned from the smoke of two cooking fires. Cuscus skins, still moist, stretched over vertical slits in the bamboo walls. Hanging from strips of bark, a bunch of small bones played with the smoke, like wind chimes. Sleeping mats--grimy with sweat--blended with the dirt floor. A pile of gourds and a blackened clay pot carved a corner at one end of the hut. No other possessions were apparent to me, except the smells of a lifetime.

The nauseous combination of sweat, dried skins, pigs, and singed possum fur made me regret going in there to get out of the rain. The smell overpowered my desire to communicate, photograph, or even smile. The rain started to ease. Humidity thickened the air. My eyes watered from the stench created by the warmth of the fire.

Women and children stood watching us, as motionless as the small possum sliced open near the fire. We must have looked like aliens with bare legs attached to elephantine boots. Our ponchos hung on us, slimy and dripping with rain. Eyes focused on our hunchbacks, not realizing we had blue vinyl protecting our backpacks. A grey-haired woman spoke with authority to four girls squatting with their knees touching their shoulders, hiding their developing breasts. "What is she saying, Mom?" Katherine said.

I said, "The girls won't look at us. I hope the experienced old woman is suggesting they return our smiles."

Singing in the rain seemed like a much better option to me than waiting out the storm inside with the suspicious women and the disgusting, overwhelming odor of their hut.

Our boots were heavy with mud, and we were exhausted. It amazed me how, even after all the time we had spent in this country, we could still feel horribly inadequate to our circumstances. To think that just that morning I saw our day's journey as not much more than a hike in the woods, and later I stood in a hut, filled with pig droppings. Desperate to be dry and warm, and desperate to lie down, we realized that it would not happen here in this place!

The rain let up, and I felt overwhelming relief. Simply the ability to leave the stench of the women's hut was a gift more welcome than air conditioning or a dry, clean hotel room. As we moved on following a shortcut Julius knew through the virgin jungle, a thicket of thorn bushes stopped me, stabbing and snagging my skin and clothes. I looked at Julius with annoyance as I attempted to get myself untangled, and he didn't need an interpreter to understand I did not care at all for his shortcuts. The entire experience was wearing down my physical and emotional reserves.

My boots made deep imprints in the muck as we slogged on: left foot inhale; right foot exhale. Mazes of burnt green wilderness claimed every bit of my energy. The reveries of yesterday played in my mind, helping divert the thoughts of my current physical discomforts.

Periodically, Julius would hear my shouts and walk back to check on me. Drenched in mud and sweat, the group made intermittent stops for leech checking, slowing all to a tortoise-like pace.

You can spot leeches while naked, but clothing and boots offer leeches many dark places to hide. Checking to make sure no leeches had worked their way into shirt buttonholes or into the lace holes of my boots took our guide's time, and when the black, gooey spot on my leg turned out to be a hungry leech, I screamed, which brought Panus running. By now I was used to all kinds of little creatures crawling about; but the exhaustion from dealing with the mud and rain drained my patience with even the tiniest of problems.

"Only a baby leech," Julius explained, laughing at me while reaching for my matches in Panus's bag of cooking utensils. He lit the match, touched it to the leech, and the slimy creature fell off.

The trip had trespassed on every known necessity of my life except fresh air. It tested all my senses. I felt enough distraction from fleabites without adding in the stinging and itching brought about by leeches. Julius returned the matches to the pack, and our party once again moved on.

Like an umbrella, the tree canopy slowed the rain. The resulting mist had radiance, illuminated by the vertical shafts of sun. Could the sound of a waterfall spilling down into the valley forecast a bath? Covered in mud, we all looked like we mourned for some dead soul, and I could imagine how cool, clean water washing over us could lift all our spirits. An algae-smeared log bridge no wider than my size-ten boots came into view. We concentrated on a scary silence, disregarding the rush of water below. The porters walked across, dropped our previously green but now gray-black packs in the slosh, and crossed back again. I wish I had not seen Amir's foot slip. Catching himself with perfect balance, he anchored his toes around the log, a display that troubled me even more. No way would I be able to navigate that log with such skill. Surprising me completely, Amir reached under the log for a large dragonfly and ate it.

Tightrope walking never did appeal to me, and the algae slicking the log added more tension to my already jangled nerves. With Amir in front and DenDee in back holding Katherine's hands, she made it across without faltering. Amir and DenDee positioned themselves in front of me, leaving Julius and Panus to get behind me. My grip on their hands turned their black knuckles white and must have told them, "If I fall, catch me."

Once we reached the other side, I thanked my adrenaline angel for crossing with me. The smelly women's hut, trekking in mud, and picking off leeches all aided in the frustration of seeing that algae-covered log bridge over the rushing water below.

After crossing without falling and breaking a leg or ruining my camera, I threw my hands in the air and ran forward. My shouts gave voice to the uneasy spirit that had bunched up in my chest and throat all morning. The bowl of the valley to our right looked like a giant's Christmas-tree farm, scattered with golden strands of tinsel. The sheltered spot we picked for lunch felt hot and still. Stripping off our grunge-covered boots and rain gear, we did not realize the extent of our exhaustion.

Coughin untied our grass mats for sleeping, and smashing down tall, prickly grass to make a place for us to rest, he spread out the mats for us. While the others prepared a fire for rice, he squatted beside Katherine, taking advantage of some rest time.

Barefooting it from the river with a bag of icy water, I thought how surrealistic Katherine and Coughin looked. A mysterious glow of protection took shape around Katherine's catnapping, almost as if Coughin's guardian light shone there for her.

The short rest revived us all. I ran the river water through my water purifier and satisfied our thirst.

The high elevation required more liquids than normal, and Katherine and I found it hard to drink plain water, even back home. The smelly, brown, river water made the task even more difficult.

After the heavy northern rainstorms of the day, Julius said, "We should stay in a schoolhouse tonight, as we could not make the village of Jiwika before dark."

Feverish puddles of leftover morning rain entertained hundreds of insects, dancing and fluttering as we walked past.

The sun rolled onto the rim of the valley, exposing stripes of white sand. From our viewpoint, the white trails looked like a ski mountain, the highways of the jungle. Worn tracks of time, like the beaches of Bali, looked fine and powdery under the blazing sun.

Rain turned them into lacquered rocks. Not wanting to succumb to the frustration of the rain slowing us down, I gathered all my patience to take notice of the gifts of the moment. If the scenery kept improving, we should arrive in heaven by dinnertime.

The air felt like flannel, warm enough to wear. The coolness of the canopy offered relief, but it meant we would now have to start watching where we were stepping.

Transitions from sand to the etched green looked like brushstrokes on canvas.

The wooded edge of the jungle with its colors of sun and shade offered few openings, even for our tiny bodies.

The mass of thorns and vines intimidated Panus, in spite of his machete, ready to cut a path. DenDee began crawling, and Julius waved for us to follow. Escaping a swamp of brown syrup, we dogged our way on all fours through a stand of ferns, overpowering the jungle with its hundreds of varieties. Crawling on the mosses, we could see baby ferns, uncurling among the lichens and fungus.

Suddenly my head ran into Julius's feet. Everyone ahead of me turned to stone in the moss. Julius turned to me, pointed and said, "Waro, waro."

Not understanding, I grabbed his foot. "What?" I asked, my eyes clouded over with beads of sweat, running down my terrified face, dripping onto the moss carpet. Distress exploded in my heart.

Julius turned again, whispering, "Shh, shh, snake!"

I froze with fear.

My muscles felt tight as metal bands as I hugged the ground in terror. The snake, a creature with a body as thick as a small tree, streamed along the earth only three yards from the spot where the men and I lay flattened to the ground. It jerked its head forward, and I found my thoughts rushing to an image of its evil fangs, slicing into my cheek.

The thought of a bite in the face by the terrifying creature filled me, yet I could not move. My only comfort was that Katherine lay protected somewhere at the back of the line.

Julius slid his machete from his belt. My arms covered my head, though I did not remember having lifted them, and I buried my face in the moss. Julius slung the machete toward the snake, scaring it back up the tree.

For a moment, the only sound I could hear was the breeze rustling the tree canopy high overhead. I lifted my eyes tentatively, and there sat Julius, unfazed by the danger he had averted. Instead, with some disappointment he said, "I hoped for dinner."

I stared at him in disbelief. "Snake makes a good dinner," he assured me with a smile. I looked back at Katherine, thinking I might find her in tears. Instead, I saw an intrepid traveler that had been hidden from me all these years.

I said, "Everything okay?"

"I didn't get to see it. What color was it and how big?" she asked.

I never thought about Katherine as a jungle trekker with the ability to live in grass huts and endure one bowl of rice a day. Invisible to me before this trip, her strengths now surfaced like her feelings toward me: unconditional. I wanted to scoot back out of line and wrap her in my arms with hugs and appreciation for not whining or complaining. I knew that she was thinking, *what fun to share this story with friends back home.* A little character building was going on in both of us.

After the snake had gone, Julius reminded us, "Watch out for the snakes. On humid days like these, they will crawl everywhere, trying to climb in your packs, wrapping around your ankles, dangling from trees."

As we moved on, vines strangled my pack, filled with a half-day's water supply, making the task of concentrating on the little details difficult. Perseverance--despite the heat, heavy packs, and little food--kept the porters' watchful eyes busy.

The slightest movement of a branch deserved a second look, for any dangerous creature could be lurking there, waiting for prey. Our porters moved effortlessly up slimy banks and over fallen trunks, their bare feet gripping the slippery surfaces as easily as my hiking boots gripped the ground beneath me.

I needed to rest, so we all came to a halt. Leaning against the huge, root supports of the trees, I recalled memories of Luis, our guide in the Amazon. He told Katherine and me how the natives use these buttresses to pound out signals.

Hollowness creates a loud, echoing sound. In the Amazon, the three of us lost our way, and Luis used these root buttresses to signal our whereabouts to the boat drivers.

Soon the denseness of the jungle gave way to the tall spindles of araucaria trees. Delicate greens in the moss forest yielded to grey-browns of the araucaria against a backdrop of blue sky.

The floor lay flat, dusted with layers of disintegrating leaves. Our boots kicked the undersides with each step. Rotting mold burned my nostrils with the smell of death.

Vacant tin-roofed shacks sat in an open field, absorbing the savage heat of the day, only to spit it out again at night. The government built the homes for sanitary reasons, hoping to avoid the insects and filth that thrived in the wood huts.

The Dani used the cement-block shacks as storage or corrals for the pigs, so the government abandoned the idea. Locals could not adjust to modern techniques even as simple as changing the structure of their homes. Their thatch-roofed wood huts, the better option, kept out the heat of the day, and double outer walls retained it at night.

Not wanting to stay out in the open jungle, Julius showed us our wood shack for the night next to the two cement structures. Belonging to a schoolteacher away teaching children in a more remote area, the shack had a double bed. It had no mattress or pads, just a horizontal surface of tree branches balancing on log supports.

Surrounding villagers treated the schoolteacher as a foreigner and offered a cement shack for his living quarters.

He apparently didn't like the heat of the enclosed cement and chose the wood hut instead.

Panus cut up a pineapple to share for dinner. Without the protection of a village, Julius did not want to attract outsiders, so a hot meal was out of the question.

Fire would bring attention to our location. In this black, open space, I could sense the strength of the jungle dominating those who feared it, welcoming those who respected it.

Any subject would do for a bedtime story, but the stories about their people remained the ones closest to Dani hearts.

Hypnotized by the fact that we were witnessing a place in time we would never see again, we listened to the men talk for hours. Exhausted, we had played ourselves out. Katherine stared at me as if she had not enough energy to close her eyes.

"You look like a statue with not even an eyelid blinking. We'll share the bed. Try and get some sleep," I said to Katherine.

The night turned into another no-sleep night. My body sagged into the little gutters between the barkless branches called a bed.

Hard bumps tortured my skinny hipbones, legs, and arms, making lying on my side impossible. I lay on the first bed I had seen in weeks, wondering about my obsession for travel.

Was I losing my enchantment for this type of travel after sleepless nights and days of discomfort from insect bites and intense heat?

This life belongs to the Dani and as much as we want to fit in, we are still newcomers or outsiders: strangers who have no way of blending in. Would finding some kind of commonality in those blank stares satisfy me? My anticipation for a month-long getaway from responsibility had lingered for a whole year, prior to departure.

Anticipation always exceeds the results. I also knew from previous travels that culture shock after returning home would remain the same, no matter where my adventures would take me.

I realized that a part of me never returns. Reinvented, the other half of me becomes apprehensive about unveiling my true values and desires, creating a fabricated reinforcement. I knew I would have to work hard at not allowing society's interpretation of what and who I should be. Travel returns feeling to the human journey.

Travel allows me to peel back my own layers while observing other people's values. I watched those around me doing silly things like Julius, wearing outfits that clashed. He accepted the teasing which made me think twice about the importance of always looking perfect.

Those invisible facades built on fear of rejection exhibited a distortion of my true self.

By challenging my self-esteem, I could remove that mask of security. Standing still, we invite stagnation, but through the restorative powers of travel, we become ourselves again, gathering new strengths. Escaping from my Midwest-American reality for long periods allowed me to look at my own self-worth and realize nothing would ever look the same again. Re-examining travel and its experiences provides me the direction for my next step forward. All night I squirmed, trying to find a place away from the knots of the branches poking me from the teacher's bed, but not succeeding.

Within hours my aches and pains had convinced me: never again would a tree-branch bed, with no mattress, look like heaven to me.

*"Anthropologists say you must immerse yourself in an unfamiliar world in order to truly understand your own."* **The Nanny Diaries**

## Chapter 12: Off to See a Mummy

Awakening, I felt adrift at sea, confused, and off course. I stared at the smallest details in the shack, trying to regain my orientation. Triangular-shaped chips of bamboo held scribbled notes to the wall, where rusty rain dabbled its colors. A crude table with a wobbly top sat alone. Deformed by its uneven tree-branch legs, the table stood too tall for us to use while sitting on the dirt floor. Panus should have cut our pineapple on this table last night. He told us that nanas, or pineapple, brings good luck.

I had propped my bag of dwindling foodstuff in the corner the night before, and now I searched for the schoolteacher's. I was disappointed to find that he had left no personal items lying about, let alone food. No clothing or dishes cluttered the room. An opening in the wall allowed nature, with its music and players, to enter at will. Light, sound, insects, and small creatures co-existed with us this morning as I could see they hosted the teacher when he was here at home.

Two porters laughed outside at something funny that had happened the night before. I listened, feeling contented here at this time and in this moment. In almost three weeks, two cultures--the Dani's and ours--had blended into one; or at least that is how it felt to me. The Dani had gone beyond simply answering our questions, as they had done when we had first arrived and were only visitors. Now I knew that they had reached the point of allowing us into their lives, allowing us to absorb a small portion of their heritage.

Living with the Dani had turned back evolution's time clock for us. A brief moment of pausing reflection swept through the recesses of my mind, and I wondered if my ancestors of thousands of years ago might have lived in a similar manner.

We headed out onto the trail again and Coughin, with his pied-piper song on his mouth harp, carried the most weight. The oldest and perhaps the wisest of our group, he managed to remain two steps ahead of the rest of us.

I heard Panus speaking with Julius, and I looked at Julius questioningly. He translated Panus's message: "The rice is almost gone; one bowl each today."

Only a few days back, I thought the packs were heavy with rice. Was Julius selling rice to earn extra money? I nodded understanding, thinking I should have been more aware of my rations myself. On past treks, my guides had made the same statement close to the end of the trip, and my light-as-a-feather rations bag felt empty as well. Oh, well, I thought. Today our energy would come from the sun and within.

On we hiked, south to Jiwika. The fading slivers of orange and pink from the blazing sky said hello to a blue-on-blue horizon. This valley made me think that the earth had turned its pockets inside out, wanting me to see everything it had to offer. I stood in awe of the beauty that surrounded me, not wanting to miss a single sliver of golden light or the way that clean, so-blue sky filled me up inside with an emotion I could not explain.

***Different body art***

I had read about places like this and watched the specials on television.

But glossy, digitally altered photographs could not compete with the majesty I witnessed.

Photographs and movies showed me only the very crust of the world.

As I stood there, I experienced the depths, the shadows, the breath, and the heartbeat of beauty itself.

Prior to this adventure, life appeared to me as one of those puzzles of hundreds of sections in myriad colors, all different yet the same.

Staring at the pieces, shifting and adjusting them, I had been unable to find connections that fit together, except for the edges, perhaps. The edges consisted of pieces made up by my research, planning, and preparation for this trip.

Now, as the adventure engulfed our lives, puzzle pieces of self-confidence and assurance changed shape, looking for new places to fit in the puzzle. Grandma's patchwork quilt covered the valley we viewed from our bird's-eye perch. The Dani had stitched together folktales, secrets from generations past, and knowledge of survival over the rugged beauty of the land. Our walk, as slow as a lazy cloud's shadow, stirred up a flurry of ragged moths prancing in a light tunnel amid the desolate forest.

Katherine sidled up alongside me, and I smiled at her serious, young face as she said, "Doesn't it feel a little like we're lost in here?"

"We're not lost, Honey," I said.

Katherine hesitated, thinking. She seemed unconcerned about her footing in the tangled mass that was the forest floor, and I could see her searching for the right words to express her feelings.

"Maybe what I mean," she said slowly, "is that I feel like we're wanderers, lost in our surroundings. Like we're intruding on nature, without even realizing we're doing it. We don't belong here, yet here we are, stomping along."

I thought about that comment for a bit as Katherine and I tromped along together in silence, listening to a strange bird song and picking through roots and fallen branches at our feet.

After a bit I looked up, seeking Julius, and asked his back, "Are there a lot of snakes here?" In many ways, I didn't want to hear his answer.

"If I were a snake," he called back to me, "this is where I would be."

Movement in the brush caught the party's attention. Naturally, my first thought was snake, but no, it was just a female cuscus about the size of a possum. Startled by our voices, the cuscus was hurtling among the low branches of the forest floor, her baby clinging desperately to its mother. While my heart rate slowed, DenDee chased her; but after a few moments she climbed to familiar territory high in a tree. Curling her strong, prehensile tail around a branch far from DenDee's reach, the cuscus and her young one hung from the tree, smirking. Her brown fur blended with the branches, but the white spots of her head and body caught the sunlight. The Danis prized her wool-like fur for decorating armbands and headbands. The fact that the Danis knew her kind made a delicious meal made her worth catching. Katherine and I, glad that she got away, had no interest in seeing her skinned for dinner.

I noticed as we walked on that Panus was fiddling to clean his teeth with a root he had carried for days. His conversation with Julius sounded pleading.

"Does he have a problem, Julius?" I asked.

Julius said, "Panus wants to borrow 25,000 rupiahs from Katherine and you against his wages to finish paying for a pig, a gift to his parents. He had already paid 70,000 rupiahs ($35) to a friend and wanted to complete the deal while near his friend's village that day. He had never given his parents such a nice gift."

I felt that giving in to the pleas for money could have a negative effect on the porters and any foreigners they would cross paths with later. I tried to explain about the money, and I reminded Julius he had already borrowed quite a bit from us. We had no more to give them. How could we decipher their fierce grins? Were they pleading smiles or thanking us in advance? We could not tell if they had a real problem or wanted to take advantage of wealthy foreigners who did not know better.

With several days left in our journey, we could not afford to upset Panus; but at the same time, I hated parting with our rupiahs. It wasn't the twelve dollars I was concerned about, but the fact that rupiahs could possibly get us out of an emergency. I looked at Katherine. Her slight nod encouraged me to say yes.

A savage "Wha-hoo" from the thicket of trees ahead surprised everyone.

"Wha-hoo!" DenDee howled suddenly, startling Katherine and me. Amir cried out as well, "Wha-hoo!"

All our guides joined in the cry, and I heard the cry answered in the distance. It became clear to me that it was a form of greeting, not a war cry, as children came running toward us from the direction of the Jiwika village. Jiwika, pronounced Yiwika, twenty kilometers' northeast of Wamena, bustled with activity.

As we entered the village proper, women bundled potatoes and carrots into net bags as the Sunday morning market moved into high gear. Not until the market crowd disappeared did I ask Julius what Panus had bought for our dinner.

Embarrassed to tell us that they had spent the food money on other things, Julius told me that one bowl of rice for each person remained, with no options.

My disappointment in Julius left me speechless. Fresh vegetables and potatoes were all bundled up and on their way back to some small village.

Out of embarrassment alone I could never spend someone else's money on myself without their permission. I couldn't think of a way to explain to him about his mistake of spending our food money for other items for himself.

Jiwika took pride in its two jungle hotels, called losmen in Indonesia. One was made from panels of distorted tin. The walls looked like they might collapse at any minute like a house of cards.

The other hotel bore the name of La-uk. Lauk is a word used only by women to say hello. Different from any huts we had stayed in, the doors of La-uk stood six feet high, as if the builders decided they did not like crouching any more. Each had a tiny brass lock hanging with its key.

By that time, we took for granted the natural toilets of the jungle. Katherine came around the corner with a look of happy surprise. "You won't believe the clean toilet area," she said.

I couldn't wait to see if the toilet was a tile floor with a ceramic hole or a crude hole in the dirt floor. In a village hotel, a mandi consisted of containers of water for bathing and washing hands and a hole in the ground for a toilet, with simple dividers or walls offering privacy.

Its proximity to the western influence of civilized Wamena changed Jiwika only in the ways of sanitation.

Penis gourds and spirit boards decorating grass huts as well as no utensils for eating indicated the ways of ancestors were still alive.

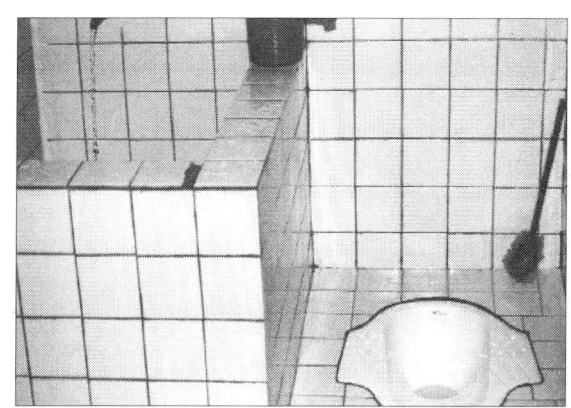

*The mandi or cubicle has water to flush toilet or for sponge baths*

Memories of our first day, when we saw our room at the Sri Kandi Hotel in Wamena came back to me. Katherine had said, "Where am I supposed to take a shower?"

Neither of us had ever seen a hole in the floor with porcelain footprints to show where to put your feet and a three-foot tall basin of water with buckets hanging nearby.

Several children tiptoed trying to hide behind Katherine's legs.

My thoughts changed from toilets to children. Our gift from every village included the greeting of children, with their welcoming smiles and laughter. Receiving them with open arms always provided comfort.

At first, they responded with caution at the sight of our light-colored skin, hair, and eyes. We returned their smiles and reached for their hands, and these simple acts removed all barriers; the children began to swarm, each wanting to participate in this most eventful moment.

In America, the type of greeting we received from the villagers would best compare to the treatment received by celebrities when they walk into any public place.

Americans are excited by the arrival of actors and want to touch them, speak to them, and tell their friends later that someone special smiled at them directly. It was that way for us when we met the tribal peoples of Indonesia.

I have to admit the attention we received in Jiwika--as in every place we visited that entire month--felt wonderful.

Happy, excited children tugged at our sleeves, pulling us into a circular compound protected by a wall of huts.

We met Chief Kurulu, longtime chief and once a powerful man in the valley. The local government named the district after him in his honor.

He talked to us, expecting an answer; however, we could not find Julius anywhere in the crowd, so we could not understand a word the chief said.

*New friends in Jiwika*

Three Dani women, very old but strangely beautiful, sat in the shade on a wood bench. Opposite, three women stood in perfect posture, like statues or a scene from a postcard. "Julius, are these women mother, daughter and granddaughter?" I asked.

"Yes," he replied.

*Three generations in Jiwika*

The chief kept pointing to the circular hut behind him, nodding and shrugging his shoulders. Confused, Katherine sat with the four women while I photographed two worlds side by side.

To capture and convey the fragility of the moment, I needed to reach into my heart to understand at a deeper level. I lowered my camera and took in the scene, wanting to absorb the rich simplicity of the women's lives. The old women sitting beside Katherine lived in similar ways of their grandparents.

Their contentment showed in their welcoming smiles. Without embarrassment, one woman reached for Katherine's hand and wrapped the other around Katherine's shoulder. I knew at once that my writings could convey my passion for travel to encourage others to do the same, but like the taste of something special, mere words would never substitute for the taste of the journey itself.

*Jiwika and the 100-year-old mummy*

At this point a tribesman inside the hut brought a mummy out to the chief. Warrior leaders did not receive the typical cremation after death. Instead, the village desiccated their bodies and kept them in the men's hut as a channel to the spirits for prosperity, health, and safety in warfare. No one knew the age of the mummy--it could have been one hundred years old, for all we knew; but it had been positioned knee-to-chest, with his mouth wide open, as if the man had been frightened just before expiring. We felt an eerie presence, difficult to explain, for I had viewed mummies only in museums. This mummy portrayed something more than a dead body, and I felt as if it might, in fact, represent a portal to the spirit world.

Julius appeared suddenly and whispered, "Pay the chief two dollars for seeing the mummy. You didn't bargain with him."

*Jiwika chief showing off the mummy*

And in the same breath, pointing to the thatched roof, he said, "Look, penis gourds growing."

Through interpretations of hand motions, Julius pointed to the gourds on the roof and the gourds worn by the men.

Julius explained, "The individuals grew their own personal gourds. They straightened or curled the ends as the gourds grew."

Vines wound in and out of the yellow-grass roof. Some of the brown gourds, darkened from the sun, waited for their harvest.

Instead of paying the chief, I snapped more photographs, deliberately giving him the clear understanding that we had seen enough of the mummy. His men carried it back inside the hut.

The mysteries of the simple, everyday lives of the Dani revealed themselves to us village by village. Our journey unfolded day by day, according to our needs.

The remoteness of the jungle created an environment of simplicity, taking away the social complications of my Midwestern lifestyle. Halfway around the world nobody could save me, for I had nothing to fall back on. And yet I found a powerful self-reliance.

Children calling, "Lauk, lauk," got our attention. They wanted to go up a steep mountainside to the saltwater spring called Iluwe, about a thousand feet above the valley floor.

The Dani, Jale, and Kim Yal tribes visited the spring often, as the pool offered the sole source of salt for the villagers. For many, the pool requires a laborious two-day walk.

Julius and two teenage boys led us to the rocky path. We trusted the porters to stay behind with all our gear, except for my camera pack which never left my sight.

My camera hung around my neck, leaving my hands free for grabbing handholds of brush and for keeping my balance on the steep trails.

A mixture of seasons revealed their colors in the trees. The brilliance of tropical hues such as mango orange and blood red complemented the richness of the earth's rust, chocolate brown, pine green and ochre palate.

Katherine and I had come from a place of high technology, of skyscrapers and sleek cars, of DVD players and shopping malls. The beauty of this place struck us with its simplicity, its peacefulness, and its breathtaking splendor.

*Relaxing along the roadside*

At times the inhospitable jungle floor, full of potential danger, disappeared. Did its insects carrying fatal diseases, vines home to armies of ants, and impenetrable walls of plants harmful to touch all belong on the page of a book I read years ago? We skimmed that hidden heart of darkness, replaced with a place similar to the jungle canopy, a place full of light and exotic flowering trees.

As we climbed, columns of smoke signaled the location of inhabited villages. The music of nature, our footsteps, and the gentle rush of water played melodies for us.

Quickly my perspective of the beauty of the jungle bounced out of focus again, when off to the side in a cleared area of reddish limestone soil, poles stuck out of the ground in the shape of a teepee. We saw brown, dried grass stuffed in the middle of the intersecting poles. Rat bodies turning to skeletons filled the nests. This was a mystery I just had to unlock.

Julius said, "Those are mokat aku, or spirit carriers, used to control and guide the spirits. Aku means the poles used for people to walk across rivers or ditches." He explained, "The rat poles would attract and transport away the spirits that might cause harm to the pigs or gardens. Villagers often used rats in ceremonies. For a wounded man, they cut a rat in the stomach. If the bamboo knife damaged any internal part, the wounded man had no future. If the internal parts of the rat remained intact, however, the people would hang the rat by the fire in the wounded man's hut to ensure quick recovery."

Satisfied with Julius's explanation, I put many of his words to pen and paper in my pocket-sized notebook. Taking my time writing, I realized the significance of my weariness. Singing and talking, trying to ignore my aching knees, I might have overlooked the rat poles, so I thanked my young guide for bringing them to my attention.

We received unique and often abstract gifts. Often I had to remind myself that what appeared complex or perplexing, such as the story of the rats, resulted from my background, not theirs. The opportunity to observe what I considered the unconventional signaled that one more important piece of the mystery of the Dani had fallen into place. Stepping stones about a foot tall grew taller as the climb continued at a pace too hurried for me. The midday heat and lack of food depleted my physical resources. Within minutes after resting, I felt the need to stop again. I gasped so loudly that the boy pulling me up onto the next slippery step could probably hear my heart beating. The terrific heat of the equator silenced everyone on the climb. I wanted a gust of wind to blow the humidity away from this wild climate.

Although challenged, we fought to overcome our limitations, knowing it takes strength from within to gather energy and courage.

The boy pointed to an ordinary-looking cluster of rocks. I could not understand, so I asked Julius, "What is so different about those rocks?"

Julius said, "Those rocks are an old woman bent in half on her way to the salt pools, but the spirits turned her into stone."

When we had started up the mountain, my backpack felt innocent enough, but it eventually bore into my back as if an evil spirit had filled it with heavy logs.

A trickle of a stream fed the porous stones on one side of our path, giving vitality to a variety of plant life, including the plant I named the "keep-cool plant." Its leaves, when held under the icy water for a few seconds, took on the coldness of the water. My young guide laid the leaves on my arms and cheeks. For a moment, the coolness overshadowed the intense ache in my legs and wobbling knees and fought the heat, which seemed to pierce every pore of my body.

There were two people between Katherine and myself. Attracting everyone's attention, I yelled to her. "Have you tried the leaves, dipped in the cold water?"

She turned to face me and had leaves stuck on her forehead! I laughed so hard it hurt and wished I had the energy to dig out my camera.

She said, "I love them and am going to remember this trick."

An hour's climb turned into two, while the compact canopy above us turned day into twilight.

*Silora at the salt pools*

We emerged, finally, from the infernal trail, squinting from reflections of sunlight bouncing off the tops of hut-sized boulders. Glowing with perspiration, we prayed the scorching sun would leave us alone. Streams of sweat burned my eyes. Weariness disappeared as I saw the silhouette of a Dani playing his mouth harp in the pool of water. Plumes of bird feathers moved back and forth like white flames in the center of the mirrored formations. Massive rocks surrounded the small pool.

The teenager pulled me up the rocky path with a jerk to help me maneuver over the last high rock. The silhouette came to life. A Dani, covered in designs of white paint, tucked his harp behind his ear and jumped from his rock to mine. His arms spread out like a bird for balance, his bow and arrow teetered back and forth. A white, fluffy, feather garland topped his head. A single red feather came out the back, and two long feathers pointed to his eyes. White lines painted under them stopped at his flat, broad nose.

He moved energetically, almost dancing, and began humming on his mouth harp again. I stared at him eagerly, wanting to see everything about him. He never looked up at the diversion our arrival caused. I drank in his features: his wild, black eyes, his dull, yellow teeth, and the curves of his muscular arms and legs. This tribal man's presence felt out of place. Whether he was watching the activity at the salt pool to pass time or had a reason for being there, nobody in the group understood.

Finding the salt pools made the difficult climb worthwhile. We had overcome the jungles of New Guinea and felt as if we sat on the rim of an earthen cup of hot tea.

*Jale man at the salt pools*

In the bottom of this cup stood three men in knee-deep, dreggy water.

Julius said, "Two of the men are from the Jale tribe, and the other is a Dani." They did not acknowledge our presence.

"What are they doing?" I said. With a sharpened slice of stone, one of the Jale men cut thin strips from a piece of banana trunk about six inches wide by a foot long. The other two men soaked the strips in the salt water, squeezing them like sponges, forcing the water to impregnate the strips. We rested and watched them at their task, and after a half hour or more, they carried the soggy strips back home in net bags.

My interpretation of the next steps came from Julius. The next day they will hang the strips over fences or thatch to dry in the sun. They will burn the strips when dry and collect the ash on banana leaves. A young girl would then wet the ash, form it into balls, and wrap it with the leaves. Villagers could then use the salty balls for seasoning, an important trade item.

Beneath the towering watch of the forest formations, the cool dampness of a rock offered a relaxing place for me to watch the amiable Dani interact with Katherine. She climbed the rock where he sat. His legs spread apart, allowing full view of his privates.

Julius, with the other men, left to find a jungle toilet, I guessed, or maybe to share a handful of betel nuts to chew. Would this man lift his bow toward Katherine or continue to play his harp? Like me, Katherine possessed a level of daring courage and the will to take chances. We did not expect to own and then lose this power.

The manner in which Katherine dealt with this strange Dani defines our personalities.

We discovered a new trait in our lives, not tested at home, but relied upon in our new world. She would never have thought to approach a stranger dressed to kill back home, but then she would never have been in a situation to need or want to.

Trying to make friends with this tribal man helped her discover her capabilities to use unknown resources.

With my smiles and by getting my camera out, I encouraged her initiative to approach the Dani.

Teenagers struggle with their changing sense of identity. Here in a faraway place, Katherine could be herself, whether silly or serious, without peers judging her behavior.

She moved closer to the wildly painted and feathered Dani and tried to ask him his name.

His words, untranslatable, did not matter to her, as the purpose of her communication succeeded, and she could ask him to play his mouth harp.

He reached for her hand as she tried to move closer. A buzzing sound, mixed with a funny little tune he hummed, brought smiles to all. Katherine, on her own, had made the decision to approach this wild man of the jungle, hoping to shake his hand. I could almost see her sense of self-esteem building before my eyes.

*Silora excited to pose for photo*

This entire experience of meeting this man and seeing how these people figured out how to make salt overwhelmed both of us.

I felt gratitude for the Danis' acceptance of our inquisitive nature and for their gracious welcome. No doubt we appeared more like aliens than mere strangers.

Total immersion with these people seemed to block out the monotonous everyday life we had left behind.

Reflections on thoughts of home brought to light the differences of those common, routine tasks we could perform in our sleep: making coffee or pouring salt from a shaker.

*Silora our new friend*

The Dani represent real stories of humanity. Despite an extensive amount of research and planning, I had never read any book that conveyed the stories, wonder, or intensity of their lives. Imagine learning to dance by reading a book. Yes, you might learn the steps; however, you will never taste the rhythm or the spirit that dancing provides for the soul until you get on the dance floor. That's how it was for me, and that's how it was for Katherine.

We had read the books, now we were really dancing. As an eyewitness to Dani tales, we allowed the Dani spirit to entwine with ours. The heat of the Indonesian jungle slid under my wet clothing and sapped every ounce of energy from my pores. My water bottle was empty. My knees buckled when I stood and thought about the trip down the steep path ahead, but I heard the birds, singing along with the Danis who had begun the trek down. I allowed their harmonious rhythms of song to saturate my senses and to place me on the dance floor of their lives.

I had what I would call a cultural breakthrough. It occurred when I had to place my independent attitudes aside and lay bare my vulnerabilities and limitations in this strange new world. Independence in our American society often provides an invisible shield of protection against others, wanting to take advantage of us.

Self-preservation in the Dani culture depended on a feeling of trust, allowing other people to see your weaknesses and limitations. This strengthening and binding of the human spirit help us create a balance with the power of nature.

Julius climbed the rock where I sat while taking pictures of the Dani tribal man and Katherine. "Can you ask him his name?" I said.

"I don't speak his language, but he understood and told me 'Silora,'" Julius said.

While talking to Julius, Silora pulled out an extra bamboo flute that he had tucked in his armband of leaves, and he offered it to Katherine in a wordless gesture of, "I'm happy to have met you." It was a generous act on his part. He showed her how to move the pieces while humming to create a sound. She tried but could not hear any sound except for her own humming.

I tried to give him a handful of one hundred rupiah notes, but he pushed my hand away.

He did not want payment for the flute. While putting the money away, I saw out of the corner of my eye that Silora had noticed the clove-flavored cigarettes I kept in my waist pouch for bartering with the Dani. He smiled and pointed at the cigarettes, and his face lit with joy when I gave him a couple. He followed us all the way down the steep trail, taking care to help my wobbly knees make it to the next lower step; and I figured he really appreciated my gift of the cigarettes, and deserved more.

Indonesians should win the world record for having the biggest smiles. Silora's face looked as if it had a permanent pinkish-grey grin. In hindsight, I think the intensity of his smile developed because he wore no masks to display misleading impressions.

His vibrant sincerity and personality sprang forth through his body language.

Without a common language, people provide communication by amplifying the traits common to all humanity. Communication in these circumstances occurs through body language.

The sharing that takes place far outweighs the content of the words. The spirit of man becomes interpreted through the body.

Silora touched my deepest essence with his heartwarming nature. His strength of character, along with that of the other villagers befriending us, would operate as the backbone of our memories. The Dani, with their simplistic, primitive lifestyle, offered practical examples of the facts of life. Their teachings emerged not through the conventional means of classrooms and lectures, but through living life itself.

*Dani women walking to the fields*

Allowing us to live as they live, the Dani opened for us the doors of learning in Indonesia. Upon our return to modern society, the real test of courage would begin. Would we have the strength to live what we had experienced in Indonesia, those things that had pushed us to our limits of adventure? Or would we lapse into the same old habits?

For now, I could not think much of what we would do when we got home. I was exhausted and famished and still had a long way to go before reaching the foot of the mountain and the village there.

I was relieved when we finally arrived to see Panus, excitedly waiting with a huge pineapple in his slender, brown hands. I didn't know if he had traded something for it or if he had stolen it, and I didn't ask. Katherine and I had cravings well beyond the munchies.

"Yes!" we both said in unison, before Panus even got the chance to offer us some of the succulent fruit.

We sat down under a tin roof draped over tree supports for more years than anyone there could remember. The roof provided shade on an area of ground, worn bare from hundreds of years of tribal people, selling and trading. I craved a salad with grilled chicken strips, but the pineapple tasted like participatory heaven.

Before a trip, I try to change my eating habits by eliminating foods not available while traveling, such as caffeine or sugar products. Waiting until late afternoon for food fit with my new reality. Prior to an off-the-beaten-path trip, I put my body into training for the physical changes I will face while on the road. I exercise, concentrating on my legs. As a busy housewife, I'm not used to walking six hours a day, so it's important to condition myself as much as I can before setting out for tribal life. Otherwise, I would never survive three days, let alone thirty, in places like Indonesia.

A couple of weeks before leaving on a trip to a Least-Developed Country, I also limit my diet to staples of carbohydrates. I had learned to take things as they came while traveling, without expectations, remembering that if a person can't bend, he may break.

Food is one of those things I learned could be here now and gone in an instant: I always packed food wisely, but I also knew that food could be lost or stolen.

Animals or bugs could get into it. It might be needed for trade in an emergency. Food might be offered to me that I found inedible, and I might crave types of food I could not acquire, such as meat, for instance, or salad with grilled chicken strips.

I knew I had to go with the flow, though, and bend so I wouldn't break: eat the pineapple and forget the chicken. Maybe thinking I have a need for nutritious food becomes part of the emotional detachment you have to make before a remote trip where the basic food is rice. As we free ourselves of those things in life that we take for granted, we learn to trust that Mother Nature will provide for the body.

*"Most travel, and certainly the rewarding kind, involves the kindness of strangers, putting yourself in the hands of people you don't know and trusting them with your life. The risky suspension of disbelief is often an experience freighted with anxiety. But what are the alternatives? Often, there are none."*
**Paul Theroux**

## Chapter 13: Ring Around the Rattan Hoops

How do mosquitoes know where to find you when they have the whole jungle to search? Slapping ourselves until it hurt, we dispensed the hundred-percent-Deet repellent to cover our faces and hands, draining the bottle dry.

Julius lit the ends of two mosquito coils, and blew out the flame, leaving the ends glowing. The coils burned like incense, giving off a strange odor in the billowy smoke that most of the mosquitoes did not like.

Some brave souls among them continued to buzz around our heads, though. Nightmarish thoughts of malaria flashed through my brain along with the annoying drone of mosquitoes in my ears. I lay awake, swatting and slapping.

Deep inside my sleeping bag, my feet kicked at the bag, hoping to knock the devil keecus to Timbuktu. Those little mice lived in every village and somehow knew that strangers meant food.

Julius knew we carried snacks in our packs and always tried to serve our meals away from where we slept, but the protein bars sealed tightly in foil wrappers gave off a smell that brought the little creatures in before we even had said goodnight.

My flashlight blinked on and off as I tried to find the sneaky mosquito that had found its way inside my bag, creating a ringing that was hard to ignore. Distraught by the obviously poor forecast for a good night's sleep, I wanted to lose my balance and fall into my fantasy world of magic carpets and medieval castles.

I shuffled the bag and netting the next morning after another sleepless night, finding that the bright morning light always rejuvenated me.

"What are we waiting for? It's been two hours sitting here doing nothing," Katherine said.

"Listen, I hear something," I said.

"That truck looks like it just lost a bullfight," Katherine said. "Julius is suggesting we hitch a ride to the next village."

"I can't believe that clanking, choking pickup could carry all of us," I said. Julius and I scrunched in with the driver after Katherine and the porters found a spot to share on two bundles in the open back end. The two bundles of synthetic, imported rice bags held our sleeping bags, wrapped around the wok, our two plastic bowls, two red cups, and our spoons.

The backpacks now contained net bags, animal-skin bags, fragile penis gourds, several cassowary feather headdresses, and an assortment of gifts of bark-string armbands, which left no room for our sleeping bags.

"Are you okay back there?" I yelled back to Katherine.

"Yes. Panus propped the soft rice bags for me to lean and sit on. I guess that gives us a clue as to the comfort of the ride ahead," she said. DenDee's monotone voice to the others lacked enthusiasm and concern. Wasn't riding in a truck less strenuous and faster than walking?

The ride would have been bumpy in any event, but it seemed the driver aimed at the potholes, trying for the local record. A flat tire came almost too quickly, and I had to ask Julius, "The next flat is inevitable, so what do we do, since we have only one spare under all our stuff?"

He shrugged. Everything always works out, he seemed to be saying. I learned that you needed a certain mindset when traveling in Least-Developed Countries. Uncertainty becomes a norm. A person from our society must learn that delay and doubt should not frustrate, for it comes with the adventure. To believe anything else results in anxiety. Anxiety devours the joy of the journey.

The driver changed the tire, and about an hour later, we got started, singing our favorite Dani songs and delighted to ride in such luxurious transportation instead of walking. Katherine and I tried to teach others our own songs, but the words never came out right when the Dani tried to repeat them. I suspect our music sounded too complex to their ears. Our lyrics speak stories that may or may not relate to our own lives, but the Dani songs represent lyrics of the heart. Therein lays the difference between our peoples.

Reflections of the silver fibers in the distance turned the grass fields into shimmering lakes. The truck headed south with the jungle far to the east and west. The land looked like an unruffled emptiness. Morning rain showers ungraciously left behind sticky humidity.

Our cramped quarters further compounded the discomfort. Dust, entering through glassless window frames found a home on our skin, providing a crunching grittiness in our mouths that made simple swallowing a major task.

Someone's stomach started growling, and I was not sure if it was mine. All of us rubbed at chapped lips, and mine felt like brittle parchment.

Katherine and I sought relief in our limited supply of purified water, and the men with us, not understanding our need for purified water, reached out for our bottles, expecting us to share.

With no food and two liters of water remaining, I hoarded the water like gold and tried repeatedly to explain to the porters and to Julius that Katherine and I were not trying to be mean, but that if we drank their water, we would get sick.

None of them carried water or personal items, except Julius, who carried one small bag with one extra outfit.

I felt bad about it; but afraid of not finding water the rest of the day, I kept the water swaddled in the safe outside pouch of my camera pack. I had to think of Katherine's health as well as my own.

Katherine yelled, "I'm starving."

I wanted to satisfy her hunger with words, but found none that qualified.

Sitting in the front seat, I shrugged, not able to explain to her that real courage and self-respect came from setting the hunger aside. Often, we needed to tell the mind to fulfill the pangs of hunger with visions of a new world or experiences from a sharing people. Having our pineapple one day and not the next cultivated risk-taking. But I couldn't relay this information to my child.

I could accept the hunger, for I had conditioned my mind to accept it. What I had not prepared for was overcoming my natural instinct to provide for my young.

A consuming desire to furnish Katherine some sustenance took my mind off my personal emptiness, but my wishes afforded her little comfort.

What caused this lack of preparation? I wished I had a couple of sticks of beef jerky to offer her. I should have asked Julius how long the truck ride might take, so we could have planned for lunch.

A brief moment of calm reflection reminded me of how this inward look might shape another step for our path. I could create a diversion with a story or tell a funny joke to help all of us stop thinking about food.

Before we traveled, I tried to explain to Katherine the reality of hunger as a potential problem. Back home, we take so much for granted that hunger while traveling never seemed a real possibility.

As I thought about what I might be able to do to ease Katherine's discomfort, the second tire blew and brought everything to an immediate halt. We all sat where we were, in dead silence, the songs we had been singing to cheer us dying on our cardboard lips. As the air escaped the tire, we felt the joy in spirits cease.

"Everybody out," said Julius abruptly.

"What now?" Katherine asked no one in particular, and I could hear both the tiredness and the annoyance in her voice as the men chattered and disembarked.

No doubt Julius had prepared himself for this process. He hummed again, motioning for Amir and DenDee to take all the bags out of the truck. In the confusion, I heard Julius calling, "Jackie!"

*Goonin Su Su or mountains called woman's breasts*

He touched my shoulders, pointed to the two small mountains beside us, and called them a name. The men laughed. Katherine and I did not understand, and we failed to see the humor. A woman with a heavy load walked past us, and again Julius touched my shoulders to get my attention. He cupped his hands on his chest, pointed to the woman, and then to the mountains.

"Woman's breasts," I said.

Nodding, duplicating our words, he repeated in Dani, "Goonin SuSu." All the men laughed.

The men pushed the truck over to the side of the gravel-worn-smooth road.

Although we had not seen any mode of transportation other than our own feet in three weeks, Julius said, "Another vehicle will arrive soon to pick us up."

"How are you going to contact another truck to find us?" I asked.

He answered seriously but not argumentatively, "The truck will come soon, but we don't have radios or phones." Below his black-as-coal eyes and brows of the same color, his betel-stained mouth ballooned into a submissive grin.

I adopted an impatient tone, signaling my own hunger. My patience with Julius was coming to an end.

"Julius, how in the world would another truck just happen to know that we would have two flat tires?" I said in an irritable voice. In the last twenty-four hours, a few slices of pineapple and a bowl of white rice did not give me the pick-me-up my body needed. While waiting for his answer, I noticed my hands shaking. My glucose levels were dropping. With only a few days left in the trip,

I should have known to save a few snacks for emergencies. As soon as we got back to some type of store, I would buy some biscuits or crackers.

Katherine remembered the foil packets of nuts she had squished into her book bag on the plane. The little foil packets represented a real treasure.

Before, the beauty of the land and sharing treasures of the people's lives had filled our stomachs. We sat on the side of the dry, river-bed of a road and chewed the few nuts we had while the heat created a mirage around the silver grass.

A small area of shade blanketed the road along the side of the truck. Of the five men, Coughin alone wanted to share our peanuts. Grateful, selfish, and starving, we savored each morsel of our one-third share, slowly.

On the edge of the vast blue horizon, a tornado of dust gave me hope of an oncoming truck.

We wanted to see a festival in the village of Wesaput that day. The day before, many feathered and painted tribesmen walked south. They scheduled dancing and games at midmorning.

My main concern was getting some kind of food, although the festival was almost as important. I knew we might see some unusual tribal people different from previous villages.

Our anticipation for rescue grew as the billowing of dust moved toward us. Crossing our fingers for space for seven plus packs, and not caring how much it cost, we all stood and began to wave at the oncoming truck.

The truck driver, delivering two newly-elected government officials to the district of Gondura had space and time and offered his services for the fair price of 4,000 rupiahs (about two dollars).

Visions of grilled cheese and hot chocolate, which might be served at the Flowers Cafe in Wamena, danced in my head. The café was only an hour's walk from Wesaput, and I was determined to get both Katherine and myself there today.

"Julius, where will we find a place to sleep tonight?" I asked.

The description Julius had given of the lone hotel in Wesaput had a magnetic pull. He said, "The hotel should have a clean bath, comfortable mattress, and foods other than rice."

That idea felt like heaven to me right then, and I knew it was important to get Katherine there as soon as we could.

Those attending the festivities might occupy all the rooms, but Julius proclaimed he owned it, so we were anticipating a comfortable night's sleep and no hunger pains. As it turned out, I would find I'd misunderstood Julius's claim to own the hotel.

*Entrance to village*

    The truck slowed at an arched entrance, and we disembarked and paid the driver his two dollars. As we walked along, rows and rows of fuchsia led the way to the first sign of life in the village. Our pace quickened.
    Immersed in a pocket of evergreens rested a capacious cottage designed like a hut. Meticulous flowerbeds wound beside the walkway to the cottage door. The coolness of the shadowed yard felt refreshing, and the luxuriant green of the jungle surrounded us. Vines, reaching for their turn in the sunlight, clung to the front of the large two-story building.
    Julius directed the men to watch our bags while he talked to someone about rooms. I had to duck at the short entrance, built to save wood apparently, although some of the Dani men were taller than I was. Inside everything looked black. As my eyes adjusted, I made out the masks, headdresses, and cowry-shell bibs that adorned the walls. Around the corner from where I stood, a wood picnic-like table was stuffed into a small room. I saw no reception desk. The ceiling touched the head of the boney man talking to Julius, but the man didn't seem to mind, as his posture showed no signs of constant bending over. A puff of sunlight tumbled its way through various openings of the wood-slatted walls and rested on the floor inside.
    Katherine said, "Standing on this floor, I feel safe and clean."
    "Dirt floors, fleas, keecus, white rice, and dirty river-water for tea were all part of the adventure and behind us at the moment," I said. Dreams of a mattress to sleep on and hot food were a reality.
    Mumbles heard above us somewhere left Katherine and me crossing our fingers again, since it had seemed to work earlier. I pulled out two tree-branch stools from under the picnic table and waited for Julius who had disappeared. Loud voices and a few thumps replaced the whispers. Feet protruded from the opening in the ceiling, feeling their way to the hand-cut stairs.

Calloused and bare, a foot found the top step, worn smooth from use. As if working their way out of a tunnel, a young boy, followed by Julius, shimmied down the eight or nine vertical steps. No Dani had a wider grin than Julius that day. The young boy moved close to Katherine as if to study her or hoping to start a conversation. I did not understand his questioning look and turned to Julius for interpretation.

He said, "They want 10,000 rupiahs for two rooms and hot tea with biscuits for breakfast."

I responded, "We need only one room, but we will pay the five dollars anyway."

Without another word, Julius walked outside for our bags. It took two people to shove my heavy bag up into the opening in the ceiling.

As I watched the men muscle the luggage up through the hole, I thought of the fragile items I had in my bag, especially the penis gourds, which could easily be cracked or broken in the hustle and bustle.

One of our bags slid back down into Amir's arms, almost knocking him over. Julius stepped forward, looked at me with raised eyebrows, and lifted the bag over his head. He balanced his feet on the narrow and steep log ladder and gave a hard push to the bag through the small opening into the second-floor area. The strength of this skinny guide once again caught me off guard as it had the time he picked me up and carried me across the river.

Julius waved me toward the steps. My heavy boots barely fit the rungs of the ladder. I put all my weight on my toes as I climbed up, assuming to find a normal second floor hotel room. The opening into the next floor touched me on all sides. Somehow, I managed to get my long body up into the area. I yelled down to Katherine, "Oh my gosh!"

The hallway and height of the second-floor ceiling were both hardly four feet. Six baby doors surrounded me, with two of the doors wide open.

The small space meant I had to crouch to move my bag forward and into one of the rooms. Inside, on the floor, I saw a twin mattress touching the walls on all sides. No wonder Julius thought we needed two rooms.

I did not like the idea of Katherine staying alone in a room, but I could hardly see how we could share a room. Our packs alone took up a fourth of the bed.

"You were very lucky to get sleeping space for tonight. More than a thousand Jale tribesmen are coming here for a festival," Julius explained.

I said, "I know this is the only hotel in the area, but tribal people don't stay in hotels, do they?"

"No, but government officials from Wamena are coming to watch the dancing and might have wanted the rooms," he said.

Overwhelmed by the excitement of getting rooms, we put aside our thoughts of food and a bath.

A tribe, singing and playing musical instruments, sauntered past the hotel, and their songs brought to mind the day's festivities.

I grabbed my camera and roused Katherine, who had already collapsed on her mattress and lay napping. We could sleep later. We double-checked the locks on our luggage. Neither of us could stand up in the room or hallway, so we scooted along to the hole in the floor, leading to the first floor.

I doubted if a person weighing more than 120 pounds could get through that hole. Our group of porters and guide were not in sight so we walked outside in the direction of the music and crowds.

*Jale men walked many days to reach festival*

Jale tribesmen and women came into view as we walked closer to the festivities, and their numbers could cover a football field.

Not wanting to appear obtrusive, I contemplated my movements. The members of each group of twenty Jale danced to a particular tribal song, aware of the gawking visitors. They sang lyrical harmonies, like the sound of magic.

The Jale people had cast an alluring spell that I did not want to break. I looked forward to re-awakening my memory of this transitory moment when, at a future time, I would review these photos.

The Jale, also known as the Yali, come from the isolated Silimo Valley, about thirty kilometers southwest of Wamena. Unlike other tribes, they wore hoops of rattan around their waists.

To dress, they first step into tight hoops that act as a support for larger ones. The men adjust the hoops so that their penis sheaths stick out from underneath the rattan hoops.

We could see the penis sheaths, long and thin, with decorations of cuscus fur or red fabric, dangling from the ends. I never found out if the decoration was for fun or how they protected the penis gourd while repairing a roof, or sleeping.

*Jale men wear the hoops and gourds day and night*

The name Jale came from the Dani word jalemo, meaning "lands to the west."

Arduous terrain and rough mountains kept missionaries and the government away from the Jales until the late 1950s. In 1961, the first Protestant mission came to the area and decided it needed an airstrip. In those days, the Protestants paid a wage of two cowry shells per Jale working the airstrip.

Protestant traders offered steel axes to the Jales in exchange for land and pigs. Villagers received medical advice from the missionaries, including a cure for a skin disease.

The missions built schools. Maize and peanuts, along with lessons in animal husbandry, came to the Jale tribe through the missionaries, along with other signs of progress the foreigners brought with them.

By 1964, however, the villagers had had enough of the Good Word. The Jale burned the missionaries' houses and ate the preacher and twelve of his assistants.

In 1968, two Protestant missionaries met the same fate. Despite pacification from religious groups and the government, pagan traditions in the isolated villages of the Jale remained strong.

After a few hours of exchanging stares with these people, Katherine needed relief from her pounding headache. She needed food, and the promise of real food in Wamena called our names.

I walked her back to our rooms, thinking the hotel staff might find something to hold her over until we could start our walk to Wamena after dusk.

My soul had not yet reached its saturation point when it came to absorbing the sights and sounds of the festival and the Jale, and I wanted to get back outside to live with them for a while longer.

After giving Katherine a boost into the ceiling hole, I came back down to the lobby and inched my way into the different rooms at the back of the hotel's first floor.

Trying not to act guilty while wandering through the hotel unattended, I surprised a teenage boy who was coming around a corner.

Communicating with chewing motions, pointing to my stomach, and shrugging my shoulders, I used my version of sign language for hunger, which ended up making us both laugh.

The boy rewarded me for my antics with a loaf of koti or sweet bread. I offered three one-hundred-rupiahs notes, or fifteen cents, and said, "Terima kasih, terima kasih."

He acted as if I had given him twenty dollars and responded, "Baik baik baik terima kasih, banyak!" Meaning, "Okay, okay, okay! Thank you very much!"

He beamed at me, his grin telling me how happy he was to have helped me, and suddenly he threw his arms around my neck and hugged me hard.

Gently pulling away and pointing to my chest, I declared, "My nama Jackie." I could not remember how to ask for his name, so touching his shoulder with my forefinger, I asked, "Nama, nama?"

He replied, "Muhammad." I had met several other Muhammads in Wamena during our initial days in Indonesia when I was trying to find a guide.

Climbing up to the second floor with the steaming loaf of bread made me think of the haylofts in Iowa when I was a kid.

I recalled Aunt Dorothy's homemade bread smothered in fresh-from-the-barn butter with peanut butter dripping off the sides.

I knocked on Katherine's door, let myself in, and said, "Katherine, want some warm bread?"

I crawled onto her mattress and found her just rousing from sleep. "Can you think of any packets of peanut butter we stuck away and forgot about?"

Her eyes grew wide and she smiled, grabbing her backpack from the end of the bed. Lost in the mumble-jumble of the backpack, one tiny one-ounce packet of peanut butter surfaced.

"I think I found some," she said.

Food from home never tasted so good.

Katherine's headache had returned, so I left my waist-pack next to her and prepared to head back out to the festival.

Our passports, traveler's checks, local currency, and pepper spray were right where my daughter could get to them, far from pickpockets lurking behind trees.

This allowed me to concentrate on the colorful, jubilant people in the fields. "Lock your door after I leave," I warned her as I turned to go, "and don't open it for anyone. I'll be back in an hour or so."

"The edge of the world does not look far away; to that I am on my way running." The words of an old Indian song I remembered singing with the kids on camping trips came back to me.

My strange clothing, skin color, and gender made me obvious. It took skill for me to blend in. It was important for me to keep the subjects of my photographs interested in their routines, so they would not stop and go into soldier stances.

The ethic of the journalist to tell the truth with the photograph far outweighed the artistry of creating images, as far as I was concerned.

Photography interprets and documents simultaneously, and reward comes to the photographer from the involvement she shares with the subject.

Past enterprises have taught me to move in to new environments slowly, take the shape of a rock, and find an inconspicuous spot from which to observe new people without distracting them from the activity of their normal lives.

I had found that the novelty of my presence would soon wear off, and the people who had noticed me and felt self-conscious or threatened would relax again, and the situation would return to normal. Wandering abstractly, my body took shorter steps, testing reactions to my camera among the people.

The lemony sun traveled slowly across the sky, and I mentally calculated how much time I had to circumnavigate the festival.

The men, showing extraordinary displays of tribal rituals, danced with vigor, knowing that dusk signaled the end of the festival.

Crocheted hats made from tree fibers much like the noken bags the Dani women wore on their backs, covered men's heads. The shell decorations hanging on their chest were a sign of prosperity.

Unlike the Dani, their bodies were free of paint and elaborate decorations of feathers and furs. The dozens of hoops around their waist were enough to catch anyone's attention.

I knelt by a group whose outstretched hands were swinging bows and arrows. Research told me that many clans feared those of us with pale skin. I used caution approaching the Jale, who had little exposure to cultures alien to their own.

*Taking turns climbing the tower*

*Potential enemies can be seen from top of tower*

There were no bushes or logs to hide behind, and Julius and the others were not around. I then noticed a kaio, or watchtower, behind me, towering above the festival. The kaio served as a lookout for enemies.

Twenty-five-foot lengths of liana branches gave the tower its height, and wide vines circled the branches, creating a stepping tool for climbing. Next to the kaio sat a thatched-roof shelter, a place for retreat from the sun.

At the top of the tall branches, a platform rested just wide enough for one man to stand guard.

I moved toward the empty hut for a little privacy after a few photographs, catching a glimpse of one of the few children with her mother trying to tighten the girl's fiber skirt, which was hanging loose.

The girl immediately hid behind her mother when she realized I was watching them. I found the supernatural world of dancing completely entrancing. Enveloped in a world time had forgotten, the Jale people gave me a visual statement about what mattered to them.

Angry shouts broke my train of thought. I looked up to see two men trying to out-yell each other while pushing at each other's shoulders. They stood at the base of the kaio, right next to the hut where I pondered my next move. I trained my camera on them and snapped pictures of their struggle.

The more powerful of the two men scampered to the top platform of the kaio and stood like a palace guard. I decided to stay where I was, photographing the men, but keeping myself and my expensive camera out of breaking distance.

Neither man looked like he would appreciate my stepping in to capture their moment in pictures.

"The traveler who returns from a journey may tell all he has seen, but he cannot tell all."

This Ashanti proverb reminds me of how little we can bring back from our journeys in stories and photos.

Would the changes within me last, quenching my thirst for remote discovery? Or would the changes fire the desire for another adventure in yet another, more distant, forbidding land?

Time holds the ultimate answer to this question, but certainly travel includes more than transit. It develops into a way of life. I realize that the adventure does not need to involve a specific goal; the adventure helps me find myself, for the adventure reveals my abilities and limitations. It functions as my escort and my guide, teaching me with every step the infinite values of living.

The real journey stays inside as I taste a thousand ways of living. As experienced adventurer, or simple traveler, I return with more memories than yesterday, less than tomorrow.

*"Once you have traveled, the voyage never ends, but is played out over and over again in the quietest chambers. The mind can never break off from the journey."* **Pat Conroy**

## Chapter 14: Removing Our Cultural Masks

*Girls wear grass skirts until they pass through puberty*

The sun made preparations for the highlight of the day. Shades of brilliance accentuated the redness of the earth. A chill crossed my path, maybe my own spirit expanding. Some of the more curious walked in my footsteps as I strolled back toward food and shelter. My motto for the trip was, "A smile invites smiles." How many times had I heard these words in my head over the course of my travels here, heard the words playing like a needle stuck on an old record player?

Tired as I was, those words forced me to hand out a few more smiles before finding Katherine, and sure enough, the beautiful brown people around me returned my smiles. The smiles warmed me, yet worry over Katherine's ever-more-frequent headaches lingered in the back of my mind.

*Transportation in Wamena*

Fifty minutes after walking from our hotel, we entered Wamena, and climbing into a bicycle rickshaw, I told the driver where we wanted to go. The Flowers Cafe sat on the other side of town. My having a vague idea of where the café was did not help the becak, or bicycle-rickshaw driver, and, lost, we ended up back at our first night's hotel, the Sri Kandi.

While checking on the safety of a backpack I left stored at the Sri Kandi, we ran into Rita, a woman we had met our first day in Wamena. Rita had "escaped" New York to write children's books while traveling the world. She suggested a little restaurant well known for its giant crayfish and so busy that they required reservations. Rita arranged for our dinner, sharing with us the one crayfish it had left, along with some spaghetti. Being able to eat something other than rice or peanut butter was a treat, and being able to speak with someone who did not require an interpreter and understood our cultural references was a delight as well.

Each of us had an overabundance of stories, hers sounding very different from ours. She had left at the same time we did to visit the remote Asmat tribe. The Asmat's reputation for cannibalism and headhunting, plus the disappearance of Michael Rockefeller in the area in 1961 silenced any ideas of my own about trying to travel there with Katherine.

Rita told us she had spent most of her time trying to get back from that inhospitable area. Weeks went by as she attempted to get out of there by radioing for a plane. Tangles of thick vegetation, malarial mosquitoes, and crocodiles filled her memory. I don't have a major concern about disease and insects when I travel alone; however, my parental responsibility for my daughter's health limited the choice of destinations.

Back at the Sri Kandi, Rita showed us her miracle contraption: a baby-sized tent made of mosquito netting that fits over your head while your body rests in safety inside your sleeping bag. Its fiberglass poles folded into a twelve-inch pouch, weighing only a few ounces. It was something I will consider purchasing for our next trip into the jungle.

During the hours of exchanging tales, Rita read the beginning of one of her new stories, one that she was just getting under way. To say I envied her lifestyle would amount to a gross understatement.

Without her knowledge, I adopted her as a soul mate, a role model, and an inspiration for me to write of our travels. I wanted to jump into her skin, and I spent countless hours thinking about her adventurous, romantic lifestyle. Rita showed me how capable she was of taking care of herself with her heavy investment in experience.

I wanted the world passageways to shock me, change my perspective of my past, show me how to believe in the impossible, or find some order in our confusing world. I loved my family. But like Rita, I simply wanted a few more days of not organizing around the needs of others. Meeting Rita gave me the confidence that if I opened myself up to the world, I could have complete trust in the experience.

I will always thank Rita for touching my life, reaffirming the bond our gender feels when we confide in each other as Rita, Katherine, and I did during those fleeting hours of kinship and sisterhood.

At 9:30 that night, Katherine and I sat in the lobby of the Sri Kandi Hotel when an eerie feeling crept over me. Alone, the two of us needed to find our way across the runway and under the arched entrance that led back to the hotel in Wesaput. By day, the runway created a separation between the primitive and the materialistic. In the moonlight, spirits of the past and the present danced on the runway, causing anger between the two. With the black sky came thoughts of Wosi's spirit, still lost.

We both felt cold, and like the Dani people when chilled from the weather, we crossed our hands over our chests. The wind whipped and cried, and the mournful sound mixed with the distant chanting we could hear from the primitive village. We felt pursued by unfriendly spirits, and I could feel the racing of my heart.

Freaked, I grabbed Katherine's hand, encouraging her to run with me all the way to the archway of Wesaput. Not until we had cleared the arch did we feel safe again, and we stood panting and gripping each other fiercely while our painful heartbeats slowed.

Travel guidebooks warn you to have your teeth checked before traveling. It didn't dawn on me to bring wire cutters for a potentially broken bracket from Katherine's retainer or some denture cement.

Earlier in the evening, Katherine satisfied her sweet tooth with some hard candy and pulled out a chunk of white. Was it part of a tooth or cement holding a retainer? Flashlight in hand, several men at the Wesaput Hotel tried their luck at figuring out her problem.

Julius heard a rumor that a European dentist had checked into the Mariana Hotel. Julius would try to bring him to the Wesaput Hotel after his dinner about ten o'clock in the evening.

I returned once more to my feelings, the language of the soul, and decided to shelve the end of the trip. Yearning to erase the coming of that night, our last night with the Dani, my soul begged for more time to understand that which is not understandable.

Moss, lichen, and velvety ground-cover shared our thinking spot outside the Wesaput Hotel. "Sit down and let's talk," I said to Katherine.

Katherine sat, knees pulled up to her chin with her shoulders touching mine. Her shivers were contagious. "Do we really have to start for home? Is our trip almost over?" she said.

I dreaded this departure on the same level as I had longed for it to begin. "I hate to admit that the moment is upon us to say goodbye to this unique place," I said to Katherine as I hugged my knees, trying to ward off the chill. The spell of New Guinea caused shivers. Thoughts of going home almost hurt.

Branches shifted, making odd sounds, as if invisible Dani wished us a safe journey home. Sitting skin to skin with my daughter, I felt a sense of belonging with the Dani people sharing pieces of their lives and Katherine, opening the doors to her heart. Within a few days, our enchanting spell would find a special place in our hearts

Squishing moss between my toes, I silently reflected on the previous four weeks. I turned to Katherine and said softly, "This trip gave me the opportunity to throw all my masks overboard, including that of mother."

In all cultures, man wears masks, whether that man hails from the Fulani tribe with its tradition of wearing heavy, gold jewelry over their bodies, or the Mursi tribe, with its ever-present lip discs. The Tuareq wear indigo turbans, and the Colorado-tribe members paint their heads red. The Hamar wear animal skins, and the Dayak tattoo intricate designs on their bodies. At different levels of civilization, masks serve to communicate and assist in conducting business.

After numerous travels in primitive societies, I made my best discovery: finding that my masks create no value or consequence. Strangers give me the opportunity to speak my mind and act unpredictably, exposing myself. I challenge my expectations. I suspect that the primitive peoples I have encountered do the same. With us, Julius lost his mask as a guide. Intrigued with our openness, he found the freedom to reveal himself. If we can seek the commonality of humanity, our avenues to communicate will broaden as we erase our self-imposed boundaries.

Katherine and I had removed our masks of the conventional mother-daughter relationship, thus providing a new, much closer relationship of companions or peers. The strength of our relationship has continued to grow. Over the years, we each learned that our relationship has a rare strength or quality that other mothers and daughters envy.

I have found it takes energy to keep our masks in place in order to retain proper appearances. Conflict exists between the conscious and subconscious when we are trying to appear to be someone we aren't. What would others think if they saw the real me? More importantly, my treasured experiences deep within my soul need protection. I want nothing and no one to scatter my precious memories. On the other hand, seeing and experiencing two divergent worlds and how each could benefit from the other, I sensed an obligation to deliver messages from the land that time had forgotten.

My message lies behind my mask. Sharing those emotional and spiritual discoveries that we made on our trip to Indonesia has required considerable, deliberate effort on our parts. Removing one's mask requires trust.

My heart seeks understanding of why we wear masks. Do they protect a fragile sense of self-confidence? If I had this understanding, I could live within my own world with a similar sense of personal freedom to that I obtained in remote places.

We gave ourselves an occasion for gratitude.

Lying awake that night, I thought that if I had visited some hinterland and met only Coughin, I could have fulfilled my richest dreams of a successful trip.

Would all the countless treasures of the heart, buried deep within, eventually surface? Had we found what we were looking for? Answers to these questions would emerge in time. At the beginning of the trip, the vision of our destination seemed concrete; however, unaware of time moving forward, and now close to departure, we recognized those visions ceased to matter.

*"In the world through which I travel, I am endlessly creating myself."*
**Frantz Fannon**

# Chapter 15: Cannibal's Hide and Seek

The loudest sounds came not from humans as the first slants of sunshine burrowed through the hidden cracks of the hotel walls, all of them stuffed with glossy photographs, torn from magazines. Tethered hens scuffled outdoors, disturbed by the noise coming from the scratchy throats of the roosters. Birds, dancing energetically, flittered in leaves with aspirations of bewitching a mate. Young lizards crashed among the pastels of rhododendron. These were the images and sounds that signaled the beginning of the end of our journey.

A cup, floating in somewhat clear water, waited for us in the red-plastic five-gallon bucket in the bathing area. Neither Katherine nor I would miss using the hole in the floor for a toilet. We would not miss the slimy wood planks around the toilet hole or the rot that had found its way up the sides of the bathroom walls.

As we entered the bathing area, naked and shivering, roaches scurried from us, and mosquitoes delighted at the thought of an easy conquest. They had found quick access to our hands and faces in the jungle over the past few weeks, and the more intelligent among them had feasted on entire naked bodies inside the toilet area. No, we would not miss the mosquitoes finding us unarmed in the mandi.

Once clean, Katherine and I crawled into clothes we had been wearing for two days, and the feeling bore no relation to a clean-sheet feeling. We both hoped that a late flight to Jayapura might offer a hotel with a place to wash our clothes in preparation for the three-day maneuvers toward home.

Our porters had disappeared like ghosts by the time we came into Wesaput. While in the hotel last night, I didn't recall seeing Panus, DenDee, or Coughin. Maybe a home-cooked meal lured them to visit their homes.

In the morning, though, here they all were again, carrying our bags for the last time. They smiled as they went about this final, but familiar, task for us. Together we sang the songs the Dani had taught us, spending our last hour sharing the gift of music.

Julius interrupted the singing to give me a message. "Panus says he wants to buy Katherine for five hundred pigs." We all laughed, but even more when Julius added that all the boys would like to marry her.

I said, "Katherine, maybe I should consider the offer. After all, seldom will you meet a man who will carry you across a river or over pig poop and then offer five hundred pigs to your mother to marry you!"

"Mom!" she almost yelled.

The runway felt wider as we crossed with apprehensive steps from a world standing still in time toward materialistic Wamena. Tons of subsidized goods and gasoline land there every day, weather permitting.

Old Japanese minibuses that sell for $300 arrive in Air Force Hercules cargo planes. While we wandered from village to village, our adventurous spirits had given us a new perspective of the world. The memory of a lost culture in all its simplicity carried us across the runway, the edge of unforeseen change.

Fortunately, our bodies had not forgotten how to sit in the chairs of the Sri Kandi lobby. We tried, in awkward English, to explain to Julius about how much money he had borrowed on the trip, which left us owing him only a few thousand rupiahs (about ten dollars) to split among the other four men.

If Julius wanted to gain credibility as a guide, we needed to educate him with delicate negotiations. He had difficulty in comprehending my explanation of how he had spent all the money we had given him along the way. I wanted him to understand better how to deal with money issues for future guiding experiences.

Julius and the others worked hard to make our trip rewarding in many different ways with much success. Although an advance on wages for a month-long trip did not seem out of place, I knew Julius felt those loans were long forgotten. I thought about the generous purposes for which he borrowed the money. The porters and cook reappeared, expecting their wages. The four men stared at us politely, not able to communicate except through Julius.

We could scarcely imagine what Julius had told them about how he would pay them for their help or why there was little money for them. I looked at Katherine long and hard and said, "What do we do? It's not the porter's fault that Julius spent all their wages on his own personal affairs."

Kind-hearted Katherine said, "Do we have enough money to give them each a nice tip?"

A big part of my life is teaching responsibility and respect. The logical side of me wanted the cook and porters to learn from working with Julius. Would they want to trust him for future trips with their wages?

"At fifty cents a day they each earned about fifteen dollars. Should we give them the whole amount even though we already gave that money to Julius to spend?" I said.

"How about giving them each ten dollars," Katherine said.

"Instead of giving it to Julius, I will get some change, and you can hand it to them individually," I said.

Julius asked if he could have my cassette tapes and Sony Walkman. He could not comprehend our long journey ahead, including the two and a half days of layovers and flying. We needed that music to help get us back.

"How much would a tape player cost in the market?" I said.

Julius thought for a few seconds and then said, "Maybe two thousand rupiahs."

I looked at Katherine and she nodded. "Okay, these three thousand rupiahs should get you the player and a few tapes," I said.

We chatted with Julius, recalling funny stories from our time together. I told Julius to thank Panus for offering to buy Katherine for 500 pigs. The others laughed. The light on the group, sitting in chairs, had a different intensity, compared to our first-day greeting.

These black-as-night men in penis gourds were now our friends. Each of us understood a little more about another culture and ourselves.

Our goodbyes brought tears from Katherine, Coughin, and me. We could not put our feelings into words, but we did not need to. The group of men stood to leave the hotel lobby. Wondering if we would ever see them again, Katherine and I gave them each a hug and watched them step out into the sunlight, and start down the dirt road. We lived in a world apart, not bound by customs, language, color, or knowledge, but linked together. For the Dani, an endless cycle of life; for us, the beginning.

"And your trip. Is it good?" We looked around to find the source of the near-perfect English. Outside, a young man in his twenties waited for our approval to enter the hotel.

To keep beggars, homeless, and unemployed guides from entering the building and annoying guests, the hotel required guests to have an invitation.

How could we refuse, for it was Atmin, whom we'd first met upon our arrival at the airport in Wamena, along with numerous other entrepreneurs? A transmigrate schoolteacher from Sumatra, Atmin was paid by the government to teach in a remote village sixty kilometers away. Visions of loud music, designer jeans, and four-wheel drive cars enticed him to spend time hanging out in Wamena, hoping for that rare opportunity to make some money.

Our flight didn't leave until late evening, and I remembered reading about a place not far away that I wanted to experience. His borrowed car offered us a chance to see a different type of jungle at a higher elevation than we had ever trekked on foot.

"A place where nomadic cannibals hide from the advances of church and government groups," he said with a glint in his eyes, as if he was offering us diamonds. "And I will only charge you sixty dollars American to take you there."

"Your price is too high. Do you have any other jobs waiting for you?" I asked.

"No, I'm just hanging around town," he said.

"How about we will give you English lessons during the drive and pay for your gas?" I said.

My bargaining power won as he quickly answered, "Yes, let's go."

With Katherine's headache coming back, we could not do much but sit in a car. I assumed he wanted to learn more English and the magic of our stories might interest him. We stashed all our gear behind the hotel desk, checking and rechecking all our locks. We ran a wire cable through all handles, loopholes, and locks, to keep anyone from running by and snatching a piece of luggage. Although someone could cut the cable, he would have to find something to cut it with first, which would not be easy. We stopped at the Flowers Cafe for some takeout grilled koti with white cheese. Then we headed out of town for our scenic drive.

I sat in the front of the jeep-like vehicle, thinking Katherine could have that place on the return trip. Children playing in rivers squealed at our greetings. Old women lowered their heads, not understanding the reason for the automobile passing them. The road to Tiom Pass, dotted with Dani life, wound its way toward the mountains.

Atmin asked, "And Julius. Did you like him for a guide?"

Thinking for a while, I replied, "It's easy to like a person, but building a relationship depends on the person's integrity."

Atmin answered, "What's integrity?"

I paused again and replied, "Julius and Katherine." I wanted to say, their inner beliefs of honesty, stability, sincerity, trust, and compassion are revealed in the way they choose to live their lives on the outside. They won't sacrifice who they are as they decipher the layers of expectations from others. They believe in themselves and their own voice. Different environments have shaped their destinies in their own ways and as a tribute toward life.

Atmin sometimes understood my questions and answers but often just smiled. Instead of the long explanation I simply said, "We trusted Julius, and he worked hard to make our experience more than we had hoped for."

Atmin smiled.

A young python slithered across our path. Atmin jerked to a stop. One of his many part-time businesses included collecting pythons in the jungle and transporting them to Jakarta for sale to zoo buyers.

Oddly, he explained his fear of even the tiniest of spiders. He told us that he wished he could forget the memory of a python, stealing across his bed in a Jakarta hotel room after escaping from its jail-box. Atmin showed us how to pick up a snake, using as a subject the lifeless baby python we had accidentally run over.

The road ahead was blanketed in mist, and I had a feeling of foreboding, as if we were about to enter a world more hostile than any I had ever known and become prisoners there.

"Tribal men here wear their ancestors' fingers on strings around their necks. Stone implements are their tools. They would run if they saw their own face in a mirror," Atmin said, and Katherine and I sat in silence, almost holding our breath.

Would he let us get out and take a walk in the jungle? Impenetrable tree islands provided an air of nebulous mystery. Hawks coursed above the comatose canopy.

"Villagers talk about the cannibals living deep in this jungle; it is unsafe to walk in here," our timid driver said, shivering.

I looked at Atmin and said, "Who do they kill?"

"The locals say they cook the bodies of other tribes which releases their spirits," Atmin said. He took his hand and pretended to throw a spear in the air.

Katherine, in the back seat, leaned forward with, "Please, oh please!"

Atmin slowed for some boys walking from a construction camp. He poked his head out his window and spoke to them in words I couldn't understand. After his conversation with them, Atmin explained that he took no responsibility for our safety, and the boys agreed to take us in. Atmin trembled.

I had made peace with living on the edge many trips before, but my imagination never has boundaries. My heart does not always pay attention to good intentions and logical adult thinking.

The tree line at its crest wavered with gloom. As eight hands clasped together, we glanced back at Atmin apprehensively. We had difficulty seeing him in the exhaled breath of fog from our guardian spirits.

We took a few steps over a deep crevice. One of the dark corners of the island walled us in with its choking humidity. The jungle did not force itself around us. We barged in as uninvited guests. One of the boys described our floor with hand motions as layered limbs, vines, and roots taller than my head. He pointed to a black hole, an opening down to the real floor of the jungle. His feet led our feet. Solitude seemed natural.

The openings between tree branches became wide enough to allow us a view into the next walled-in room of growth. The air smelled of fresh rain on thick foliage, and breathing became difficult but invigorating, not like breathing the decaying smells of a few weeks earlier. A yellow spot flickered past, a butterfly, representing an entire population living somewhere among the trees and the one and only sign of bright color. Clear, liquid-like rhinestones simulated necklaces around the leaves. Chunky scales of bark played with the tangled youth of trees, trying to find a home.

The evolution of life turned itself inward. Seasons ceased to exist. Cycles in this bit of forbidding jungle revolved upon the living replacing the dying. New blossoms of leaves replaced the bronze ones, fading in the same plant. The varieties and shades of green raced with each other to see which could produce the most color.

"Watch out for those sharp plants. The branches have red stripes on them." I said.

"Those are tiny red ants. Anyone can read about the jungle in a book but we get to use our senses to experience this," Katherine said.

This place represented a paradox, compared to the Amazon jungle, a place where the life lives high, and death tumbles down to conceal the dirt floor. Stimulated by one of the smallest wonders of the world, we spoke not a word. Nothing moved around the group. Sweating and apprehension, concerned with the unseen activated feelings of fear. A cascade of images took shape in the vegetation.

After a few minutes, branches, breaking and cracking with our passing, broke the silence. Something moved in the underbrush, and we were startled. We quickened our pace. Katherine whispered in my ear, "I think I heard that sound before. It makes me think of bows and arrows when they clack in their quivers when the warriors are walking."

I began to sense the strength of the jungle. Dripping with fright, all four of us halted. The sound moved away, prompting us to shift directions.

We hoped the young boys planned to head back toward the road. The twenty minutes it took us to come in did not prepare us for the two hours it took us to find a path out. Screeching monkeys and alien sounds made us quicken our steps. Maybe we heard the rare cassowary bird which scientists say may be the closest living approximation of a dinosaur sound. We were not lost in our surroundings, but obvious intruders to the natural environment, encompassing us.

"Katherine, we are completely dependent on these boys to get us out of here," I said.

"Mom, don't worry we can trust them. Look up! I can see the sky," she said.

We emerged just where the boy in the lead calculated we should arrive.

The wet mist lifted long enough for us to see Atmin's car. I paused for a moment, trying to absorb some of the untamed spirit the jungle had to offer.

Icy fluid straddled a rocky wash as it came sprinting down from a high cliff, dividing in half at the road. Spraying a footbridge, trying to conceal itself underneath, the clear water still needed purifier treatment before finding its way into our bottles. We gathered the water and ate some white goat cheese mixed with sweet bread. It tasted strange to us, but with the icy river water, it was edible.

*Atmin and Katherine before first driving lesson*

The easy downhill drive back to Wamena gave Atmin the idea to teach Katherine how to drive a stick-shift car.

He moved to the middle, with Katherine and me on either side of him.

While I tried to talk him out of the idea, innocent women and children flanked the chugging car.

Selfishly I wanted to think about the interconnectedness of the jungle with other places that dwelled in my mind, but the startling stops and starts of the car--as Katherine figured out how to work the clutch--kept my eyes and mind on the road.

After much laughter, Katherine found Wamena at which point she switched driving places with Atmin.

Atmin was always on the lookout for foreigners. He imagined that one day someone would have a scheme to help him get out of town.

He wanted to see the world, he told us, and asked for help in writing a letter so that he could respond to an ad he saw in a magazine for cruise-ship employees.

He did not possess correspondence talents equal to that of an American schoolteacher, but we put together a nice application.

Katherine remarked, "The energy here has never been touched. In such a remote place, you become more aware of your own existence. With your reality gone, you can fully experience this place."

*Plastic comes to Wamena market*

Having a couple of hours before flight time, we walked, which brought us to the exciting half-and-half market in Wamena.

By half-and-half, I mean that half the people wore clothing and half didn't wear much.

The clothed lived in Wamena and traded steel axes, plastics of every color, watches, flashlights, and cassette players with batteries.

A thirtyish man traded for souvenirs of bark-string bags, carved masks, and even penis gourds to send to the larger islands, keeping the fruit and vegetables for himself.

The mostly unclothed half of the group, in their costumes of fiber skirts or penis gourds, walked for miles with goods from a variety of different tiny communities.

It was not uncommon to see pairs of men, carrying pigs between them that had been strapped upside-down to long poles.

My fifty-inch beaded string wrapped around and around my wrist drew added attention to Katherine and me, as we tried to remain invisible in the crowded marketplace.

When Chief Kusaw had wrapped it tight around my arm, I wanted so much to hear his story of its meaning.

Besides good luck and good health, the bracelet reminds me each day of the place that stands still in time, but moves forward with contentment.

*The clearest way into the universe is through a forest wilderness."*
**John Muir**

# Chapter 16: Impossible to Leave-Impossible to Stay

Strips of plastic bags secured my bow and arrows together. We had three sets given to us by chiefs along the way. I valued the tiny set Chief Kusaw used to show us how his tribe dealt with malaria.

Handling luggage at airports has always caused me a lot of anxiety because I never turn down a gift. Even a twelve-foot-long spear can be part of my belongings when returning from a trip abroad. Katherine and I hand-carried all our gourds, masks, and penis sheaths, along with my camera equipment. Our net bags bulged with newspaper-wrapped treasures. No questions were asked of us by Garuda Airline officials, directing us to our transportation, which bridged the gap between the old world and the new.

The sky blazed a white light from flood lights, highlighting entrances to planes and runways. No jet ways at this tiny little airport. To me the whole world stood in the shadow of that plane. Strangers, neglected by time, watched as new relationships left for faraway shores. An ephemeral gust carried my straw hat close to the village side of the runway. I reached for my hat while maneuvering carry-ons. Unable to interpret a faint wind's whispers, I felt a lump in my throat. Village faces filled with timeless dignity peered over the grass crest of the fence.

Reaching, I extended my hand to accept one last handshake. The engine vibration rebounded like a collision with the valley and its past. Reality barged in. I gulped one last deep breath to absorb this scene before boarding. Ralph Waldo Emerson said, "We must travel the world over to find the beautiful; we must carry it with us or we carry it not."

An invisible seamstress with her green thread of growth left us a tapestry of red plastic bowls, brown river-water tea, people black as night, and songs with magical tunes. Colorful experiences from villagers crowned my trip, where I became what they were convinced I already was.

No direct service to catch our international flight back home meant a layover in Sentani for the night. Nothing intimidates me more than leaving the baggage area at a foreign airport and walking outside.

At that moment, the locals descend like vultures upon foreigners. The fear I experience arises from the potential misplacement of heartfelt treasures. Before you can get your hand on your luggage, someone speaking gibberish picks it up for you and carries it off toward the door.

"Stop, put it down!" you shout in English, but it means nothing to these people as a second man grabs for your remaining bag, already hoisting it up over his shoulders and out of your reach.

After you rescue your bags from these "helpful" souls, you hand them the ransom money they were planning on when they first snatched your luggage and then try and find an honest driver. You have the name of a cheap hotel that you found in a guidebook, but the taxi drivers never seem to know where those places are. Instead, they offer to take you to an uncle's hotel or a friend's hotel.

The Sentani Airport, forty kilometers from Jayapura, offered us a group of yelling, fighting young men whom neither Katherine nor I could deal with.

The 40,000 rupiahs--twenty dollars--they would charge to take us to a dinky hotel around the corner could not match the two dollars we could pay simply by walking out on the road, lugging all our gear, and waving for a taxi.

Danny, our taxi driver, said he could not find our hotel and drove us instead to a cheap replacement, as they often do, going in with you to check in, to claim their commission. I then asked him to drive us into the mountains to find a batik factory I saw suggested in a guidebook.

The road wound up around the valley of Jayapura, overlooking the Pacific Ocean. By the time we reached the factory, Katherine's headache had worsened. The two-hour drive back to our hotel made me uneasy, as Katherine developed the chills. That night, Katherine continued suffering from chills, and she developed a high fever. The severity of her headache did not abate. Could this be the beginning stages of malaria?

I knew that malaria takes about three weeks to develop the first symptoms. The math was easy: instead of contracting the disease in the jungle, she must have met that dreaded mosquito in Jayapura on our arrival there.

Then again, Hepatitis A, dengue fever, typhoid, and bilharzia all share the same beginning symptoms with malaria. In time, we would identify the real culprit. Nature's instincts completed my transformation from explorer to a nursing mother, seeking to provide Katherine with as much comfort as possible.

Fear of the unknown came along and stabbed us both right in the heart. Fear, a trip's true opponent. One-minute life is perfect and the next doubt comes in and plays a game in your mind with its playing pieces called misery, weakness, desperation, and anxiety. I tried to estimate the level of Katherine's fear by embracing other possibilities of causes for her illness. She willingly wanted to understand the truth behind these fears which I felt impacted greatly on her overall health in the long run.

The next morning, Katherine surprised me by rising and feeling great. It was as if the last couple of days hadn't happened, as if the fever of the night before had done its work and killed whatever bug she had. She was her old self again.

Back at the airport, I handed over seventy-two dollars to the clerk, and he handed me two tickets for our morning flight to Biak, our last stop before the long journey home. Katherine still felt wonderful.

When we landed, our cheap hotel offered wood beds with one-inch mattresses and one blanket on each. There were locks on the doors, but a fury of mosquitoes harbored in the mandi. We felt closer to home when our tea, not brown, river-water, came in a white china teapot in the hotel restaurant. We had purchased some canned pineapple, peanut butter, and chips in a can from a grocery store across the street and had smuggled them into our hotel. These items definitely enhanced our white rice and white bread feast.

*Love that peanut butter sandwich with chips thrown in*

Young boys waited outside the hotel to offer us tours of the city and local market or take us on side trips to the islands. They knew the international flight did not leave until early morning, which gave them plenty of time to earn money from the perceived wealth of foreigners. Several more of these young entrepreneurs came out of the cracks when we started talking money.

*Sailboat coming to Small Rubes Island*

*Fish for lunch*

We made a deal. A double outrigger, outboard-powered canoe (a boy called it a Johnson, though powered by Yamaha), would take us to Small Rubes Island, where we would spend the day snorkeling, swimming, and sailing on a small out-rigged canoe with a handmade sail.

It seemed a wonderful way to spend our last day before starting home in earnest.

Katherine still felt great. Relaxing and reflecting felt like the perfect prescription before regaining consciousness in our former reality.

Within the hour, we walked on a dock with wood slats so far apart that one could clean a fish and scrape the bones into the water twelve feet below without mucking up the slats themselves.

Our boat driver lived in a two-room, tin-roofed home on stilts. As we entered his home to let him know we had arrived, I noticed rolled woven reed mats on end in a corner of his front room.

Less than a handful of clothes hung on crooked nails. His nighttime entertainment occupied a corner where a blackened oil lamp weighted down piles of ragged newspapers and magazines.

*Home of our boat driver*

While he went outside to prepare the boat for passengers, I creaked my way into the next room.

Overcome with the odors of rotting fish, my mouth had to take over the breathing.

Bushel baskets, woven of thin branches, overflowed with dried fish. Empty sockets for eyes stared at me from the soot-veiled iron pot.

On a piece of metal scrap, a crusty grate protected red and gray coals ready for duty. A blue, five-gallon bucket full of water and floating blue plastic bowls begged for a handful of soap.

A narrow plank, wrapped around the ocean side of the house, led to the toilet, a three-foot cubicle of vertical wood slats with a foot-in-diameter hole in the floor.

Outside, the boat driver started the motor, and we headed out to the dock again. The driver spoke no English.

We could not even figure out his name. He helped us down into his canoe, a craft maybe twenty-five feet long, with two areas covered by uprights and blue tarp. Thirty minutes after leaving the city of stilts, we saw a small island of palm trees.

It looked safe in the horizon of waves. Azure blue lapped the marshmallow sand.

*Small Rubes Island beach*

In the excitement of leaving, neither of us thought to bring drinking water. Once back in the city, we had already stored away the worry of food and water for the next trip.

Thirst nagged at us like a constant companion for several hours of shell searching and snorkeling. Katherine said the salt water chilled her. I crossed my fingers.

*Chopping a coconut for some much-needed liquid*

We drew pictures in the sand, trying to communicate with our companion. Fortunately, his translation of our coconut-tree drawings saved our day. He disappeared into the palm fronds, spreading their shading coolness.

Lifting our chins, we saw two coconuts flying toward us, and we scrambled into the safety of a group of tree trunks as several more coconuts crashed to the sand below. The coconuts, green, satin-finished, and the size of bowling balls, battled with the boy and his machete.

Warm coconut milk, though wet, sounded about as thirst quenching as salty peanuts, but Katherine was dehydrated, and so was I.

Eventually the boy nicked a slice off the top of a coconut and exposed the clear liquid within. Imagining a coconut flavor made it easier for me to force down the warm, unflavored nourishment.

The hour arrived for a repeat of the prior day's matinee, with the return of Katherine's headache. Her skin had also become quite red, which made it difficult for me to tell if she had fever or sunburn.

An inviting homecoming, the bed in our room turned into Katherine's melting spot for four or five hours of nightmarish chills and fever, during which time she became confused about where she was.

Her pain felt as real to me as if someone had injected it into my bloodstream. The Hotel Mapia offered no English-speaking employees, and I had a terrible time making them understand that I had a sick child who needed help. A boy brought several blankets after I coaxed him to the room to see Katherine's condition.

Obviously, our mission to live among the tribal people of New Guinea had ended, but our mission of bonding, understanding ourselves, and bridging the parent-child generation gap would, hopefully, continue for the rest of our lives.

I seriously suspected malaria. The challenge of dealing with a life-threatening illness loomed in the darkness of that room. Ghosts held hands, swirling their legless bodies around my head. Were they trying to cheer me up or haunt me?

We never know what will happen when we offer ourselves to a place. I tried to recall the substance of how we found ourselves here in this position.

I didn't want to taxi back into the shelter my life had constructed for itself. The humidity, mildewed walls, and Katherine's sweat brought out smells of past guests in those wool blankets, controlling Katherine's shivers.

Even the cockroach crawling on the wall above Katherine's head didn't cause me to flinch from my dream-like state. I found myself drifting back to my first thoughts of taking a trip like this.

> *"Knowledge of what is possible is the beginning of happiness."*
> **George Santayana**

## Chapter 17: Before the Trip, a Volcano under My Feet

A tremendous sense of anticipation blanketed my life. Like early morning dew, the feeling soon burned away as I pulled cool, damp laundry from the washer and tossed it in the dryer.

Obsessed with the challenge of travel to remote places, I had the yearning to break free of burdensome housewife boundaries. A single ember of desire glowed deep within my heart. My belief in my ideas and abilities heightened the desire for adventure.

Breaking away from the desire for an adventurous sojourn became more difficult each day. The challenges of meeting new cultures and living a more primitive lifestyle would boost my self-possession. Could some remote island in Indonesia satisfy my hunger for the strange mix of emotions, emerging from connections with distant cultures?

Language barriers, the chance for independence, the intrigue of walking among unfamiliar tribal men, and the freedom to roam the world unbounded by time or people summed up the dreams I lived and breathed.

As I unloaded groceries, vacuumed dog hair, and finished making the bed, my mind drifted to the wild jungle alive with cannibals, deadly snakes, and spiders, a place more eternal and sensuous.

Had someone dared me to close my eyes so I could face the endless uncertainties? I wanted to shout to my family and friends the passion, excitement, and apprehension I had for the challenge of these confrontations.

Attempting the unpredictability of this type of journey tested my courage. Could I discover a tribe that had never seen white skin? Would an elderly Dani medicine man save me from a dreaded disease with his magical potions? Could my presence in the midst of the cannibals of the Asmat tribes ignite enough curiosity for them to take the time to get acquainted?

Months passed, and my ringing telephone, school car pools, and piles of laundry replaced fantasies of becoming delirious with fear halfway around the world.

Growing up near the wheat fields of Kansas, I dreamed of distant lands. Childhood vacations consisted of visiting relatives in the farm country of Iowa.

Braniff Airlines, my first job after college days, gave me the first opportunity to travel the world.

After six months with the company, I won two tickets to anywhere on TWA, and unlike most employees who would invite a friend for a weekend to New York City, I chose to begin my trip from Kansas City toward the west and come back around the world from the east.

Circling the world, I photographed the fortifications of China's Great Wall, touristy camels in Jerusalem, the iron lady of Paris at night, and the wild cats stalking the Coliseum's ghosts from executions and animal hunts of 80 AD.

With my second ticket, I motor-biked the jungles of Thailand, witnessed the birth of a giraffe in Kenya, explored castles by train outside London, ambled along the countryside of Portugal, and feasted on gyro sandwiches in Athens.

I worked on my days off and double shifts so I could sample the capitals of Europe for a few days, every other week. TWA had a familiarization fare for five dollars round trip. Hotels and airlines use "fam" fares to encourage employees to recommend their businesses to potential clients.

My employer, Braniff Airlines, did not fly to Europe. TWA hoped I would recommend its service, since it treated me to almost-free fares to sample the world.

For the next several years, nothing could stop me; I traveled to foreign lands as much as I possibly could. I loved every minute of it.

> *"Our greatest natural resource is the minds of our children."*
> **Walt Disney**

## Chapter 18: Trading Free Travel for Family

Little girls dream of white picket fences surrounding babies in swings. The responsibilities and diversions of marriage and motherhood moved my travel priorities to the bottom of my wish list, but when Allie, the youngest of my four children, turned three years old, I explained to my husband that I did not want our children to believe that the world existed only around Nintendo and soccer games.

I wanted them to know there was a wonderful undiscovered world outside the confines of that white picket fence. That year, my husband and I packed up our three youngest and headed to Guatemala, a place so unknown to us I had to check the map to see which countries bordered it in Central America. While there, we hitchhiked in the beds of pickup trucks, going from village to village for several weeks. It seemed a wild country with military personnel carrying guns along the main arteries.

The next year, we took "the train from hell," as we called it, from Nogales to Mazatlán with no water, beds, air-conditioning, open windows, or food; well, I did bring a jar of peanut butter and one box of Ritz crackers. It felt like a twenty-four-hour endurance test.

One day on a local bus in Antigua, Guatemala, a woman turned to smile and Allie said, "Mommy, why does that lady have black teeth?"

What an opportunity to explain about poverty! Important factors I wanted my children to learn through these trips included appreciation for the life they lived and personal responsibility.

Living out of a few suitcases kept everyone busy with keeping track of their own clothing and where they put their toothbrush or favorite book to read before bed. Within days of this kind of trip, the obvious realities of no electronic entertainment, ready-made food, or personal space hit even the youngest. Each of us began to see the others in a different light. We had no more sibling disagreements. Sharing the last package of crackers encouraged smiles instead of tantrums. The children seemed to recognize qualities in their brother or sister that made life easier. One would get out a box of crayons and make up some game that involved drawing. Often during a long hike, Brennan, barely seven, would sing a favorite tune, inserting his own rhyming words.

Before long, the whole family joined in with more laughter than I could ever remember hearing. We relied on each other for entertainment, instead of the outside world. For security, we all slept in the same room, often pulling a double-bed mattress to the floor with half of us on it and the other half on the box springs. The majority of the time the girls lucked out with the comfy mattress. That two-week adventure included horseback rides to the caves of the Tarahumara Indians and meeting a family that lived in a cave. Andale, meaning "let's go" in Spanish, and used often on the horses, became our mantra as our slow train climbed the steep mountains of the Copper Canyon.

During the spring that our oldest daughter, Carrie, was making plans for college, my husband and I were making plans for another summer vacation abroad. Allie, our youngest daughter, in an outburst of wanting more time for summer fun, disagreed with the painful immunizations for travel. Her brother also took issue with having to leave our lake house with its fishing boats, jet skis, and sailboats. Allie scrambled to her father's lap and suggested her mom and sister go to the jungles and leave her at home with her father and brother. So that's what we did.

Prior to announcing our planned endeavor to loved ones and friends, I sought some means to present the idea so they could believe our traveling to such a remote destination made sense. I hoped the idea of a mother-daughter bonding, similar to a father-son camping trip, would justify our 9,000-mile journey into snake-infested jungles of New Guinea, living with tribal people who once practiced cannibalism.

*"I had hoped that the trip would be the best of all journeys, a journey into ourselves."* **Shirley MacLaine**

## Chapter 19: Dancing Your Own Dance

Trekking the previous summer through the jungles of the Amazon, meeting the wildlife of the Galapagos, and even riding the roof of a train offered a glimpse into more remote cultures for Katherine and me.

An old Chinese proverb says, "A journey of a thousand miles begins with a single step." Katherine and I, with resolve and determination, had taken that step with the help of each other. To live our dreams, we had to start walking in their direction not only with the first step, but also with all the steps separating us from our goals.

In the Amazon, we spent ten days with Luis Garcia, a guide, studying the secrets of the jungle in hopes of becoming a medicine-man like his father.

I felt the special bond, developing between Katherine and the environment. With energy, she focused on everything Luis could teach. Sleeping under mosquito nets and bathing in muddy piranha-infested rivers, she showed me her level of patience and adaptability.

The Amazon taught us a new way of living, without the wonders of our modern world back home in Kansas City. The simplicity of the Haurani Indians' way of life turned into an extraordinary memory for us. As I challenged my expectations, my confidence and strengths began to surface.

Months later, after we returned from the Amazon, the unconscious notes I had taken in the jungles or while lying in my simple bed under mosquito netting so many weeks before had an impact on my life. The greatest reward of my travels narrowed down to the journey of self-discovery. While making my own rules and learning to trust myself, I began to redefine my individualism.

Gertrude Bell, a Victorian explorer, once pondered, "Are we the same people, I wonder, when all our surroundings, associations, and acquaintances are changed?"

Television ads preach that our strongest attribute lies in our outer landscape. We step out into the world well-dressed, manicured, and pampered.

To evolve, we need to turn inward to understand who we are. Traversing our inner geography requires discipline toward an unknown exploration.

To help Katherine grow and become the woman of her dreams, I needed to be stronger myself.

By feeding my soul, I realized the importance of the inner landscape. While expanding my world, I knew I would begin the process of changing within, changing in ways only I would notice at first. Would the invisible changes catch me off guard?

Like a tree, I wanted to bend with the wind, not stand tall and erect. During this trip to New Guinea, I expected to develop a deeper relationship with my daughter, to observe her perceptions of life in the jungle while they happened. Would this experience change how she sees herself in the next few years?

Letting go is the beginning of a new life, and both mother and daughter need an open mind and confidence. Admiring Katherine so deeply, I wanted her to recognize she had the right to her own dance.

By leaving behind the burdens of yesterday's doubts, we were both plunged forward into a very different way of understanding the world.

*"Once you have felt the Indian dust, you will never be free of it."*
**Rumer Godden**

# Chapter 20: Pieces of My Self-Portrait

Would another sip of tea cool the anticipation? I needed diversion from the constant thoughts of awakening in the jungle with a day of adventure ahead.

The organization of my life centered on curtains of responsibilities for children, husband, community, and even the homeless people I volunteered to feed in shelters. Journeys of the past had taught me that when I built a level of personal accountability, my self-confidence increased. Could I live two lives or divide myself into two people with one spirit? One would fulfill my responsibilities and meet the expectations of friends and society, while the other would allow me to hopscotch through the world of adventure.

Oh, to find release from the restraints that had grown like clingy ivy around my soul! I could then live life all the way. I needed to find a new dimension within myself. An internal journey began after I made the decision to break from social barriers. By removing self-imposed limitations and escaping from a materialistic world, I could experience serendipity. Expectations of uncommon connections danced in my head, sometimes clouding the feeling of apprehension that came with the onward mental challenge.

In my imagination, I could see a tribal man, wearing a feather headdress, his body painted with ancient symbols. He smiles at me. To ensure a soft landing, Dad used to say, "Consider the consequences before making important decisions;" so I searched my schedule for hours to spend in research, preparation, and planning. The daylight hours hung around as if they owned those summer days before our August departure.

"Mom, is it worth my reading about this culture when I don't know what is important to share with you?" Katherine said, after we decided the trip was a go.

Her offer surprised me, as she had a summer job to think about as well as squeezing three months of summer fun into two. "I'll do the heavy research on which villages feel safe, and on our long journey there, I'll share with you the culture," I said.

To avoid the heavy feelings of guilt I would get from spending too much time on trip planning, I wanted to give a hundred percent to my children and husband. I tried to hide my feelings of anticipation for late-night reading about how to plan an expedition through the claustrophobic jungle, with its poisonous plants waiting to touch bare legs.

Research on finding amiable tribes and packing necessities for a primitive lifestyle into one backpack took hours away from sleep time, but careful preparation was imperative to guaranteeing our safety. The extensive research I was doing made me aware of the potential dangers in trekking on an island of naked cannibals, bloodthirsty insects, slithering reptiles awaiting a misplaced step, and a host of vermin lurking in the underbrush. With quiet calm, my head told my heart to slow down. My level of anticipation exceeded the speed limit. To make the idea work, facts and figures would have to come into play along with emotions. The joint effort of wishing--while accepting reality--provided courage to move forward on calculated risks.

There was simply no way to get around the research I was doing and not feel strongly about its necessity. I knew that to ensure our safety in an untamed land, to have a rewarding and enjoyable experience, I needed to gather facts, sometimes very disturbing facts, and I needed to keep my emotions in check at the same time.

On the other hand, it was all right for me to wish, to hope, to imagine, to anticipate the wonder we would find on our next excursion into the unknown; but it was also important that my excitement not cloud the reality of the dangers that awaited us.

Two women, traveling alone, face the possibility of danger. Newspapers, the six o'clock news, and our mothers teach us that fact; however, an old saying pulled at my heartstrings: "With greater risks come greater rewards."

> *"Travelers' prized souvenirs are the strands of different cultures they decide to knit into their own character."* **Rick Steves**

## Chapter 21: Reality Better Than Dreams

The scary red "check engine" light came on during the 3:00 a.m. drive to the airport. My close friend Paul didn't flinch as I pondered what I might say to my husband and two children, ages seven and ten, at home, fast asleep. If we missed our no-refund flight from Kansas City to New Guinea, my family would want to know why. Paul volunteered to drive us to the airport so my husband would not have to get the rest of the family out of bed for the one-hour drive.

My family wrapped me in a cocoon where I felt safe and secure as wife, mother, and community volunteer. It took a year of planning for that metamorphosis so I could wriggle free of responsibilities, like the butterfly struggling to break free of her chrysalis, fill her wings, and fly. My friend Paul, the same generation as my father, ignored technology, so none of us had cell phones to call for help if the car should die in the middle of that lifeless highway. Katherine and I were in the custody of Paul and his trusty vehicle. Somehow, we made it to the airport. Trust would play an important role in the upcoming month of jungle trekking. I believed the world filled itself with kindness and that trust would always take the place of fear, helping turn strangers into new friends. External changes to our world would call on internal changes to happen, as well. A new pattern would emerge of Katherine protecting me as I had always protected her.

Katherine's ideas and beliefs in moving toward independence rapidly changed over the years. Our trip to Indonesia created a rite of passage, moving her beyond questions of self-doubt. We discussed situations where we might reach an outcome that we both accepted. While Katherine tried to be her own person, sometimes her viewpoints did not fall in line with mine.

For one month, this teenager had to live in concert with her mother. I loved those times when I could not see the big picture because of fleabites, controlling my every thought, and Katherine, playing out her ideas. Sometimes it was hard to reach where Katherine really was. As she took youthful steps forward, hoping to discover more, I would take two steps backward, reflecting on my past.

During this time of reflection, I thought about parenting in the broader sense of all four of my children, and how best to help Katherine convey her personal discoveries to her siblings. They would soon see the experience through the eyes of Katherine and me. Each of us would have an impact on their lives, either as a parent or a peer. What an opportunity to leverage our special time together for the benefit of the entire family!

Katherine's uniqueness shined during those moments when I surrendered to her authority. I traveled to teach Katherine about the world and its beautiful people. After returning, I would realize the deeper education came from her teaching me how to let go of fears. We think we know our children, but when we embrace them as they move into society as young adults, we learn startling things about ourselves. Living in a middle-class suburban community teaches children things such as materialism, ownership, jealousy, dishonesty, and competition. Children need a strong background for morals, respect, and responsibility.

"Alone time" allows for nursing one's own needs. Conflicts with ideas encourage us to find the answers. Our endeavors find their way with the help of challenging obstacles. Taking a trip to a place without the distraction of computers and telephones helps develop introspection, maybe for the first time. We were at a time in our lives where we needed to face those demons and find answers. Not having to meet the needs of others, we could lose ourselves in a longer trip away from our normal routine. We could let go of attachments that no longer define our new transformation. We often fear how others will react to the new person we have become.

I hoped my friends and family did not think I wanted to ignore them. I hoped they understood that the trip resulted in a claiming of my self-image. After returning, I would have the ability to step outside my old comfort zone. My summer's absence would be an informal step toward teaching my children the meaning of independence. I knew the inspiration from the trip could be leveraged during future months to benefit all the children.

*"There is a great hunger in our culture for meaning, for things that connect us with the world and with other people, things that really nurture the soul."*
**Bernadette Murphy**

## Chapter 22: Barefoot in a New Guinea Hospital

My dream-like state, where I found myself drifting back to the first thoughts of taking a trip like this, was no match for the reality of the scene before my eyes.

Katherine was so sick in the Mapia Hotel bed that she agreed to let me find help, so I locked her in the room and headed out into the street to find someone who could speak English.

I would not have wanted this trip to test our bonding and commitment to each other through the challenge of a serious illness. So, her willingness to let me find help instead of being brave gave me the courage to let my mothering instincts take over alone. I had a map of the city that showed an immigration office, a bank, and the Garuda Airline office a block away, but I could see no sign of a hospital anywhere. I thought someone in one of those offices would speak English, but as it was a Saturday afternoon, all those businesses had closed.

I walked to the pleasant Titawaka Hotel and thankfully I recognized a friend we had met in Wamena, sitting in the shade of a palm tree. Jonas, a seasoned, world traveler, found us a taxi driver familiar with the location of the hospital. Three blocks back to the Hotel Mapia felt like a hundred.

When I unlocked the door to Katherine's room, she was sitting on my bed. She stopped reading, looked up, and smiled. Symptoms of malaria come and go. She thanked Jonas for his help and agreed to go to the hospital. Jonas stayed in the taxi after it dropped us off so he could return to his hotel.

A white-coated man of thirty stopped us at the hospital entrance. He asked us, in perfect English, to take off our shoes and socks before entering the hospital. We complied in silence, entering as if into a cathedral. He led us down a long corridor, stopping in the first room: a spacious, white, meticulous, and empty room. Two narrow beds covered in crisp, white sheets had been set at one end of the room.

Thoughts of my standing for days, piling blankets over Katherine's chilled body, wiping her feverish brow with cool rags, intensified. I marveled at the strange sight of a reflection on the floor, mirroring Katherine's dangling feet.

The floor looked cleaner than anything we had touched in the previous month. My imagination had envisioned an overcrowded hospital with screaming or dying patients, crowding the halls. This place was so quiet that our voices echoed down the hall. The hospital was eerily silent. To a man named Dr. Dicky Effendi I said, voice cracking, "Here are the symptoms. What do you think is wrong with Katherine that has caused her suffering for several days?"

Without even a pause, Dr. Effendi diagnosed, "Malaria."

My heart skipped several beats, while tears welled up in Katherine's eyes. I had a million questions, and I was suddenly asking them all at once.

"What does that mean? What form of malaria? Does she have to stay in the hospital for a long time? Will she recover or have symptoms the rest of her life? Can I stay here in the hospital with her? Did it start four weeks ago when we were in Jayapura? Is there medication here at this hospital or do we have to fly to Jakarta? Will there be more pain?" Frightened, I wanted to yell, "How can you be so sure it's malaria? You hardly took time to hear all the symptoms!" I didn't say it, though. I could not find the nerve. Dr. Effendi left the room, and I hugged Katherine.

"What is he going to do? I'm scared," Katherine said.

I said, "This is a hospital, and the doctor knows exactly what to do. He sees these symptoms all the time. He already recognized the signs of malaria." He came back with a needle and a microscope slide, explaining that he wanted to rule out the fatal Falciparum strain of malaria. Minutes later, though it seemed like hours to Katherine and me, the doctor came back with a smile and a piece of paper with indecipherable words written on it. Sitting beside Katherine, he reassured us that three Fansidar tablets would kill the parasites in the blood.

He told us it would be perfectly fine for us to leave for the States as planned, as the medication would cause her to sleep for hours. I did not want to offend the doctor, but I remembered that Fansidar is taken for malarial symptoms when one is alone in the jungle and can't get to a hospital. I also knew the New Guinea mosquito had considerable resistance to Fansidar, but the doctor convinced me that after the symptoms disappeared in about a week, Katherine would be fine.

"Doctor, I don't understand what I'm supposed to do." Katherine said.

Dr. Effendi said, "You will start to get over the malaria as soon as you get on the medicine. Your chills and headaches will go away very quickly. The medicine makes you want to sleep."

"But, I'm scared they won't give me the right drugs. We only speak English, so how will I know how much to take?" she said.

Dr. Effendi said, "I will go with you to the pharmacy and help get you started on the Fansidar. I can go with you back to your hotel and stay with you until you feel comfortable."

"Our windowless hotel doesn't have a fan and the mosquitoes are as thick as the hot air. We could go to the hotel of my friend Jonas and let Katherine rest there till flight time since his room is air conditioned," I said to the doctor. Still a little nervous, I accepted the doctor's willingness to go with us. The trip would give me a chance to ask more questions, and I could tell Katherine needed more assurance.

Our total hospital and pharmacy bill came to almost three dollars. A man in a white coat must have lots of influence in a pharmacy. He walked back to the taxi, wearing a smile and carrying a small, white package.

"Thank you for helping me, Dr. Effendi," Katherine said.

The blank look on the taxi driver's face caused the doctor to ask, "What is the name of your friend's hotel?"

"Titawaka," I said.

Jonas opened his hotel-room door with a look of I'm here to help.

I explained the situation, and he quickly pulled back the blankets on the bed, plumped the pillow and made a gesture for Katherine to crawl in. The white, crisp linens invited company, but I doubted if Katherine thought much about melting into fresh linens or fresh grass, filled with fleas. Her head turned in my direction as she said, "Mom." Without blinking, her eyes sent me a message of Help me please; I'm afraid.

The bed was narrow and short so her heels hung over the end. There wasn't room for me to sit beside her, so after tucking a sheet around her feet, I knelt on the floor beside the bed. Jonas handed me a cool wet washcloth for her forehead. I leaned over and gave her a tight squeeze.

"The doctor told me your nightmare is over. He doesn't think you will have any more fever or chills, only sleepiness," I said. One of her tears wet my cheek as I gave her a good-night kiss.

The medicine worked like magic. Katherine was asleep in about fifteen minutes. We each have our own scale for happiness. Success, customs, and sometimes health can tip that scale.

When Dr. Effendi left the Titawaka Hotel, I felt comfortable that we had put Katherine's scale back in balance again. Katherine slept. Jonas bought me dinner at the hotel. We had been living in places where sanitation was not a top priority, and the dishes here looked too clean, the food tasted too incredible to eat.

The steam from the hot vegetables fogged my glasses, hiding my eyes, swelling with tears. I never understood the real meaning of comfort food until I tasted that baked chicken breast smothered in white gravy.

I looked at Jonas and said, "If only Katherine could enjoy this high protein meal which her body needs desperately."

"The medicine made her too tired to think of food," Jonas said.

The walk back to the Mapia alone to arrange our bags for return brought necessary solitude my way. Had we reached the end of our journey?

The sky, pleats of purple velvet stitched with sequins of silver, invited me to sit outside the Mapia in a colorful, decorated outrigger canoe on display. Staring at the sky, I buried myself in the dark shade of the folds of clouds. Between sunset and moonrise, penetrating colors wrapped the earth.

The stars seemed so close that I felt if I just reached out with a finger, I could touch one and make a wish.

My journey enveloped me with whispers from brown-eyed children, unknown words of songs, and the wind, answering the call of my own spirit. The emptiness of that dark night filled my mind. Halfway around the world, we had traveled to explore remote Stone Age people, but came as well to know our own innermost world. We had lost our old lives and yet found them again in something new and fresh and real. Our mirrors were removed for a while, and when we looked into them again, we could sense change. We had satisfied ourselves in another culture and had matured within ourselves.

Our observations allowed us to reflect insights and understanding into our own souls. Travel incorporates all the living elements that welcome, share, and protect things that will remain with you always.

*Travel not only stirs the blood...it gives birth to the spirit"*
**Alexandra David-Neel**

## Chapter 23: Which Color to Slide Down on the Rainbow

The time came for us to board our flight home. Red clay, reluctant to stay behind, clung to our packs as a flurry of strangers reached for the handles of our luggage at the airport terminal. Taxi greeters included an assortment of porters, beggars, tour guides, becak peddlers, hotel well-wishers, and thieves, all wishing to practice English.

A group of young boys wanted to try on our boots, offering us a dollar for them. I waved them all away, forgetting to get Katherine's bags. One boy of about eight came to my rescue, snagging my sleeve with one brown hand and offering me Katherine's bag with the other. Despite her lack of complaining, I still wished the malaria happened to me instead of to Katherine.

Green-uniformed Customs officials told jokes among themselves and didn't trouble us with inspections of our bags. Inside the terminal, we saw the usual form fillers, money exchangers, fake souvenir hawkers, and airport tax takers, plus all the folks who loved charging foreigners twice what a local would pay for the cheapest of items.

Finally, ticket takers and baggage weighers glanced at our pile. They tagged the spear and bows with a different color code from the rest of the luggage. Later, at customs in Los Angeles, we found out why.

The dangerous weapons rode first class in the cockpit. After boarding, I moved us to a row of four empty seats in a middle section, hopeful for Katherine to have three seats to stretch out and sleep for the entire flight. I should have tried harder to save all the seats before a man grabbed the end seat, leaving us with only three. I explained to him that my daughter was recovering from malaria and needed to sleep, but he didn't budge. Katherine slept the entire flight, only waking for meals which I encouraged. The flight lasted close to fourteen hours.

We waited at Customs in Los Angeles while airline employees searched for two hours, trying to find our precious memories, the bows and arrows and spear.

The normal procedures did not include storing them in the cockpit which is where someone eventually found them. The dangerous weapons enjoyed a first-class ride. Patiently and without complaining, Katherine slumped in a quiet corner with the chills.

It seemed like an anti-climactic ending, but appropriate for a journey, filling the back roads of my memory. I awaited transportation back to the reality I left behind, a complex mixture of paperwork and rules that would frighten our Dani friends; and for Katherine, a Rip Van Winkle sleep.

Going home feels like trying to see that spectacular sunset again. You can't find the same home you left behind. The riches of travel, like your suitcase, come home with you. I searched for a path in my life that went somewhere beyond dead end.

The lessons of the jungle challenged me, but they gave me strength. The Dani villagers taught me that by removing my masks, I could live. The rewards of a journey include profound and abstract gifts.

You don't change forever because of the bark armband made especially for your arm or your blemished memory of seeing the remains of a hundred-year-old warrior.

You change because of the nature of the people who bring you into their lives, awaken you to the mysteries of another culture, and introduce you to yourself. For a brief period, you lose yourself in intense experiences.

Moreover, once you have traveled, the voyage never ends.

*"All journeys have secret destinations of which the traveler is unaware."*
**Martin Buber**

# Afterglow: The Rest of the Story

*Memories for a lifetime*

As we were leaving Wesaput on our walk toward Wamena for our departure home to the United States, Katherine made a comment to me. "I'm not going home. How can I go back to friends wearing Abercrombie outfits every day, wanting to smoke, drink, and do drugs at every party?

Coaches teach 'play by my rules' and teachers reward their favorites. Here, I see people who define the word contentment. If a roof leaks, the whole village helps with repairs. Everyone wears the same type of body ornaments, and competition is nonexistent. I don't want to go back to that materialistic world that needs drugs and loud music, where, to be somebody, you have to be a winning athlete."

Those comments were etched into my mind and heart for years as I considered writing this memoir, and I decided to go a step further and ask Katherine about how the experience impacted her life in the years that followed.

A mother and daughter's relationship doesn't end when the trip is over, and it's helpful to know what happened to Katherine after the trip. It planted seeds for us that would later impact our ways of thinking and living. In the years following, the seeds sprouted. Joseph Campbell's quote, "We must be willing to let go of the life we planned so as to have the life that is waiting for us," was surely written for our growth experience.

I wrote to Katherine, "How do you feel the trip changed you?"

Katherine "The trip made us rethink materialism. Why were those people so happy when they owned nothing? I was a normal teenager into materialism before we went there, but I thought I could see through it. The Danis' lives were simple. I thought about what people were doing there. I value those things more: the simple things such as gardening and living simple lives. This trip probably affected my choice of a husband, for instance, someone who has a real appreciation for nature."

Jackie "Do you think you resolved any issues you had before you left?"

Katherine "I came back with more questions. I left trying to figure out what I believed spiritually. Before the trip, I thought everyone could be saved if they had Jesus in their heart, but I met these people who know nothing about God. They were so nice, friendly, and good. When I came back, I asked my preacher why. No possible way those people are going to hell because they don't have God in their hearts.

"You and Dad did a good job of teaching me not to be selfish. We shared toys and volunteered at homeless shelters. Everything is ours, not mine. The biggest thing I've done in my jobs is help college students understand the meaning of resourcefulness, learning, and self-reliance.

"A family may be dispassionate in how the family members give: checks, for instance and non-personal contact, distancing themselves from the homeless and panhandlers. Our family shared gift-making projects for disabled children's homes and volunteered at homeless shelters on holidays.

"That's another thing. I never thought you and Dad were normal. On Thanksgiving, Brennan and I went with the bus driver to places under bridges and in underground parking lots to find homeless people to bring back to the shelter where you and Dad were serving meals. Year after year, we recognized the same faces and listened to the same stories. Remember the woman who wanted to go back to school but lived in a box? She was homeless and her home was a cardboard box in the basement of a parking lot. She wanted help in figuring out how to get money for bus fare, clothing and money to finish college.

"We had to contribute to the family. Dad paid for our gas for our little fishing boat if we mowed the lawn on time. My little sister Allie begged for her first horse at fourteen, but you said, 'Only after you have enough money to pay for the horse and three months' worth of rent for boarding him.' We worked hard for our privileges and even had to pay for our first car and insurance."

*Standing outside a local crafts market in Jayapura*

Jackie "Did you ever remember thinking you wished you were home while in New Guinea?"

Katherine "Sure, when I had malaria and hundreds of bug bites. We were so far away, though, that being home was not an option. We took that trip before I was interested in boys, or that would have been a problem. I was terrified of high school, so it felt good to get away."

Jackie "Did you ever feel hungry on your trip? Toward the end of the trip, you had saved some peanut butter packets, and my adult instincts screamed in my head, 'What a great choice for emergencies?'"

*Katherine, waiting for a travel permit in Jayapura*

Katherine "But that homemade bread we shared with melting peanut butter was better than a banana split. It would have seemed stupid to feel hungry at the time."

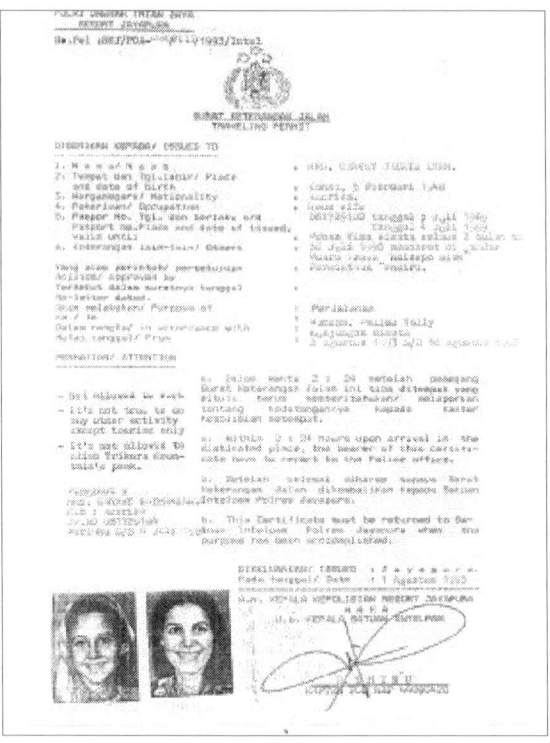

**Travel Permit**

"We were with people who had so little. Plus, we were there to see how they lived," she said.

**Jackie** "Do you think your level of communication changed between peers, siblings, and adults?"

**Katherine** "I was quiet. I came back even quieter, because I didn't know how to relate to my friends".

**Jackie** "How do you explain you lived with naked people for four weeks?"

**Katherine** "When my friends came back from summer camp, it was easy for them to explain what they did. Over time, the trip helped me be open to meeting people from different walks of life. I was a preteen, but I thought I was a lot better than they were. My friends seemed a lot younger than me."

***Jackie*** "Katherine, you were a lot more mature than your friends as a teenager. You proved that to me on our first trip together to the Amazon. While your friends thought about smoking, drinking, and expensive clothing, you were curious about the environment and how other people lived with the world. What about your worldview?"

*Leaving Wamena on a day trip to a nearby village*

***Katherine*** "The trip opened my eyes to a different kind of spiritual world. I developed an interest in other countries and their politics, ending up with a love for international business. In Muliamo, the government brought in huge trucks with movie screens. I believed the government was trying to brainwash the tribes with government policies. The government authorities were nice to us, seeing us as representatives of another country. I don't know if they were going to try to use the tribes to encourage tourism or if they just wanted to show how stuff was changing. It was random."

***Jackie*** "Regarding our brainstorming during our Indonesian trip, did that help your growth from adolescence to adulthood?"

***Katherine*** "It's hard to say, but the trip gave me confidence to make my own decisions. We already had more responsibility than other kids, so maybe I would have grown up responsible anyway. By seventeen, I was in Ecuador all by myself. Not until my honeymoon did I realize that I lived my life off the beaten path. I'm more resourceful, and if I can't afford something, I build my own."

***Jackie*** "Were you able to learn better from others, like teachers, after being in an adult world for so long?"

***Katherine*** "I never thought about being in an adult world. It wasn't like an adult world because I felt I was smarter than everyone I was around. I could read, write, and draw things. People we were around would play tricks with each other and on us. Those experiences helped mature me. I don't know if it happened immediately.

"Over the next few years, I compared my situations with those experiences. I didn't come back from Indonesia and say, 'To heck with the shopping mall.' It took a while to absorb what I'd learned abroad. One other thing is that I've never been afraid to be different. In fact, I like to be the person to present an alternate point of view. Friends say I sound like the voice of opposition when I explain things in a different way. When I worked in Kansas City as the environmental coordinator, I loved presenting to the Chamber of Commerce. Now, living in Vermont as an assistant professor, I love giving that Midwestern point of view." *

***Jackie*** *[Note: Katherine has since relocated to another University and is contributing directly and indirectly to the state by helping to improve the environment.]

"For many years after the trip, I carried a burden of guilt because of your ordeal with malaria. As an adventurous mother, did I have the right to expose you to potential dangers?" [I finally got the nerve to talk to Katherine about her feelings. I started with an apology for even suggesting we take these crazy trips together, and then I asked if she regretted any of her travels or getting malaria.]

***Katherine*** "Mom, are you kidding? You're the greatest mom in the world, and I had the best life growing up that a person could ever dream of. How many people in the world will have the experiences I had even as adults? The malaria only lasted about a week and is gone for good."

***Jackie*** "A few years later, your brother Brennan said to me, 'Mom, I made a huge mistake a few years back. I told you that I wanted to go snowboarding for a vacation that year, instead of going with you to Ethiopia for a month. Also, I didn't want to lose any summertime sailing and water skiing. Now I realize I will never have that chance again--will I? I'll be leaving for college next year and won't have the time to take a month-long trip with you. Carrie is in college, playing volleyball, and my other crazy sister Katherine is living in Bogota, Columbia, trying to avoid getting kidnapped by rebels.' Katherine, does that story help confirm your thinking?"

***Katherine*** "Yes. Maybe it was a bravery thing for me, or maybe I just wanted to do things he would never do. A few years after our trip to New Guinea, I flew to Venezuela with a hundred dollars in my pocket. I bought a cell phone, went to the university, and put up flyers, offering to teach English. For many people, that idea probably doesn't sound like fun. I read some of my first adult books, like Power of One, on that New Guinea trip, and I think reading about apartheid had an effect on me. I took a more introspective look at myself then."

*Restaurant food in Jayapura*

A mother's comments on parenting: Katherine had to make some sacrifices to take that trip. Most friends would have chosen to be lost with their moms in a mall, not in a wild, animal-infested jungle halfway around the world. Giving up pizza for a month and replacing it with rice three meals a day might be considered torture for most teenagers. In listening to Katherine's answers, I could see the growth pattern that had emerged. She had changed from a shy teenager into a confident woman.

Katherine is from me but not mine to keep. She is of herself. The trip to New Guinea was not really about living with Stone Age people, but more about demystifying ourselves. As I write, these moments live in my heart and mind as clearly today as they did the moment they occurred.

How can a few words express the intensity of those experiences? Of course, I am not a trained psychologist or anthropologist. My words are shared with other teens and parents so they may take from our experience some practical wisdom that might open doors and allow them to take some courageous risks along the path of growing inside and outside their family. One purpose of the trip was to widen our horizons and to help me get in touch with the life within my soul through living a simpler existence. Katherine most certainly overcame fear and increased her capacity for courage. Words fail to convey the positive changes I have absorbed and the discoveries of how they impacted my life.

*Indonesian carving in Jayapura hotel*

This journey was Katherine's first experience of an intimate relationship. Through the building blocks of communication, trust, reliance, and putting others' needs ahead of our own, separation and connection were tested and strengthened. Operating on a peer-level playing field built self-confidence for both of us. While exploring the world, Katherine and I explored our own identities in ourselves and with each other. In trying to help Katherine see her own strengths and weaknesses, I learned to face my own. I began seeing Katherine owning herself and her future, and I felt she began seeing her mother as an individual. Being outside one's own little world served as a catalyst for so many new layers of awareness.

The mother-daughter relationship can be one of the most powerful bonds in the world.

Travel is immeasurably influenced by our choice of travel partners just as traveling together molds those relationships by the challenges met along the way.

Katherine and I built a strong foundation for weathering the trials of life. We have gone our separate ways, but in the end, we still rely on each other. With the tools sharpened by our bonding adventure, we will travel the journeys of life.

# A Teen's Notes: Youthful Landscapes

The following pages share copies of the journal created on the New Guinea trip.

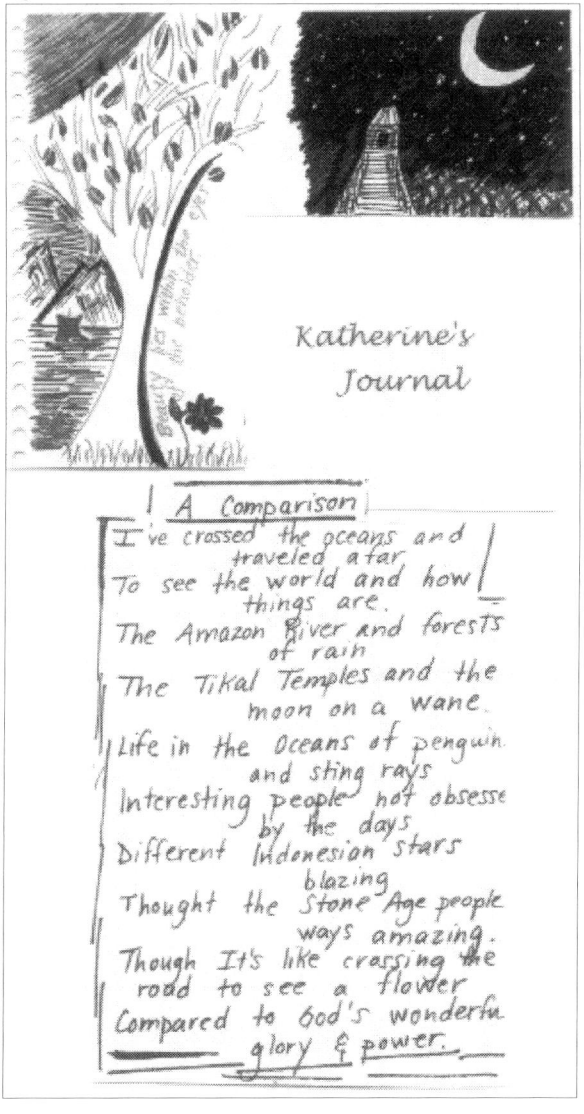

**Katherine's Journal**

### A Comparison

I've crossed the oceans and
    traveled afar
To see the world and how
    things are.
The Amazon River and forests
    of rain
The Tikal Temples and the
    moon on a wane.
Life in the Oceans of penguin
    and sting rays
Interesting people not obsesse
    by the days.
Different Indonesian stars
    blazing
Thought the Stone Age people
    ways amazing.
Though It's like crossing the
    road to see a flower
Compared to God's wonderfu
    glory & power.

1st Day (1st few pages are boring)
Swimming at home - drive to MCI from Lotawona fly to Dallas wait to next Terminal. fly from Dallas Texas to L.A. walk to next terminal. Flight is 3 hours late get fancy dinner free. forign accent hamburger guy picks up on me. We go through Security ✓ ~~She thought I was going to Australia told me I was cute about 3 times says and my Steel toed Hiking Boots make he thinks K.C. girls are cute.~~ the beeper go off. I have to get a body check so that they know I don't have a gun. Sit 2 hours waiting for late plane. This is what it takes to get ½ way around the world and 1st day I'm still in L.A. The Smog here is bad it is in Dallas too. (from the air) Well I saw Smog

2nd Day - This day is 24 hours of sunshine with no sleeping. Honolulu is beautiful - from what I see at the airport at night. - The 10 hour plane ride to Biak is fun even though the food is gross. At Biak a 19 year old Christian boy named Maxine gave us a tour of town. Then at 12 we went back to the airport and met a nice Australian who had a wonderful time on his trip and wished he could go again. We flew to Juayapura and it is most beautiful island because it so natural. When we got of the plane to get a taxi there was a big deal being made over us cause the guy we were going to go w/ went against union prices so about 20 ~~people~~ men were surronding us yelling at him. it was scary. We just took our luggage from him and started walking to catch a bus. Then the guy came and ~~took~~ us for 5000 less Rupiahs anyway. Juaypura is a beautiful town. - except for the buildings and roads being so poor the town is on this pennisula type thing kindof like this

We ate at a really dirty restaurant that night well not dirty just I don't know I didn't like it. We were supposed to meet Jonas there but he didn't show up. I ordered Spaghetti w/ Tomato sauce. and it took over ½ an hour. I was so tired and it ended up being ½ vegatables and salad stuff but after I took that stuff of it was o.k. but then they gave my French Fries and she said I could have them so I put ketchup on them but it wasn't ketchup it was Tobasco sause or something of that related hotness I thought I would puke but I didn't

4th day (I think) - it's all messed up since we're on the other side of the world. Well all the major traveling hectichness is over yesterday I was just lazy and wrote letters and stuff. We ate some really good chinese food and had good cold drinks at a seafood place. I think there was a baby octopus in my

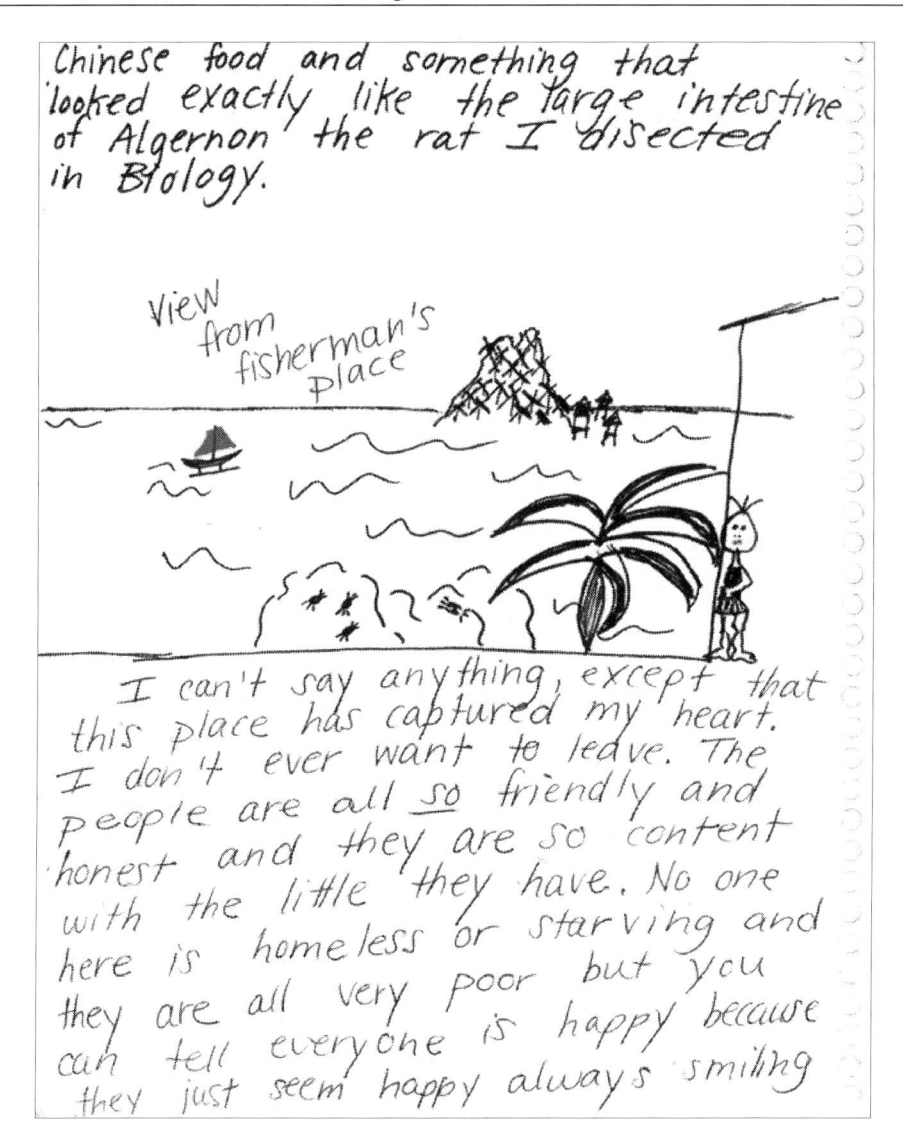

Chinese food and something that looked exactly like the large intestine of Algernon the rat I disected in Biology.

*View from fisherman's place*

I can't say anything, except that this place has captured my heart. I don't ever want to leave. The people are all so friendly and honest and they are so content with the little they have. No one here is homeless or starving and they are all very poor but you can tell everyone is happy because they just seem happy always smiling and the children get excited over the littlest things because they aren't spoiled by the luxuries of Sega Genesis. We had children running after the plane and stuff waving as we landed and it just makes me want to cry. I have surely been blessed. From a distance it would appear as poverty but up close it's a much happier place then Lee's Summit or anywhere else in the U.S. because people realize their most important values — God and family and they all have their needs met. They don't concentrate on — money I need more money. It's just simply wonderful

4 little boys carrying

Don't ask but think it's whatever you want & you know there are faces on the side.

burlap sac of wheat or something

Highlights of 1st Day in Wamena
1. A naked man tried to sell me a carrot
2. Someone was running down the street holding their penis gord. that was on them
3. I walked across a suspension bridge
4. Some boy from a barber shop blew me a kiss.
5. Someone jumped in front of me and yelled. And then I did a home alone yell. thing and did an inhale
6. Shook hands w/ a naked man that was missing 2 or 3 fingers. (These tribal people have to have 1 finger cut off for every family member that dies)-or something for mourning. 7. Smiled at at least 200 people 8. Saw the most beautiful place in the whole world.

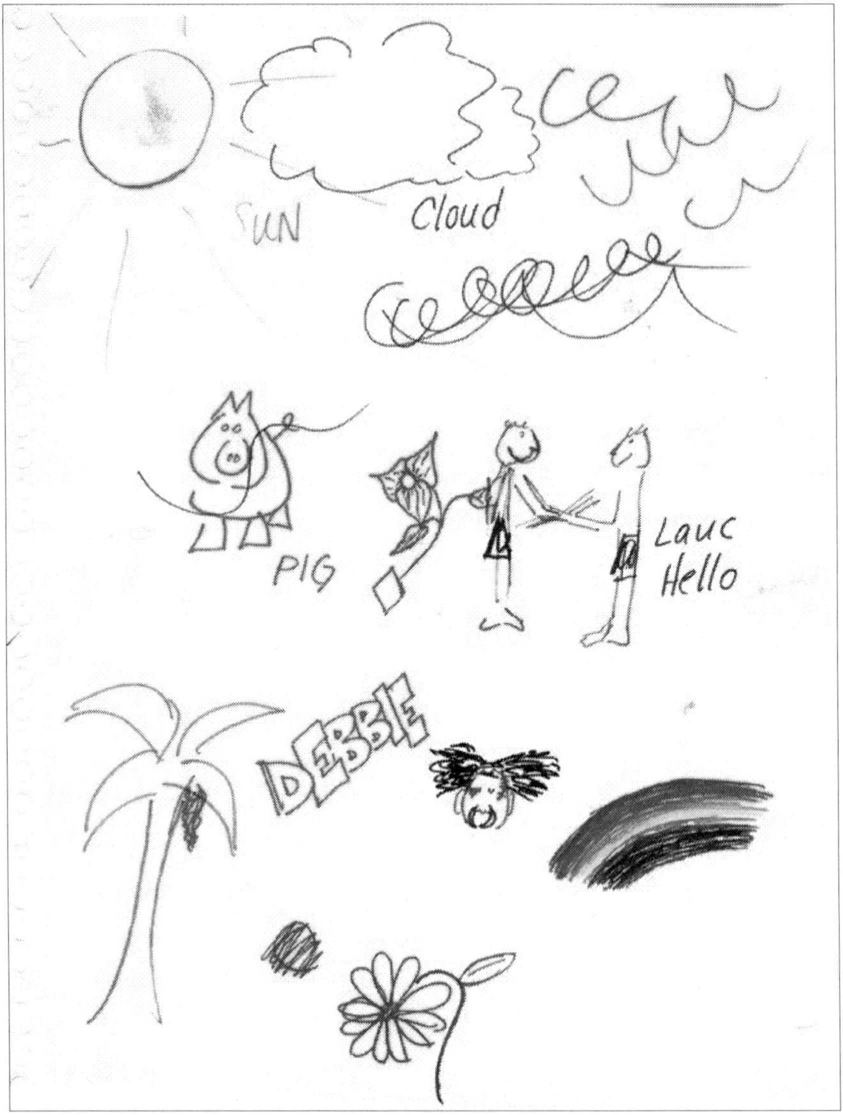
SUN
Cloud
PIG
Lauc
Hello
DEBBIE

Walking to Woot

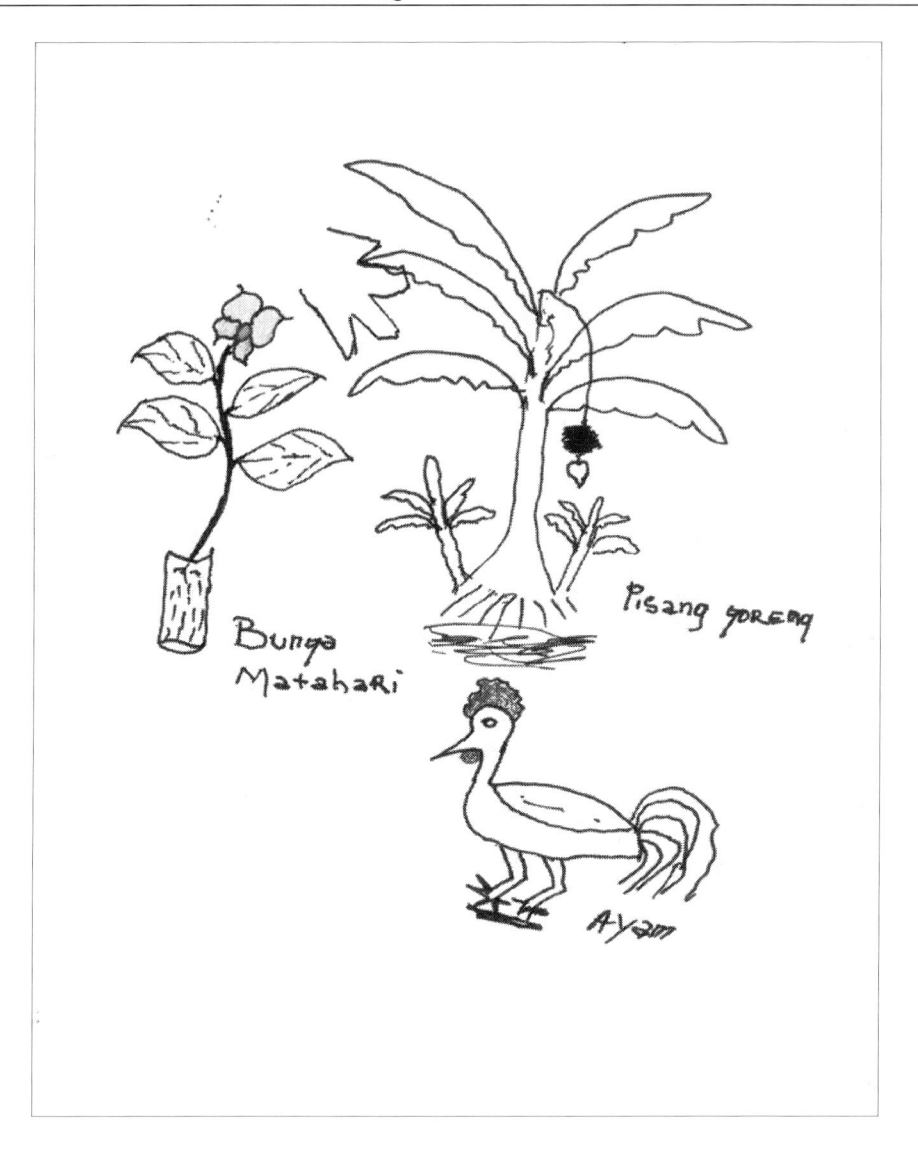

Well, I've just been asked to live in the most beautiful place in the world in a beautiful hotel w/ a man who would have done just about anything for me. He said "you can go to high school and to the University and then come here and live w/ me, we can go back to visit your family all the time"

Holy Shit - excuse my interruption and mabey shit ish't holy but I think he thinks I'm actually considering this. He says "This is our last day to walk around Wamena market together" O.K. Nevermind he didn't say for a while This is not so good I'm going to have to spend the next 6 to 10 days w/ him. Sleeping in the same hut. O.K. just be friends.

Anyway he says "it's O.K for Dani tribesman to marry American girl, and we can get a permit from Jakarta's government. I have 2 cars and this hotel and 4 mil Rup. and we can write & send pics while your at school and then you come back here and we have a big festival (probley he would have all the tribes come! and kill 200 pig and eat sweet

From 50 feet away, i look on to a tribal dance, men & women jumping around a Blazing fire in the middle of one of the densed jungles in the world. As the natural guitar pauses for a few seconds every 10 minutes everyone stops and takes advantage of the small breaks they get because they will dance all night It looks very mystical w/ the fire's smoke surrounding the dancers. And as i listen to the tribal music that is probably from many - mabey even thousands of years ago — i realize that the night before i had joined in this dancing in the darkness.

# Journey Into The Stone Age

## The Lost Paradise

We had 2 full days of traveling mostly by plane w/ a 6 hour lay over in L.A. Besides watching some on-flight movies and eating. The only thing we did was talk to people about traveling and no one could understand why we were going to Irian Jaya - New Guinea - to see and live w/ the most primative people in the world. I don't know myself - even now that the trip is almost over. Mabey it's because of the adventure - mabey it's because no one does from Missouri does this kindof thing Mabey it's because I can see happiness in the faces of people w/ no materialistic things and realize that those things aren't what make a good life.

We stayed 3 days in Jayapura waiting for someone and waiting for the plane to Wamena. We just kindof people watched the whole time and could tell immediatly the difference between these people and the average American. They are just always friendly. The main goal isn't making money to be happy, it's just trying to be happy and everyone smiles and says Hello or Hi Mister I love you to us and shake your hand. It's just amazing no one would do that back home to a complete stranger let alone everyone (except in a church or small town but that's a different lifestyle anyway.) It's like now I'm practically tired of being so polite to everyone in every restaurant hotel and on the street. I'm just not used to it I guess. Cause in my society I'm used to being impacient if my hamburger isn't on my tray in a minute. Here you go in at lunch to tell them what you want for dinner. — the reason for going to Jayapura was to get permission from the Indons. govt. to go to see these people.

  We then fly to Wamena and meet Jonas the guy we are supposed to meet and he is very abrupt takes our luggage yells for a Taxi and we get a clean hotel — well there were mice & bugs but we had a bathroom w/ river water and there were cute little Iguanas on the ceiling — there were in Jayapura too. But anyway fortunatly Jonas was a wimp and didn't want to go treking so we only had to spend 2 days w/ this rude man and he paid for everything. Actually rude is a nice way to describe him. We've also heard of him as a "rude old bastard" but we had a good time anyway. I wasn't expecting to see the tribal people until we got out treking but they were right there at the airport w/ nothing on but penis gourds or grass skirts. Quite Interesting that's all I'm going to say.

  The days we spent in Wamena or in the Beliem valley consisted of 10 nights of sleeping in huts and days of treking. The food was always crackers — Indonesian style — and peanut butter — from home — w/ an occasional bold hard boiled egg for Breakfast and for lunch & dinner always rice, noodles, and vegatables, very plain and not very good. The few nights spent in town we had canned corned beef rolls - a pleasant change and one night I had the best meal of my life. 1 plate of Fried Rice Special, 1 Fried Noodle Special, 1 Fried Vegatable Special, 1 Fried Noodle Special w/ Penut sauce, 2 Fish - just cooked sauced and put on a plate whole (I only ate one bite of fish but the best part of the whole dinner was fresh crayfish in garlic sauce. Oh it was so good. All of this food was shared between 3 people - the 3rd being a delightful lady who is a famous Children's book writer and it was just wonderful talking to her. She told us a really neat story about how she was staying alone in this small villiage and after several days of staying there she needed to get back so she radioed a plane and for 6 days she was stuck there and the whole village got together and prayed w/ her that she would get back in time and she ended up telling someone this on the radio and all the planes being missionary planes they made an extra effort to pick her up and she got back in time.

Treking for many days sometimes coming back to Wamena to stay in the Srikandy hotel and 10 of the nights sleeping in Indian huts of one kind or another. Beautiful hiking in the mountains or beside the Beliem river having one of the porters carry me & one carry mom acrost creeks or pig sludge so that we wouldn't get our hiking boots dirty/wet. It was exciting crossing bridges because they were suspension bridges w/ fallen through boards and they were sometimes 50 to 100 ft above rapid waters. Also we crossed a couple naturally) made suspns. bridges and that was fun. In the villages I sometimes felt uncomfortable because I didn't have any privacy and it was very difficult going to the bathroom. Once I walked at least ½ a mile outside of the village and it ended up about 20 men saw me go to the bathroom. Also the children follow and try to spy. Dealing w/ privacy and took a bathe in a river - I kept on a shirt but a boy saw me and did some things to make me feel very uncomfortable - It's really bad I even hate to write it down but he grabbed my chest the private part & then ran away and then came from behind me and grabbed around my waste and I screamed and pushed him

## **Katherine, 14, wrote this to her mother after returning from trip to New Guinea.**

Sometimes to live life, you have to cherish it.
To love, you have to give yourself.
To experience, you have to risk the unknown.

To understand beauty, you have to look beyond,
Even though it can be simpler than often thought, and then let your soul smile.

Before, I had said that this place has captured my heart and that I don't ever want to leave. But I do. I'm glad that I had the opportunity to sit down and think about the world and see a new culture but I am ready to go home. Probably because I am spoiled by civilized life. ~~I am~~ Especially cold drinks, ice cream, music, McDonalds, American food, just the stuff I'am used to having everyday. Private showers, American looking men. It's good to get away for a while just to realize how much I have and how much I take for grantid.

*Katherine, 13, wrote this to her mother after returning from trip to Amazon.*

To see a world full of adventure & myth.

Has made me more thankful & more than blithe.

To hear stories of medicine men & at 14 refusing coffee & gin.

For galloping through an ~~untraveled~~ mountain.

To see a natural water fountain.

To learn the importance of the trees & the air.

To hope people's traditions will always be there.

To learn patience from a country not as busy as our own.

To go for a while without using the phone.

Eating Tapir, Lemon ants & Dragon's blood.

Under leaf umbrellas, hiking through the mud.

As the only blond on the plane getting special dishes.

Swimming with pirannah, seals, penguins, & fishes.

Thanks not only for my life & birth.

But for showing me the wonders of the earth.

Katherine
Jarvey 93'

## Map of New Guinea

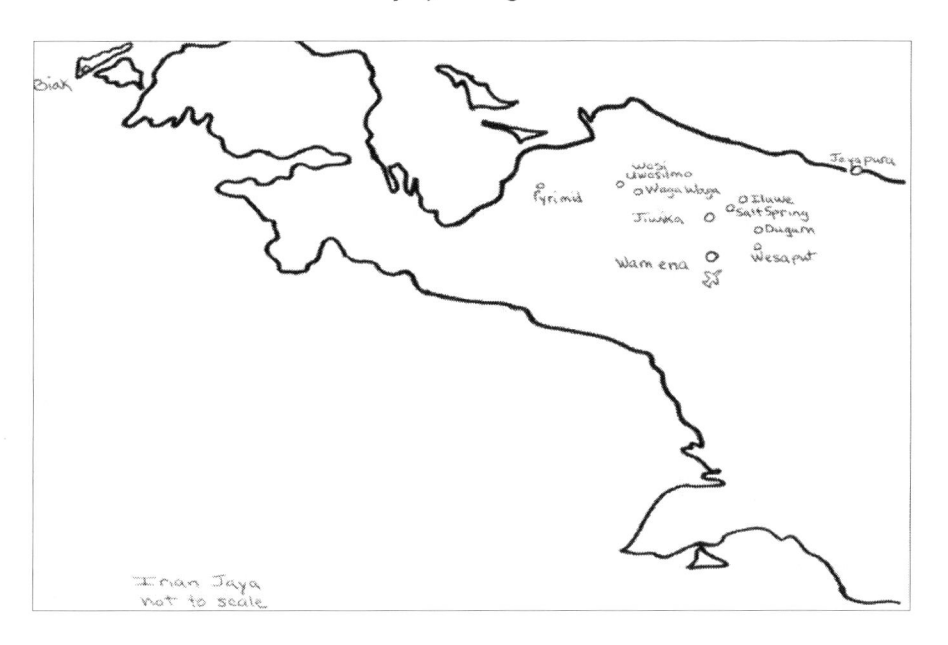

# Appendix: Two Approaches to Packing

### Packing List for Jackie Chase

Canvas duffel bag with straps for wearing backpack or one with handles for carrying clothes, One pair long nylon pants which zip off into shorts, One pair cotton knit pants, One long sleeved nylon shirt, One cotton short sleeved shirt, One cotton button down cotton shirt, Three pairs panties, Two bras, one with double lining sewn in to hide money, One pair hiking boots, One pair flip flops, One rayon sarong, One polyester travel towel, Three pairs of heavy-duty cushioned socks, Lightweight cotton jacket, One hat, Travel-sized rain poncho, Waist belt for hiding money, Waist pouch for outer wear to hold daily necessities, Watch but no other jewelry, Camera with extra batteries, Cassette player, Batteries and four tapes to play, Blank journal, One dozen extra pens and color markers, Two books shared (City of Joy and Power of One), Water purifier to share, Twenty-foot length of small rope for clothesline or to tie bag together if zipper breaks, Sleeping bags with mosquito net attached.

First Aid and Personal Hygiene to store in one-gallon-sized zip-lock bags, Four-oz-size toothpaste and one toothbrush plus dental floss, Enough tampons for one cycle, Three-oz-size bottle shampoo, Three-oz-size bottle of conditioner.

To share: Half dozen hair bands for pony tails, Two tubes of hydrocortisone for itching, Handful of small boxes of matches, Flashlights and extra batteries, Half dozen Band-Aids, Half dozen foam donut shaped pads for blisters, Malaria pills, Bottle of Ibuprofen, Imodium, Two dozen personal sized Kleenex packages, Six-oz-size sunscreen with high numbers, Pepto Bismol box of 24, Vitamin B complex daily tablets, Deet (100%) insect repellent in four three-oz-size bottles, Two dozen insect repellent wipes, Alcohol wipes for sanitizing hands, Small tube of Neosporin for infections, Two containers of pepper spray with clips for waist belt attachment, Handful of large safety pins to tie things together if they break or to hang clothes to dry, A needle with long piece of string attached for repairs, Small jar of Tiger Balm for sore muscles, Three razor blades for shaving legs, Two Blistex or Chapstick, Two water bottles for refilling for daily use, Two extra one-gallon-sized zip-lock bags for wet or dirty clothing,

Food products to share: Five-dozen high-protein bars, each having over 30 grams of protein per bar, Two-dozen travel packets of peanut butter,

For personal-sized backpack, always locked: Passport, International vaccine certificate, government permit for travel, six extra passport-sized photos (each), Photocopies of all documents in zip-lock bags, Notes and maps on what villages to visit, US money, Travelers checks, Credit card, Addresses and contacts of close family and friends, Small locks and keys with extra keys carried inside waist belt with passport, Sunglasses and one extra pair of reading glasses.

### *Nellie Bly's Packing List*

For comparison: Nellie Bly at the age of twenty-four traveled the world alone. Nellie Bly, born in 1865, wanted to turn the fictional Around the World in Eighty Days into fact for the first time. With two days' notice she began her 25,000-mile journey which she completed in seventy-two days. She said, "Packing that bag was the most difficult undertaking of my life; there was so much to go into such a little space."

\*\*\*

Nellie Bly's Packing List:

Three veils, silk bodice, two travel caps, slippers, toiletries, inkstand, pens, pencils and paper, sewing kit, dressing gown, tennis blazer, flask and drinking cup, hankies and fresh ruchings, cold cream. She put these into one tiny bag called a gripsack.

## Author Page

Meet Jackie Chase, Photo/journalist at websites: www.JackieChase.com, www.WorldTravelDiva.com and www.CulturesOfTheWorld.com, where you will meet a woman who has traveled to over 100 countries and specializes in staying in remote villages in order to use her keen observations and photo-journalism skills to share her insights with her reader fans. She has traveled alone, with a child, with family, and with friends; she has earned 29 awards from international book contests to date of printing; she shares with the public many of the travel secrets she has experienced in her book titled, "How to Become an Escape Artist" A Traveler's Handbook. The Handbook was tested for several years with students in a college evening, class, and they soaked up Jackie's hints and the many ways to avoid disappointment, reduce expenses and frustrations, navigate the issues of visas, language, customs, currencies, accommodations, transportation, attitudes, danger, travel alone, and other problems all covered in over 190 segments in the book.

Her "All Hands Working Together" Cruise for a Week: Meet 79 Cultures book treats cruising in a unique way to learn about cultures; the reader experiences personal contact with crewmembers from many of the 79 countries they represent, and from many skills they possess.

Jackie Chase has written definitive books on "People to Meet" in contrast to "Places to See". She convinces her readership to look beyond mountains, lakes and buildings to see world inhabitants as potential friends and shows how much we have in common. She shows how to bridge gaps created by custom and language in "100 People to Meet before You Die: Travel to Exotic Places". This book, [as well as the others], are available in color, grayscale, and with life-like images on eBooks that come to life on backlit screens. This anthology contains 321 story-telling images and her adventures in twelve countries. For her fans of a particular country, she has twelve "singles" in print and in eBook format, plus at least one (Panama) translated into Spanish.

For children, from small up through teens, a "winner" of a book is "Giraffe-Neck Girl" Make Friends with Different Cultures. It is about a ten-year-old girl in Thailand who warms the hearts of young and old as she shares her different life and customs.

Jackie Chase's 2016 book, "Walking to Woot" A Photographic Narrative Discovering New Dimensions for Parent-Teen Bonding has won awards in the genres of Parenting, Multi-Cultural, and Travel areas and contains both poetic descriptions and visual ones with its 180 images of life with stone-age tribal warriors who haven't changed customs in a thousand years. The New Guinea villagers welcomed Jackie and her blond 14-year-old daughter to pig roasts,

customs, and dances. Jackie Chase loves to hear from her fans and to see copies of reviews they submit to the web. Contact her:
JakartaMoon@hotmail.com, or Publisher@AdventureTravelPress.com

BOOKS BY JACKIE CHASE: 2014/17
All Hands Working Together: Cruise for a Week: Meet 79 Cultures (2014) & (2017)
How to Become an Escape Artist: A Traveler's Handbook (2014) & (2017)
Giraffe-Neck Girl: Make Friends with a Different Culture (2014) & (2017)
100 People to Meet before You Die: Travel to Exotic Cultures (2014) & (2017))

AWARDS (14) FOR THE FOUR BOOKS LISTED ABOVE
Royal Palm Literary Award; National Indie Excellence Book Award; FAPA President's Book Award; Readers' Favorite Book Award; International Book Award; USA Best Book Award; Beverly Hills Book Awards

BOOK BY JACKIE CHASE: 2016

AWARDS (15) For *"Walking to Woot" A Photographic Narrative Discovering New Dimensions for Parent-Teen Bonding*:

Beach Book Festival; Beverly Hills Book Awards in 3 Categories; Eric Hoffer Grand Prize Awards in 2 Categories; Florida Authors and Publishers Association (FAPA); International Book Award, Montaigne Medals; National Indie Excellence Award; Next Generation Indie Book Awards in 2 Categories; Paris Book Festival; Reader's Favorite Awards in 2 Categories; San Francisco Festival Awards

## What is inside her other books?

The following excerpt shows how a Midwest mom of 4 could tackle the dangerous areas of the New Guinea jungle plus the tangle of preparation, regulations, and rules needed for travel these days and teaches you how to save money, avoid problems, and plan an inexpensive and enlightening trip or vacation.

Her book *"How to Become an Escape Artist" A Traveler's Handbook* has been updated annually and the following is an excerpt showing not only the titles of the 192 segments that will be your best traveling companion, but samples of the 113 internet links that would be difficult to find without a ton of work. Note the many telephone numbers that can save you time, money and disappointment! There are many more of these hints in the book along with the stories that prove the need for this info and that help you remember the secrets she shares.

### Introduction
### I. PLAN

**1. TOURIST OR INDEPENDENT TRAVELER?** Your Options; Which World do you Choose?

**2. LEAVING FEAR AND CAREERS BEHIND** Preparation; Basic Needs; Obstacles; Traveling Alone; Removing Masks; Fear of Other Cultures; Fear of Foreign Languages; Meeting with the Unexpected; Words of Encouragement; Careers

**3. THE WHY AND WHEN TO RESEARCH** Traveler Tastes/ Interests/ Personalities; Gathering Ideas and Choosing a Destination; Ancestors; Alternative Travel; Relaxation; Volunteering; Internet; Friends; Magazines; Newspapers; Television; Libraries and Other Resources; Tour Operators; Languages; Tourist Offices; Adventure Tour Operators; Guidebooks; Climate; Length of Stay; Getting Away for a Week or Two

**4. MONEY What Can You Afford?** Before You Go; Hidden Money; Cash; Traveler's Checks; ATMs; Personal Checks; Bargaining; Nitty Gritty; Record Keeping; Credit Cards; Budgeting; Bartering; Black Market; Run Out of Money? Become Familiar with Local Currency; Emergency Stash; Traveling for Free; Returning Home

### II. PREPARE

**5. HEALTH AND INSURANCE** Preparations; Food and Water; Where to Go For Vaccinations; First-Aid Kits/Health Supplies; US State Department Travel Advisories; Common Diseases Contracted; Medical Tests Abroad; Stress; Jet Lag; Toilets; Laundry; Sun; Altitude Sickness; Motion Sickness; Exposure Extremes; Care of the Feet; Cuts, Bites and Stings; Ticks and Leeches; Your Physical Condition; Broken Bones, Sprains and Strains; Swimming and Bathing; Travel Insurance

**6. TRANSPORTATION** Many Options; Airlines; Couriers; Trains; Buses; Automobiles; Taxis; Hitchhiking; Motorcycles and Bicycles; Walking and Miscellaneous Travel; Boats and Cruises

*III. ON THE WAY*

**7. FOOD AND SHELTER** The Adventure of Eating; Staying Healthy; Fancy Restaurants or Cafes; Rules of the Table; Street Vendors; Eating Alone; Remote Situations; Water; Hotels; Home Exchanges; Hostels; YMCAs; Other Types of Shelter

**8. DOCUMENTS** Passports; Visas; Tourist Cards; Immunizations and Medical Records; Insurance; Driver's License

**9. SAFETY NETS** Travel Safely; Extra Foresight; Flying; Pets; Smoking; Choose a Safe Hotel; Preventing Theft; Money Scams: Jewelry; Pepper Spray; Airport Scanners; Luggage; Rental Cars; Taxis; Hiding Money or Documents; Laptops and Miscellaneous Electronics; Phone Cards; Foreign Laws; Homeless Children; Personal Space; Giving in to Crime; Take a Positive Attitude

**10. ETHICS AND COMMUNICATION** Responsible Travel; Body Language; Tipping; Begging; Communications; Telephones; Cell phones; Laptops, Notebooks and iPads; Global Positioning Systems; Faxes; Mail Services; Measurement Units; Time; Calendars; Calculators; Foreign Languages; Finding Help; Do Not Forget

**11. TRAVELING SOLO** Pros and Cons; Dealing with Loneliness; Women Alone; Companions

**12. PEOPLE** Cultural Differences; Culture Shock; Respect; Bringing Back Great Moments, Digitally or on Film; Scrapbook Memories; Journaling; Tape or Audio Recorders

*IV. SPECIAL SITUATIONS*

**13. TRAVELING WITH CHILDREN** Patience; Sleep; Flying; Cars; Getting Lost

**14. SENIOR TRAVEL** What is a Vacation? Changes in Travel Methods; Physical Changes

*V. CHECK IT OUT*

**15. PACKING** Packing Ideas; Types of Luggage; Lost Luggage; Carry-On Luggage; Baggage Allowances; Excess Baggage; Clothes; Shoes; Tips for Packing

**16. CUSTOMS AND GOING HOME** Customs; Going Home

**17. RESOURCE LIST 1** Reference; Reference Books/Publications; Customs; Emergencies; Freighter Travel; Gear; Insurance; Medical Concerns; Student Travel Organizations; Travel Organizations for Singles; Travel Organizations for Seniors; Travel Warnings, Reviews, and Advice Websites

**18. RESOURCE LIST 2** Lists; Carry-on Packing List; Standard List for Three-week Adventure Trip; List of Basic Toiletries; Camping List; List of Additional

Basics; List of Basics for Cold Climates; Basic First Aid Kit List; List for Longer or Survival Type Trip; Document List; List of Other To-Dos before Leaving Home

**SAMPLE EXCERPT:**
**"REFERENCE BOOKS/PUBLICATIONS**

From the Superintendent of Documents, U.S. Government Printing Office, Washington, D.C. 20402, you may obtain many publications for $1.25. Examples include "Your Trip Abroad," "Safe Trip Abroad," "Tips for Americans Residing Abroad," "Travel Tips for Older Americans," and many publications on specific parts of the world like "Tips for Travelers to the Caribbean."

Background Notes offer you detailed information about a particular foreign country. Each booklet contains information on 170 different countries and geographic areas with descriptions of people, culture, geography, history, political conditions, economy, and government. Include the specific country or area you plan to visit, and $2 with your request to Background Notes, Superintendent of Documents, U.S. Government Printing Office, Washington D.C. 20402, or check the web site at www.state.gov.

Key Officers of Foreign Service Posts booklet has valuable information on all American Embassies, consulates, and missions in foreign countries including names, addresses, and telephone numbers for $3.75. Use the same address as Background Notes (above) or call 202-783-3238.

**CUSTOMS**

"Know Before You Go" Booklet available free from the U.S. Customs Service, Box74077, Washington, DC 20044

"Travelers Tips on Bringing Food, Plant, and Animal Products into the United States" is free from the U.S. Department of Agriculture, Washington, D.C. 20250

**EMERGENCIES**

To find travel information for emergencies, consider the following website: www.travel.state.gov.

Overseas Citizen Emergency Center will help with any legal, financial, or medical problems occurring while abroad. They will help notify relatives at home, help with medical support, or help you receive money. Their hotline provides information on entry requirements, crime and security conditions, and areas of instability related to travel for a particular country. They issue travel warnings when the State Department recommends deferral of travel by Americans to a country because of civil unrest, dangerous conditions or terrorist conditions, and when the U.S. has no diplomatic relations with the country or cannot assist Americans in distress. The Policy Review and Interagency Liaison (PRI) Agency provides guidance concerning the administration and enforcement of laws on U.S. citizenship and documentation for traveling and living abroad for Americans. Reach them at this same number. The State Department's Office of American Citizens Services and Crisis Management (ACS) office administers the Consular Information Program, which informs the public of conditions abroad that may affect their safety and security. Useful information includes Country Specific Information, Travel Alerts, and Travel Warnings.

To contact Overseas Citizens Services from within the U.S, call 1-888-407-4747 and from a foreign country call 1-202-501-4444, or write Overseas Citizens Services Department of State Washington, DC 20520, or find the online site at www.travel.state.gov/travel/travel_1744.html.

Global Assist can help American Express Card members. They have a free hot-line to assist with medical, legal, translation and professional problems. In the US, the phone number is 800-333-AMEX and abroad, call collect at 715-343-7977.

### *FREIGHTER TRAVEL*

If you plan to visit the Panama and the Suez canals, you're going to have to spend a considerable amount of time at sea, since the Panama Canal is in the Western Hemisphere, and the Suez Canal is in the Middle East.

Try checking out Maris Freighter & Specialty Cruises (www.freighter-cruises.com, or toll-free, 800-99-Maris) offers a 15-week voyage that includes both canals, but it begins and ends outside of the United States. Trips sail every month from Dunkirk to Le Havre, France, then across the Atlantic to Cristobal, Panama, and through the Panama Canal to Tahiti, then on to New Zealand, New Caledonia, Fiji, Vanuatu, the Solomon Islands, Papua, New Guinea, and then to Singapore, followed by a passage through the Suez Canal and the Mediterranean, ending in Hamburg, Germany.

The same company also offers an eastbound cruise starting and ending in Texas. This voyage lasts 18 weeks. The itinerary starts in Texas, moves up the East Coast of the United States, and then includes Hamburg, Germany, Belgium, Italy, the Suez Canal, India, Indonesia, Singapore, Vietnam, various ports in China, Korea, Japan. The return to the States, stopps in Southern California, passing through the Panama Canal, and ending in Houston, Texas.

For a variation check out Strand Voyages: See www.strandtravelltd.co.uk/voyages/destinations-and-prices/

Freighter World: www.freighterworld.com/ or 800-531-7774

TravL tips: www.travltips.com or 800-872-8584; Freighter trips for tips and info: http://www.freightertrips.com/.

## GEAR
Campmor 1-800-525-4784 or www.campmor.com.
Magellans 1-800-962-494 or www.magellans.com.
Sierra Trading Post 800-713-4534 or www.sierraTradingPost.com.
Travel Smith 800-770-3387 or www.travelsmith.com
REI 1-800-426-4840 or www.rei.com
Columbia Clothing www.columbia.com
Ex Officio 800-644-7303 or www.exofficio.com

## INSURANCE
Insure My Trip 800-551-4635 or www.insuremytrip.com
Global Travel Shield 1-800-332-4899 or www.globaltravelshield.com
Travel Guard 800.826.4919 or www.travelguard.com
Assess America 800.826.4919 or www.assessamerica.com
CIEE (Council on International Educational Exchange) 1-207-553-4000 or www.ciee.org.
Healthcare Abroad 800-237-6615 or www.wallach.com.
International SOS Assistance is helpful at www.internationalsos.com.
Travel Trip (Mutual of Omaha) 800-228-9792
Travel Assistance International 800-237-6615; www.travelassistance.com.

## MEDICAL CONCERNS
Center for Disease Control (if your doctor or local public health department cannot answer your questions or problems with medical matters) 800-CDC-INFO or www.cdc.gov..

IAMAT International Association for Medical Assistance to Travelers 716 -754 -4883

Alternatively, check out www.iamat.org. This organization keeps an up-to-date chart of all the diseases and malaria for every country in the world. When you figure out where you plan to travel, you can go to this website, find the world immunization chart, and find your destination country. Each disease active in that country has a code. Look further down the chart to see whether you need immunizations for that country. The chart gives advice on the best drugs to use and how much and when to take them. I found my general doctor did not know much about malaria, and I used the IAMAT advice to help him determine how much medicine to prescribe. If you join their organization, they send a little booklet with recommended doctors for every country in the world listed. I found this information invaluable when my fourteen-year-old daughter came down with malaria symptoms while we traipsed through the New Guinea jungles. As soon as we arrived in a town large enough to have a hospital and doctor, we found the doctor recommended in the little book. Katherine and I loved the attention he gave us, including a ride to the pharmacy to help with translating his prescription, and then to our hotel to make sure Katherine found comfort for the night.

### STUDENT TRAVEL ORGANIZATIONS
Council on International Education Exchange (CIEE) A nonprofit organization helping with work, study, exchange and travel abroad 1-207-553-4000 or www.ciee.org.
Student Travel Association (STA) 800-781-4040 or www.statravel.com
International Student Volunteers www.isvonline.com.
National Registration Center for Study Abroad 414-278-0631 or www.nrcsa.com.
Hosteling International www.hihostels.com.

### TRAVEL ORGANIZATIONS for SINGLES
www.BestSingleTravel.com.
www.Travelchums.com
www.TravelCompanionExchange.com
www.SinglesTravelCompany.com 888.286.8687
www.AllSinglesTravel.com 888.286.8687
www.SoloTravel.org

### TRAVEL ORGANIZATIONS FOR SENIORS
My Travel Companions (free membership to find travel companions for seniors) www.mytravelcompanions.com
American Association of Retired Persons (AARP) www.aarp.org/travel
www.RoadScholar.org 888.286.8687
www.Eldertreks.com 800-741-7956

### TRAVEL WARNINGS, REVIEWS, ADVICE WEBSITES
Consular Information Sheets and Travel Warnings 202-647-5225. You can obtain warnings at passport agencies, US embassies and consulates abroad, or access them through the Consular Affairs Bulletin Board (CABB) free. Request by fax at 202-647-3000. For each country, you will find information such as the location of the U.S. embassy and any consular offices, whether you need a visa, or seek crime and security warnings.

When friends or family of an American traveler need to reach him or her because of an emergency at home or because they are worried about the traveler's welfare, they should call 1-888-407-4747.

For emergencies, contact the Office of Overseas Citizens Services in the U.S. at 1-888-407-4747 (during business hours) or 202-647-5225 (after hours). Contact information for U.S. embassies, consulates, and you may also contact U.S. consular agencies overseas: www.state.gov/countries.

www.Advisor.com offers reviews and advice on everything related to travel, including hotels.

www.VirtualTourist.com offers advice and answers from people who have traveled your destination.

www.LonelyPlanet.com/ThornTree offers a place to ask questions and get advice on all elements of travel.

Join travel blogs like www.travelblogs.org. Check. . "

(This excerpt is only part of the book's resources).

Check into www.AdventureTravelPress.com for further info on Jackie's books.

And HAPPY TRAVELS!